To Nevill

on your 60th —

Best wishes

Camilla + Keith Jones.

Stony Gill Head

Blackstone Edge

_S w a l_

Summer Lod. Tarn

Cuddy · Currack

Bee?

Lead M

White Gill

_A s k r i g_

Whitfield Crag

Stackhill House

Lanty Bog

Fair Allotment

High Straits Lane

_L o w_

Whitfield Falls

Low Straits Lane

Garland Hill

_A b b o t s i d e_

Slape · Wath

Skellgill

Helm

Lease House

Grange Gill

Corn Mill

ASKR

Colby Hall

Dale Grange

Cotton Mill

Bowbridge

Site of Fors Abbey

Low

Old Camshouse

Old Yorebridge School

High Camshouse

Low Camshouse

_R i v e r   U r_

River Ure

Bainbridge

☐ Roman Fort

_T h e   S o u t h   S i d e   o f_

Township Boundary ▪━▪━▪━▪━▪━▪

Roads ━━━━━━━━━━

Railway ━ ━ ━ ━ ━ ━

Green Roads - - - - - - - - -

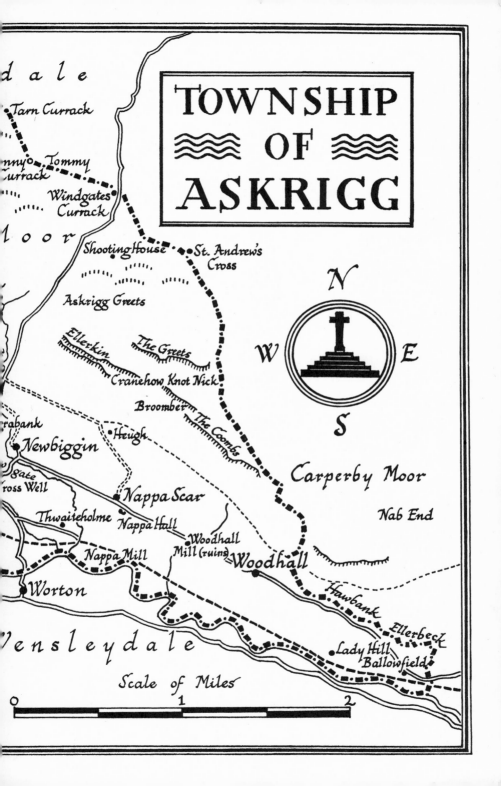

YORKSHIRE VILLAGE

YORKSHIRE VILLAGE

Marie Hartley and Joan Ingilby

Illustrated by
Marie Hartley

SMITH SETTLE

First published in 1953 by
J M Dent & Sons Ltd

This new edition published in 1989 by
Smith Settle Ltd
Ilkley Road
Otley
LS21 3JP

ISBN 1 870071 40 9

Printed and bound by
Smith Settle
Ilkley Road
Otley
LS21 3JP

NOTE TO THE THIRD EDITION

Since this book was published in 1953, it is to be expected that many changes will have overtaken Askrigg in Wensleydale. Apart from a few corrections we have not attempted to alter the text as this would blur the image of the village as portrayed in the 1950s. Therefore a brief account of the main changes is outlined in this note.

Following the reorganisation of administrative areas in 1974, we are no longer in the North Riding but in North Yorkshire, and Aysgarth Rural District Council based at Hawes has been replaced by Richmondshire District Council based at Richmond. Also Yorebridge Grammar School has been superseded by the new Wensleydale School at Leyburn, and the Askrigg Primary School has moved into part of the premises of the grammar school. The Yorkshire Dales National Park has established its headquarters in the former headmaster's house near Yore Bridge.

We have a new drainage system and a new water supply under the Yorkshire Water Authority. The railway closed in 1954. The rails have been removed, some bridges demolished, and Askrigg station yard and buildings are occupied by a building firm employing many men, which originated from an old established local joinery business. This business had been sited at Low Mill, the woollen mill, and Low Mill itself has been renovated and enlarged to form a youth centre for visiting parties and groups of the disabled.

The Primitive Methodist Chapel closed in 1971. The Askrigg Dairy has closed, and we no longer have a Women's Institute. The site of the Post Office was moved higher up the street in April 1963, and letters are no longer franked there. We have lost two butchers' shops, but retain a grocer's, a general craft shop, and other craft workshops, especially a potter's, based on the village. On the other hand a number of new houses have been built and others converted from old buildings mostly up Pudding Lane. Here the blacksmith's shop and the former cattle feed mill have been turned into houses. A large new mill for animal feeds has been built at the bottom of the village.

As experienced elsewhere, the striking change has been the influx of newcomers who have settled here, some as weekenders, some renting cottages for weekends, and some as permanent residents. Inevitably all of the old inhabitants whom we knew and from whom we gathered many recollections of former times have gone. The newcomers, of which we ourselves were early arrivals, have no doubt diluted the particular character of the village, as also have other influences, notably television. A large house in the market place (actually an Abbeyfield Home) has been used as the vet's house for filming scenes of *All Creatures Great and Small* for several years. This has drawn visitors to us apart from the general increase in visitors coming by car and motor coach that has occurred within the last fifteen to twenty years. We have two hotels, an inn, a restaurant, and many bed and breakfast places.

However farming flourishes and is all-important. Horses may be used elsewhere occasionally, but here tractors pulling muck spreaders and haymaking machinery have totally replaced them. The old system of many small barns in the meadows is under threat and poses a problem as they are an integral part of the scene, whereas the purpose-built new buildings which replace them are out of scale. Also since 1953 as a result of the application of fertiliser we have gradually lost most of our flowery meadows, once so colourful in June. An attempt is being made to recover them by the offer of grants to encourage old methods of farming.

It is obvious that these changes, whether we like them or not, speak of a thriving community. The church has a trained choir with a choir master and is used for concerts. A festival in church combined with the annual show of the Askrigg Produce Association occurs in August, and children's sports at the Spring Bank Holiday. New groups, with an emphasis on local history and Yore Club for the elderly to mention two, flourish. We wonder what changes will take place in the next thirty-five years. All that can be assumed likely is that the appearance of the village street will alter very little.

CONTENTS

ILLUSTRATIONS

Photographic Acknowledgements

Dougill family, p174–5 (Old Post Office); Fitzwilliam Museum, Cambridge, p122–3 ('Gimcrack'); A Hodgson, p174–5 (Yorebridge Grammar School); E Metcalfe, p276–7 (Jubilee); P Peacock, p174–5 (West End); Upper Dales Folk Museum, p260–1 (Old Hall fire); C H Wood, p6–7 (aerial views of Askrigg).

A spring morning

I

VIEW FROM ELLERKIN

LITTLE KNOTS of people are clustered near the school
at the edge of the village. Some collect outside the
entrance gates, others wait in the asphalt playground.
It is raised up from the lane, and those inside lean over the
wall as if on the parapet of a bridge. Although the evening
is grey, light from the western sky catches the outlines of their
features, the shoulders of their coats. A murmur of talk swells
and subsides. Here at the school earlier in the day we have
each been given a slip of paper, and after marking it with a
pencil in a wooden booth, have dropped it into a black ballot-
box. The observance would have been the same had it been
a national event, but on this occasion we are electing from
amongst our neighbours representatives for the Rural District
and Parish Councils. After a time the doors open, and people

press out. Names and numbers are announced, and short speeches made. Discussing the result we linger a few moments, then leave for homes close at hand or for outlying farms and hamlets in the township.

Sometimes a gathering with different mien is to be seen in the village. A group of sombre-clad figures, still and quiet, shows up darkly against buildings and road. Their faces are set, the white collars of the men gleam, gloves are pulled on by the women. Soon the figures file into church or chapel; and after a while a procession forms in the street to follow behind the bier, heaped with flowers, up and over and down the hill.

Or again on a spring morning there is an emptiness in sequestered corners, and a few hurrying figures head towards an animated throng near the church. The women, some pinafored, most hatless, take up near-vantage points, and the men in working clothes stand aloof at a distance. A buzz of talk and laughter eddies round the market-place, children point and shout, and a car draws up with well-known faces self-consciously smiling from the windows. There is a glimpse of navy-blue, polished shoes, well-pressed trousers, and carnation buttonholes. Soon in a flurry of white a girl steps out from a beribboned car before the gaze of a hundred eyes. The party disappears, only to reappear later to the sound of pealing bells.

Away on the fellside those currents of human emotion, rising no farther than the smoke of fires floating above roof-tops, are dissipated in the clear air. The moor road, empty of traffic, ascends steeply towards the crest of the pass; a gate through the last wall clangs behind on the man-made land-scape of enclosed pastures; and the eye roams gratefully over the untrammelled moor. Scaling a hillside we reach a plateau on the summit of the fell that makes a background to our village. All is quiet. Such traces of man as there are fail to evoke any ripple of stress or disharmony: a sheep-fold, with earth beaten hard by trampling hoofs, is newly repaired, and

a long rampart of dark-hued gritstone has been disturbed here
and there in the past by the hewers of millstones for grinding
corn.   Southwards the plateau ends where green turf slopes
upwards against the sky.

Crossing to the verge we thread a way between tufts of
flowering rush and fescue grass; bright patches of sphagnum
moss mark the boggy runnels from hidden springs; and
between gnarled heather-stems lurk yellow and red freckled
bilberry plants bitten close by sheep.   Ewes, with heavy-
coated lambs grazing beside them, stamp their feet and gaze
at us haughtily, heads erect.   As on the approach to the brink
of a sea cliff, there is a feeling of expectancy.   Close your
eyes, let someone lead you forward, open them; and there
below you lies a great green valley.

See it on a midsummer day when the air is warm and the
wind a cool caress.   The sun burns, biting into rock and earth,
its heat radiated up again.   From the sky clouds thin as
carded wool cast down a delicate shade, and others more
bunched throw shadows as sinister as those of birds of prey
must seem to rabbit and vole.   Beyond the river winding down
the dale rise the hills, marbled and veined deep blue where
gills dent their sides.   Near us limestone headlands fall away
vertically at either hand, and a black-headed gull glides below
on its way from the tarn on the moor to the river.

It is a fit time of year for long contemplation on the hills;
for here from the scars of Ellerkin, 1,600 feet above sea level,
behind the village of Askrigg in Wensleydale, are to be seen
some fourteen miles of a northern dale.   The view is so
extensive that within the narrow limits of human vision we
cannot span the whole at once.   Perhaps a mural on a grand
scale could contain it, or two tremendous canvases hold the
upper dale with majestic hills and the lower with the long
limbs of the fells stretched out into the valley.

The frame is the Pennines; the outermost edge Baugh Fell,
Whernside, Penyghent, Buckden Pike, and Great and Little
Whernsides, and the inner edge our own nearer and less

The scars of Ellerkin

formidable hills: Lovely Seat, Widdale Fell, Dodd Fell, Wether Fell, Addlebrough, Penhill, and Nab End. Their sides sweep down to the river, sometimes flowing smoothly, sometimes darting in steps, sometimes billowing in rounded ridges. Stone walls cross the contours from summits to valley, in places appearing so close together that they resemble stiff tresses of hair. Neat blobs of trees, thickest in the gills, adorn rather than clothe the scene. Stoical, austere, these are exposed lands, washed clean by storm and whipped by the lashes of pitiless winds.

In the centre where the two pictures meet, and as if a little patch of white canvas had been left, the lake of Semerwater glints in the sun. . There is a vista of a secret dale flanked by Addlebrough and Crag, the eastern end of Wether Fell; and in the foreground a knoll, topped by a few trees silhouetted against the water, makes a miniature classic landscape. Nearer to us pale crescents of blue show up where the river Ure winds down the valley. Swelled by the Bain flowing from Semerwater and by becks tumbling down the hillsides, crossed near stony runs by bridges and stepping-stones, fingered here and there with bushes overhanging deep pools, it pursues a placid course onwards towards the falls at Aysgarth.

If we look carefully we can see many villages and hamlets, perched with their backs to the fells, or tucked between hillocks, or nestled on ridges. Our eyes turning westwards, glimpse in the far distance a haze of smoke that indicates the market town of Hawes, but only a knowledgable person can find Gayle at the foot of Sleddale and Burtersett below Wether Fell End. Bainbridge, closer at hand, its houses scattered yet sheltered, is clearly visible. Shifting our gaze eastwards, and following the south side of the dale, we mark Worton on a ridge above the river, and on a still higher ridge the chimneys of Thornton Rust. Four miles down dale is Aysgarth; and here in imagination we cross the bridge by the falls, for there are no more villages to be seen where the dale curves towards Penhill. We run our eyes up the north side, look in vain for

B

Carperby which is hidden by a slope of Nab End, pause for a moment at Woodhall and Nappa Scar immediately below us, and again at the hamlet of Newbiggin. Then with a slight twist of the head that almost completes this anticlockwise circle we reach the village of Askrigg. Wedged between hillocks it has squeezed out at either end, and seen in perspective, the medley of roofs resembles a dark grey starfish.

Even from here our village appears unlike any of the others we can see. They have a rural aspect, their houses a straggling haphazard placing, whilst our more imposing buildings are grouped closely together. Walls almost appear to touch in what we know is the main street, and individual houses can only be recognized with difficulty, except those whose upper storeys rise above their fellows. The church tower, visible over roofs at the lower end, is not the tower of a little church. It is a town that we are looking at, a town that by the processes of economic change has declined to the status of a village. Beyond, spaced along a curving belt of trees that marks the course of a beck, we can see three small mills, near the lower one two newer buildings, the grammar school and the railway station; and down by the river, half hidden in trees, a farmhouse, near which Fors Abbey, the forerunner of Jervaulx Abbey, was built in 1145.

Two divisions of land that are not the same in extent radiate from the village, the parish and the township. If we draw an imaginary line round the hill summits of the inner frame of the mural, except for an area containing Lunds and Hardraw out of sight beyond Lovely Seat, we should be defining the bounds of the original parish of Aysgarth. Here, before the year 1200, was plotted one of those huge lonely moorland parishes, the largest in Yorkshire, 81,033 acres in extent, that was comparable with Halifax, 75,000 acres, in the West Riding, or Kendale in the Lake District. Now, though still under Aysgarth, we have our own independent parish that includes the township of Askrigg, Low Abbotside, and part of Bainbridge township, and when in 1930 the benefices of Askrigg

Two aerial views of Askrigg. Both show the compact nature of the village which had many yards occupied by houses behind the present frontages in the street. In the top one a lane leads off to West Mill past the West Field with lynchets plainly visible. On the very top and showing up white near the centre is the new house built on the site of the Old Hall after the fire. On the bottom photograph may be seen two pairs of council houses on the left beyond the school built after the top photograph was taken.

and Stalling Busk were united, the district round Semerwater was drawn into our orbit.

The township is our most intimate division, more ancient in our case and more compact than that of the parish. Beginning with the first Anglo-Norse settlement, growing into the Manor of Askrigg, developing within it the Manor of Nappa and drawing in the Manor of Woodhall, it became in shape a rough parallelogram, 4,700 acres in extent, contained within natural boundaries: the river on the south, Ellerbeck on the east, Whita Gill Beck on the west, and on the north the watershed between Wensleydale and Swaledale. Newbiggin, Nappa Scar, and Woodhall lie within the bounds, outlying hamlets, part of the community.

Askrigg at the south-western corner of the parallelogram is as it were the old administrative centre of what is termed a nucleated village. Surrounding it are those early divisions the town's townfields, the East Field and the High Field, easily traceable from here as elliptical shapes, the West Field farthest away not so plain to see; all now divided by walls into small irregular plats. Part too of the territories of Askrigg was the Cow Pasture, a great area of rough land at the foot of the limestone slope below the moor; it too is carved up, but into large allotments; and on the flat land by the river, the Holmes, the old hay meadows.

Much of the moorland area, enclosed by a wire fence across peat hags and heathery summits, is familiar ground to farmers who possess sheep gates, to the gamekeeper, and indeed to us. If we look round we can see the boundary marks, the nearest Cranehow Knot Nick, a broad dip in the scars of Ellerkin, behind us the Greets where the millstones were hewed, the curracks out there on the moor. One called St Andrew's Cross is lost, and Windgate, that anciently meant wagon road, is out of sight at the summit of the pass. Nor is Summer Lodge Tarn, through which the boundary runs, visible. Conny Tommy, Tarn Currack, Cuddy Currack, lead across the watershed, 'as Heaven Water deals' as it used to be graciously

expressed.   There three miles away to the west is Blackstone
Edge, a millstone grit knoll, 1,900 feet high, from which moorland height we can look more easily into Swaledale than
Wensleydale.   From there to Stony Gill Head, the western
limit, we turn back and trace the trees lining Whita Gill past
the mills down to the river.   It would be a rough ride and a
hard walk to tour the whole of the bounds in one day.

Lying out here on the turf we are lulled into silent contemplation of the scene.   Enjoyment of the present over-
powers interest in the past.   Perhaps this modern aspect is all
that the day has to give.   We have to concentrate to picture
the dale even in the sixteenth century, up above Hawes thick
scrubby woods with lanes meandering through them, and
marshes where beck joins river.   We know only too well that
now we can drive speedily that way to Westmorland, or down
dale to the Plain of York, or over the passes north to Swaledale and south to Wharfedale.

View it again on a September morning before the sun has
risen, and a dim light creeps from the eastern sky over the chill
earth.   The dew, beading the vegetation of illimitable acres,
lies so heavy that from end to end the landscape is a limpid
grey-green.   Great funnels of cloud peel off Wether Fell; from
Semerwater mist is puffed up over the flanks of Addlebrough;
and Penhill is still folded in a vaporous shroud.   A dense white
mist floating in patches on the flat bottoms, gives the illusion
of a series of variously sized lakes, as if time had telescoped into
the aftermath of the Ice Age.   The river itself winds in violent
convolutions like the aimless drainage channel in the primitive
dale.   Aeons ago the hills were broader and loftier; their
summits now are worn flat almost down to the limestone—the
limestone itself embedded with the fossils of the shell-fish of
ancient seas.   The snouts of the scars jut into the valley over
soft shaly beds; and their long limbs are glacial drift left when
a million years ago glistening ice crept slowly out towards the
Plain.   Billowing down into the valley, they meet mounds of
stony debris left as the sediment of the waters of melting ice.

Our village has chosen to seek shelter between two of these hillocks.

Changing shade and tone every moment as the light grows stronger, tendrils of rose flood the eastern sky above a sheen of primrose, green, and violet. The last star that only a short while ago shimmered in the half-light has vanished. Suddenly a flush, barely discernible, suffuses Widdale Fell. The faint glow spreads across the hills and creeps lower and lower down their sides. Our shadows fall over the edge of the scar; and turning we see the sun like a magic eye looking over the hill to our left. The crow of a cock, a dog's bark, a curlew whistling—these and the slow stirring of sheep on the pasture under the crags are the first signs of life.

Six or seven thousand years ago man and beast with nerve alert and vigilant eye wandered into this wilderness, its atmosphere so easily recaptured in the pale light of early morning. There to the right on Stag's Fell about 5000 B.C. Mesolithic man hunted and left tiny flint chippings. To the left on Nab End perhaps 1000 B.C. Bronze Age man buried the cremated bones of an ancestor in the centre of a circle of stones; beyond Addlebrough are the remains of an Iron Age village, and in the pasture below the scar tumbledown huts of these people whom the Romans found here. By the shores of Semerwater, its waters no longer icily cold from a glacial birth, men lived in huts built on piles two or three centuries before Christ was

Late-type Bronze Age spear-head
found at Semerwater

born. We can hold in our hands a bronze spear-head that was lost then, and was found by a schoolboy two thousand years later under the pebbles of the beach. It is so beautiful that it must surely have been sought for then during many weary hours until hope of its recovery died away.

During these dimly sensed times cattle with huge horns bellowed down there by the river, and in a sand-bed at one of

those looping curves near Woodhall one died; and some
thousands of years later when we by chance dig up a thick
heavy horn we call the shaggy beast *Bos primigenius*. We
have this horn wrapped up in paper, for it is not a very
attractive relic.

Or we rub with our fingers the smooth tusk of a boar, that
is to be found with many others amongst the debris in the
Roman fort at Bainbridge.   There is the fort on a mound in
the centre of the valley, brought into use by foreign invaders
A.D. 70 or 80.   The square of ramparts, grass-covered, is
plainly visible from our vantage point.   Excavators in the past
and at the present day have probed and are still discovering the
lay-out, the story of fierce burnings, and the occupation by the
Auxiliaries during some three hundred years of uneasy hold.
To the right of the fort, flinging a way across Wether Fell, a
Roman road follows a straight line, defined now as it would
not be then by parallel walls.   There are other roads if we
choose to trace them that may well be Roman: one alongside
on our right, the fell pass, in fact, eventually crossing Swaledale to Teesdale, perhaps one below us leading down the north
side of Wensleydale over Scarth Nick to Catterick, and cer-
tainly one beyond Semerwater and over the Stake Pass running
to Ilkley in Wharfedale.

The light, losing colour as it strengthens, has spread from
the hilltops to the villages.   Walls of houses in Hawes, Gayle,
and Burtersett wink like clusters of tiny mirrors, barns flicker
against the fells, Bainbridge catches the first beams of the sun,
and soon a slanting ray glances across the houses of Askrigg.

Yet other folk came.   From over the North Sea, across the
Plain of York the Angles found a way into Wensleydale
between A.D. 600 and 800; and we surmise from place-name
derivations and an early system of agriculture visible in the
fields round the village that they penetrated as far as Askrigg.
It is light enough to see the ridges in the meadows, once the
long strips of their arable land that evolved as the centuries
passed into the three town fields.

PRE-HISTORIC SITES

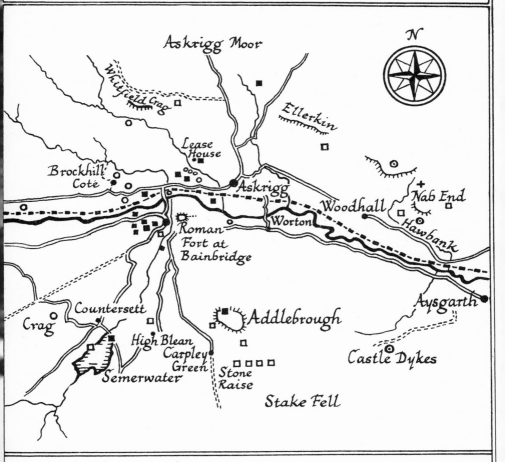

N

Askrigg Moor

Whitfield Crag

Ellerkin

Lease House

Brockhill Coté

Nab End

Askrigg

Woodhall

Worton

Hawbank

Roman Fort at Bainbridge

Aysgarth

Crag

Countersett

Addlebrough

Castle Dykes

High Blean

Carpley Green

Semerwater

Stone Raise

Stake Fell

+   Mesolithic

o   Bronze Age Barrows and Circles

□   Iron Age Farms and Villages

■   Undated

Scale of Miles

1   2   3   4

Then following these, Danes came up the dale, and in the tenth century converged in the centre with Norsemen from Ireland and Cumberland. In the valley, every place-name west of Askrigg except one is of Norse origin; but to the east a mixture of Scandinavian and Anglian names begins. Angles and Norsemen met and mingled in and about the village, and as occurred elsewhere adapted themselves to the same form of agriculture. Askrigg itself has a mixed origin, 'the ash-trees in the nook,' nook meaning a narrow corner of land or a narrow recess between mountains from the Old Norse *kriki*, and the Old English *æsc* meaning ash-tree. Other authorities make the name mean ash-ridge, but the first suits the early position of the village too well. Up the dale every hamlet, hillock, and gill was given a Norse name that appears a century or two later in definitions of boundaries: Lundesvik (Lunds Beck), Brendelecest, Stalunesbust, Crakdalewruthes (Brindley, Stalling Busk, and Cragdale): uncouth names, rough like the people who spoke them and untamed as the places they denoted, smoothed now by centuries of use.

As we look over the valley another day has begun, the same round of time with beginning and ending that to Mesolithic, Bronze Age, and Iron Age folk, Romans, Angles, and Norsemen seemed short or long according to their mood or the clemency of the weather. A wet mist coming as if from nowhere surrounds us, and swirling away reveals grey clouds that belie the earlier promise. Villages and barns have receded into their surroundings. It is six o'clock. People are pulling on their twentieth-century clothes. A plume of smoke spirals upwards to be joined by others as an hour passes.

These sensed activities make blurred images plain, as the written word of history begins to illumine the past. People press on; the canvas will soon become crowded. If we stand back, half close our eyes, and run them over the picture, the outline is almost blocked in, but a few more broad strokes are necessary to indicate the design.

Leaving the swirling mists of early morning let us take a last look on a hay-day in July. By midday the sun, high in the heavens, sends a white light beating over the valley, but it cannot bleach all colour from the gay scene. A vast transformation has taken place. The meadows, so recently a uniform sea of flowering grasses that half obscured the walls by their height, stand out patchily in shades of many yellows and greens. Some a soft lichen green are freshly strewn, others ochre mats of sere cut stems left from hay won, and yet others are chrome green with the aftermath, a forest of new sprouting blades. Down in the Holmes the meadows are spotted in rows with pikes of hay, and high up the hillsides diamond-shaped fields show up light against dark pastures.

It is too restless a sight to be beautiful, the tone values too sharp in contrast. Man pursuing his centuries-old round of husbandry is too evident. It is, however, a phase that lasts no longer than a few weeks in each year. For the rest of the seasons the pale umbers of late autumn, winter, and early spring, and the vivid greens of spring and summer, harmonize from river to summit.

Man-made the landscape is, not in the overwhelming sense of limitless cornfields in place of watery fenland, but observing a seemly balance between man and nature as we see it in the Lake District. There are those who, reflecting on Wordsworth, the Romantic Revival, and the modern influx of new settlers to Cumberland, aver that mountains, lakes, and park-like valleys reached a perfect poise in the eighteenth century. Here we may perhaps claim that the delicate adjustment still remains. The blemishes of railway and tar macadam roads, a few white asbestos roofs of barns, and two groups of council houses, not yet weathered, diminish into insignificance in the magnitude of the view. Newcomers there are, as there always have been since man peopled the valley; but saturation point has not been reached. They are absorbed, and those who are unfitted or unwilling to conform go.

Unconscious of taste in scenery, product of sophistication, Leland and Camden in the sixteenth century used words to describe the hills as, waste, solitary, unpleasant, unsightly, mute, and still.   They did not need to seek solitude, and they or their informants were, one thinks, overpowered by the sombre wilderness of the upper dale, and nervous of losing their way where lanes dwindled into vague tracks.   Above Hawes guides were still necessary to direct travellers through the forest in 1600 or thereabouts.   There was too much nature and too little man.

Two hundred years ago, although spectacular heights were lacking to attract the traveller in search of the picturesque, the waterfalls drew the few who scanned them with a fresh eye. Prosaic Dr Pococke, passing through on his travels in England in 1750, was fulsome in his praise; and outspoken Lord Torrington remarked: '. . . of Wensley Dale and its environs— a good guide-book might be publish'd'!   Twice, the second time with Mary, Wordsworth and his sister walked the length of the dale, and indeed stayed one night at Askrigg.   In 1799 Wordsworth in a letter to Coleridge described the idyllic approach to Mill Gill waterfall, but looking back from it he wrote: 'The steeple of Askrigg was not a quarter of a mile distant, but oh, how far we were from it.'

None of the early water-colourists came our way until Turner, exploring a countryside that deeply satisfied him, reached Wensleydale, and fused his own visions of wild grandeur with the comparatively mild scenes of Semerwater, and Aysgarth, Hardraw, and Mossdale Falls.   Unfortunately he left only sketches of Askrigg that are too slight to be of value.   In those days a large population, crowded in village and hamlet, pursuing in many cases wearisome industry with little reward, was perhaps out of balance with the scene.

As we look at it now the beauty of the dale depends on the tireless husbandry of man and the grazing of the herds he tends, and on the rock and soil that preserve the dominant form of graceful undulating lines of hill summits and the receding contours of rounded hillocks in the valley; and on a northern sky, rarely an overall blue, but dappled and burdened with cloud before rain, snow, or thunder. Perhaps when aeons hence the millstone grit has worn away to slip like crumbs of bread down moorland channels, the limestone flaked and scattered still farther down the screes, the shale-beds have ground away, and a small cap of hill like Addlebrough has disappeared, we shall view the scene with less satisfaction!

Down below a goods train, toy-like miniature that it looks, chugs up the long gradient from Aysgarth and disappears amongst the station buildings of Askrigg. A cream blob glides along what we know, but cannot see, is a road, apparently without motive power as if drawn by a magnet. Closer to the scar pygmy figures move from farmhouse to meadow. If we peer hard they resolve into four men, three women, and a child. In two fields tractors pulling strewers are driven by youths. They must be youths who race up and down at so swift a speed. The din of the tractors reaches us in waves of sound. Farther off near the village we can make out a horse dragging a mowing-machine round and round a lessening circle.

Some, though not all, of these people who thus trim the meadows bear centuries-old names. Men were already called Metcalfe, Pratt, Lambert, Thwaite, Terry, by 1300; and Kettlewell, Mason, Scarr, Storey, Foster, Coates, and Bell have been heard for at least three hundred and fifty years. Their ancestors built those houses, barns, and walls, tilled the fields, developed the breed of horned sheep, improved the standard of the cattle. Little wonder that they jealously hold to the land, though it has for four centuries changed hands, and still does, from lifetime to lifetime as one man by energy and astuteness gains advantage over another. That field is now so-and-so's, but someone else had it before him, and another will farm it after.

There is a unity between land and people. Even to us, not by any standard long sojourners in the village, a sense of security seems to flow from the grip of our feet on the soil, and still more strongly from the rock. The land provides for and nourishes us. If we wish to hew sandstone from the gill on our right to build a house, or grave peats to warm us from the moor behind, we may do so. These resources belong to the inhabitants by right of ownership of a dwelling-house in the township. We do not, nowadays, take full advantage of our heritage; stone is only seldom wanted for house or barn; cement and coal are brought in sacks to the door. But the soil is precious, as is every blade of grass made into hay down there in the meadows. All the land we see from hilltop to valley bottom is utilized for farming, the abiding pursuit.

This close communion between man and nature that we hold in common with other outposts deep in the valleys and moorlands of Britain is, in fact, our contribution to modern life. No great men or women, philosophers, poets, artists, inventors, or politicians were born in or indeed anywhere near our village. We have to go back many centuries and farther down the dale to find Miles Coverdale, Archbishop Thoresby, or a chancellor and an archbishop amongst the Scropes of Bolton and Masham. Our role has neither heights of achievement nor depths of ignominy, but is a decent mean. We provide a stock disciplined by its surroundings and a continuity of tradition that leaven the artificial and give stability to change. Both render less acute the tearing of man from the earth.

We could write the story of our village viewing it from here. But lest it become too impersonal, too removed from 'those currents of human emotion' we will go down to the market-place, mingle with the throng, and recapture as best we may historic memories.

Bronze Age arrow-head found
behind Stackhill House

The West End

II

A MORNING IN THE STREET

CURVING and dipping between walled pastures and meadows the moor road sweeps down to the village: a last level stretch, four sentinel larch trees, a precipitous descent, and below, on either hand, houses stand firm against a steep hillside. Here is a moorland approach, a transference of vision from open pasture to clustered habitation, a shock that may be experienced from many other terraces of the Pennines; yet surely few can offer a more sudden change or a more enchanting vista than this at Askrigg Town Head.

At the foot of the hill the high road that for twelve miles has run along the northern slopes of the valley from Leyburn, joins in on the left, and enclosed by buildings takes a sharp

PLAN OF ASKRIGG

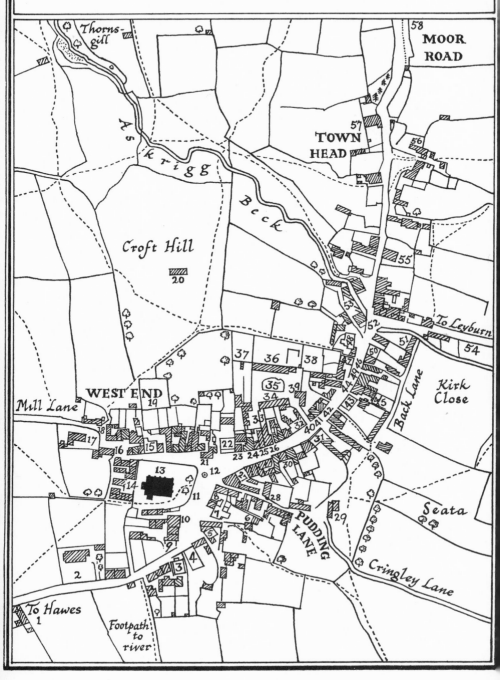

(For general reference)

1. Lowlands Farm.
2. Vicarage.
3. Methodist Chapel.
4. Temperance Hall.
5. Solicitor's house (early 19 cent.). Handley's coachbuilders (late 19 cent.).
6. Dairy.
7. Doctor's house.
8. Samuel Sykes's shop (19 cent.). Temperance Hotel.
9. Red Lion (18 cent.). Railway Hotel (19 cent.).
10. Simpson Little's forge (19 cent.).
11. Site of Toll Booth.
12. Market Square and Cross.
13. Church.
14. Hearse House (disused).
15. West End House (Scrope's house).
16. Firby's schoolhouse (19 cent.).
17. Elementary school.
18. Formerly curate's house.
19. Old Hall garden.
20. Summer House (18 cent.), now a barn.
21. Formerly Skidmore's shop. Newsagent's shop.
22. Site of Old Hall.
23. Joseph Cooper's shop (early 19 cent.). Aaron Knagg's shop (late 19 cent.). Grocer's shop.
24. Manor House.⎫ John Pratt's
25. Kings Arms ⎬ house
    Hotel. ⎭ (18 cent.).
26. Conservative Club.
27. Sign of King's Head (17 cent.). Agnes Hastwell's house (18 cent.). Grocer's shop.

28. Well in Pudding Lane.
29. Smithy.
30. Metcalfe property (18 cent.).
31. Winnville.
32. Post Office.
33. Assembly Rooms (19 cent.), with brewery adjoining.
34. Wool room, now a garage.
35. Dog kennels, now a garden.
36. John Pratt's stables (18 cent.).
37. Lodge garden.
38. Walled gardens.
39. Garage.
40. Robinson's Gateways.
41. Fancy goods' shop.
42. Shoe shop.
43. Formerly New Inn, later Queen's Arms.
44. Butcher's shop.
45. Butcher's shop.
46. Mark Bett's lodging-house (19 cent.).
47. Formerly George Inn.
48. Formerly the Mare Phoenix, the Hare and Hounds, the Blacksmith's Arms, now the Crown Inn.
49. Elm Hill.
50. John Bowman, surgeon's house (19 cent.).
51. Grenada Hall.
52. High Bridge.
53. Brewery (19 cent.), haulage contractor's garage.
54. The Gate.
55. Methodist Chapel.
56. The authors' cottage.
57. Formerly Faith and Jane Cloughton's house.
58. Formerly the pound, now the reservoir.

bend into the main street. Mounting Elm Hill, a bridge from hillock to hillock between which as we noted the village is squeezed, it curves onwards, hemmed in by stone houses, towards the market-place. A side-turning on the right leads to the West End; a narrow alley, Pudding Lane, slips off to the left, and the road continues steeply downhill, round a corner and up the dale.

The market-place is the hub of our village world. It is not a large area and of no particular shape, yet houses surround it pleasantly in the natural way that is the product of gradual growth. Here is the church behind a stout wall, hidden in summer by leafy sycamores; and the cross with a base of five high steps on a wide border of cobble-stones. Here is our shopping centre: two grocers that combine individually green-grocery and cattle food, and jutting out a newspaper and fancy goods shop. Here are the Methodist chapel and the Temperance Hall, the Kings Arms and the Temperance Hotel, but not the Old Hall that for three centuries until 1935 when it was burned down had lent a richness of expression to the scene. Here we hold our celebrations or annual events, pageants and fêtes, band performances and children's sports. Here our few daily buses stop and those for summer outings collect their passengers. None of these is new: there was a church on the same site seven centuries ago, and shops, and an inn known by 'the Signe of the King's Head' before 1700, and as far back as written word records, rejoicings, plays, and sports have been enacted there, and transport of many kinds has halted for a space.

Sheltered from the west wind under the churchyard wall are two summer seats worn smooth by constant use. In the evening they become a meeting-place for the men, the older ones sitting, their pipes alight, the younger ones standing or leaning against the wall, and in the day-time they are occupied by visitors, or a retired mason, a carpenter, or a schoolmaster on holiday at his native village. But in the early hours of a September morning no one is astir;

and from them we may watch the first activities of the day.

There is a hushed stillness round about the market-place. On either side of the road that gleams blue-black, damp with dew, buildings rise abruptly from darkened pavements, and as the light strengthens the stone-work shows up pallid, clear. Their upper windows wide open as if gasping for breath, the houses seem charged with life from their sleeping occupants: gaunt three-storeyed houses, those in the main street lined and creased by age and the stress of living, the sash windows a little askew, the courses not so even as when they were raised stone by stone in the eighteenth century. Their style over-powers that of the dated carved doorways a few of which remain from the previous century, and has so impressed itself on the many buildings of the nineteenth that it is predominant. Burdened with the joys and sorrows of generations of men, they seem temporarily loaned to and not owned by those who will shortly be stirring in them, pursuing their tasks and pleasures, adding their impress by the measure of their sojourn.

The houses are aloof, pride and independence written on their features, and it is they that have moulded the coun-tenance of the village. To some, Askrigg has not altogether a prepossessing face, a shade too stern, lacking the colourful adornment of gardens or that most admired of rural charms a green; yet, more desirable than these, it has character. It bears the imprint of men's skill, of their taste, of constant care, and is the product of environment, and of both farming and industrial growth. The village reflects the rigours of the climate consequent on a situation 700 to 800 feet above sea level, and at the foot of Ellerkin clings to the vast setting with a fitting grace.

It is five o'clock. There was a time when most of the inhabitants would have been up by now; but except for a few early risers, such as the farmers' families in hay-time and the poultry farmer who enjoys an early start, people are still

c

asleep.   Centuries ago those bound for distant places, perhaps
Richmond or Bedale twenty miles away, rose early in order
to transact business there in the forenoon.   Miners set out
along fellside tracks in the half-light or in the dark of winter
days; hay-makers began mowing at two or three in the
morning, and this century the early trains carrying away
milk dictated the time of the beginning of the working day.
Then, we should soon have been hearing the grind of wheels
and the clip-clop of hoofs, and sometimes the rat-a-tat of a
galloping horse urged on by a late-comer, as milk-floats were
driven to the station.   Cheating the day with artificial light
and daylight saving, and adjusting ourselves to the effect of
motor transport and the set hours of factory life that spread
to the country, we incline to keep a stereotyped day alike in
winter and summer.

At six o'clock the village is slowly coming to life, like an
animal uncurling itself after a long rest.   On the cobble-stones
by the cross are a milk lorry, a builder's van, and a taxi: that
they have been there since yesterday is evident by their misted
windows not yet freed from the damp chill of the night air.
Smoke from a high chimney unfurls over the roof-tops; and
soon a second fire is lit at the West End.   No other movement
is visible; for many of the kitchens where breakfast is being
prepared are at the backs of the houses.   Without the warning
sound of approaching footsteps a farmer smoking a glowing
cigarette emerges from a yard, and walks briskly up the street
in the direction of his cow-byre; shortly afterwards a woman
comes out from a passage way, and begins to sweep in front
of one of the grocers' shops; and a distant drone grows louder
as a car swerves round the corner by the Temperance Hall.
The silence of the night is relinquishing its hold as the companionable warmth and noise of the day draw near.

After seven o'clock more people bestir themselves, curtains
are drawn back; and because it is a Saturday morning a few
dustbins have been carried to the edge of the pavement, a
commonplace sight yet a recent enough innovation for us to

view it with satisfaction. A quarryman and a boy wait for a lift to work seven miles away, and a second farmer wheeling a bicycle goes off in the same direction as the first; meanwhile a board advertising ice-cream has been brought out and placed near a shop window. Rattling with empty churns a lorry speeds down the hill. It is the first of four that collect milk up and down the dale as far afield as the Westmorland border, and take the loads to Leyburn from where the milk is sent by train to London. The one on the cobble-stones soon to be driven off on its local round belongs to our own dairy situated in a yard off the lower end of the market-place. A door opens in one of the houses in the main street, to be pulled to by a postman who, setting his cap at a jaunty angle, strides up to the post office on the bend of Elm Hill. Two more postmen join him; and promptly at half-past seven a small red van pulls up, a blue-clad figure dismounts, and a mail-bag is dragged across the pavement. Before the van leaves for the upper dale ten minutes later the taxi starts off, a butcher's boy in a striped coat rides up on his motor-bicycle, and an electrician, who has come from Bainbridge a mile away, walks steadily along the middle of the road.

By this time several thresholds and even areas of pavement have been well scrubbed, door-handles and brass knockers polished, a box of groceries delivered, a shop window re-arranged, and a few housewives, clad in overalls and head-scarves, have looked out before beginning the work of the day. Here there is no concerted opening of shops at a set time. A figure appears from the side road that leads to the West End. He glides suddenly into the scene from the corner of the churchyard wall, his grey clothes merging into a background of stone house and cobble-stones, and pushing open a shop door wide enough to sidle past, after a pause he comes out thrusting change into a trouser pocket. The proprietor of the Kings Arms stops sweeping in front of the hotel entrance to wave cheerily to a passer-by. Cocks crow, starlings twitter; and closer at hand a whistling boy dressed in a bright fair-isle pullover and flannel trousers swings up the street to the garage in a yard beyond the post office.

Eight strokes sound from the church clock. Though no one as yet is in a hurry, increasing numbers of people are passing to and fro; the district nurse in uniform goes for her car, the caretaker crosses to the Conservative Club, men who work at the mill for grinding cattle food turn up Pudding Lane. A roadman and his wife, smartly dressed, come out to a large waiting taxi; a wedding, we surmise, and catch a little of their infectious excitement before they drive off in chauffeured ease. Others in normal guise and with more solemn tread enter the market-place: the dairy manager, hand in jacket pocket, turns into a yard whose narrow entrance will soon be negotiated by the milk lorry; a dairy worker clanks after him in clogs—the first we have heard, though not so long ago they were the usual footwear, and the delight of children who clattered along passages between the houses, from which testy but harmless characters rushed out to threaten them. In contrast a soft-footed slouching figure, labourer, stone-waller, rabbit-catcher, handyman skilled at many jobs, passes along with a bag of mushrooms in his hand.

There is by now a sense of urgency in the air. The first train of the day is coming up the dale, and a woman who works in a solicitor's office at Hawes walks down to catch it; and soon a girl, a bank clerk, runs after her. A taxi follows; a hoarse whistle sounds; and many minutes later we still hear the chuffing engine far away up the valley. Meanwhile the postmen have started out with the morning mail; two leave for the outlying parts round Semerwater and for Bainbridge, and one with a full bag and a sack of parcels zigzags down the street. The papers brought from Northallerton by a wholesale distributor in a grey brake arrive; and it is not long before the newsagent fills a rack by his door and is off on his round with a bundle tucked under an arm.

Like a picture in which form and colour have built up the climax of the design, or as the separate themes of a sonata mingle in the crescendo of the third movement, the half-hour before the clock strikes nine is the culmination of activities in a morning in the street. The milk lorries return, the dust-bin van backs up a lane, others belonging to haulage con-tractors start out, and some with Calor Gas, Bibby's, and Hawes Mineral Waters Company printed on them pass through. The roadman who went up with a brush and shovel over his shoulder an hour ago returns, and the dairyman in clogs goes back home. There is a medley of sight and sound of which we who live up the moor road are seldom aware. A tractor carrying milk churns appears; a farmer with back-can and pail plods along; the builder cycles off to feed his hens; the decorator in a white apron, grasping a tin of paint, sets out; housewives, baskets slung over their arms, cross to the shops; visitors hasten before breakfast to buy a daily paper; and men at intervals visit the butchers' shops at the top of Elm Hill: the black-smith, the gamekeeper, the policeman, mostly men, though the station-master's wife is going that way, and very shortly we too shall be joining them. Four girls, hair flying, race up and down and round and round on red bicycles, little boys shout, and a dog chases a smoky-grey cat out of the passage by the Temperance Hotel.

At nine o'clock the bus for down the dale, already half full, draws up by the grocer's shop, and stopping for five passengers to board it, at once moves off. It is the signal for the orderly and less frenzied routine of the day to begin; and as if in keeping men and women linger for a chat, and a farmer standing up in a low cart pulled by a pony, a little girl beside him, drives at a leisurely pace along the West End. The houses have drawn into themselves as their occupants claim them during the waking hours.

No one witnessing all this would think that the place, together with others, is suffering from the atrophy usually associated nowadays with village life. But the morning has only just begun. As it advances there is little to note. The doctor driving from Aysgarth arrives in his car. On five days of the week the children will have already gone to school; on Tuesdays and Fridays, market-days at Hawes and Leyburn, cars and cattle lorries lend a temporary bustle; and on Wednesdays the women hasten to the fishmonger's van that comes from Hawes and the greengrocer's cart from Aysgarth. By afternoon a siesta, almost as heavy on warm days as that in far hotter climates, settles over the street, and not until four or five o'clock does it lift when the children coming home from school play round the cross, and the bread and cake van arriving from Skipton, thirty miles distant, causes a last bout of shopping. Work ends for the men; and the four early evening buses and trains round off the day.

There have seemed many people abroad; yet muster us all in the township, men, women, and children, and we number 443; count up the houses and they total some 150. Then turn back to 1690 when there were 133 houses, or consider the year 1801 when 761 people lived in 200. Now, each of thirty-six houses is occupied by one person. In those days buildings were divided into two, three, or four dwellings; and behind these bland façades cottages crammed themselves at all angles in cobbled yards. Echoing once with the shouts of children, the gossip of women, the sounds of scrubbing, swilling, the clatter of pails and clogs, most of them, used as outbuildings, still remain; their windows like sightless eyes, the rooms hollow, heavy with silence, grass and weeds sprouting between the paving by the doors.

In 1609 a witness in a lawsuit said of Wensleydale that he 'knoweth of his own memory that the people are more populous than in times past it hath beene'; and if we plot a graph of births and deaths taken year by year from the parish registers the result shows a gradual rise at the end of the seventeenth century, onwards from 1717 a steady mean with the peak from 1760 to 1800, and a slow fall throughout the reign of Victoria. We have to accept the fact that we are diminished in numbers and that if the ability to support a large population is our test then undoubtedly the eighteenth century marks our heyday.

The street

Nor have we appeared to lack a variety of occupations, yet almost all of us are or have been connected with farming in one way and another, including many of the forty-eight husbands and wives, widows, and spinsters living in well-earned retirement. Until towards the end of the sixteenth century, whilst arable cultivation lasted, we lived on subsistence farming, oats, rye, barley, peas, probably our cereal crops. When ploughing ceased we had our stock, cheese and butter, lead, and stockings to barter for grain. Millers ground corn at West Mill and at little mills in every hamlet up and down the dale. Our tanners made leather, our cordwainers footwear, our tailors clothes. We brewed our own ale, and oatcake was stored in every farm kitchen. Masons brought stone from the hillsides and built houses roofed with ling by the thatchers. Glaziers melted lead into strips to fashion our windows, as later carpenters pieced together wooden frames. The cooper, the weaver, the clock-maker, all had workshops among these clustered houses. Hand-knitting, together with dyeing, was the main trade, and in addition lead and coal were mined on the fells. A cotton mill and a worsted mill in turn flourished and declined.

Besides these employments by which he lived, every man assumed a measure of responsibility for the government of the village. Until the seventeenth century, administration for want of evidence is clouded in obscurity. In Norman times and the Middle Ages the land remained outside the great lordship of Middleham on the opposite side of the valley, and was not in the lordship of the Scropes that adjoined on the east, nor in the forest that marched closely with our western bounds. Askrigg was isolated in the midst of these, a place of divided ownership for almost three hundred years, shared between the FitzHughs of Ravensworth Castle and the Scropes of Bolton. In early days the manorial courts of the Fitz-Hughs, the largest holders of land in the village, regulated the cultivation of the land and the affairs of the inhabitants; but Askrigg had no resident lord, and from the early seventeenth century was a place of many owners. Herein lie the main roots of our story.

The granting of a market charter in 1587 did not mean that we became a corporate body; 'Neither Magistrate nor Mayor, Ever were elected there,' wrote Drunken Barnaby in 1638; instead, each year we nominated the Four Men as trustees of the market tolls. We had the proper complement of parish officers, whose duties had grown from the organization of the first settlement. From time out of mind we elected a petty constable and churchwardens, and after the passing of Tudor laws we chose surveyors of the highways and overseers of the poor. Askrigg indeed was an independent body, and can show a long story of self-government.

We paid subsidies and taxes to the king, tithes to a Cambridge college, and church and local rates. We conducted protracted lawsuits, and sometimes were brought up for misdeeds at Quarter Sessions or Church Courts. In common with the Scandinavian settlement of northern England we were not serfs under feudal tenure, but free men discharging customary boons and services and paying money rents. We are free men and women still, though it is an independence of mind rather than an independent local government in which we rejoice.

Linked inseparably with national affairs certain events stand out in our story: the dissolution of the monasteries that led to changing landlords, the rise and fall of families, the Metcalfes of Nappa Hall, the Thorntons of Askrigg, the Smiths of Camshouse; the grant of the market charter, and the founding of the grammar school in 1601; the disturbances of wars, Scots raids, the Civil War, the '45 Rebellion, the establishment of a rival market at Hawes in 1700; the coming of the turnpike road in 1751 and the railway in 1877, of motor transport in this century, and above all the Industrial Revolution at the end of the eighteenth century.

Limitations inherent in remoteness, not so important in earlier days of general bad roads; our geological structure that meant lack of the kind of mineral wealth necessary to a machine age and water too harsh for the scouring of cloth; and invention and economic change brought upon us hardship and decline. Compare the ancient parishes of Aysgarth and Halifax now to mark the different development of one moorland area and another, the one divided into four parishes, the other a rural deanery with forty-seven.

As we sit on the seat in the market-place this mid-twentieth-century morning, the newsagent brings us our papers. They seem small; but they are larger than the *York Courant* and the *Newcastle Journal* that we might have been reading had we afforded a copy or indeed been literate two hundred years ago. We scan the columns with minds half averted from the woes they reveal. Yet because of world shortages that make up a large part of this news our farming flourishes. If we are a diminished community, we are encouraged to wrench all that we can from the land to help feed our fellows; and in consequence we prosper.

Askrigg from the east

III

THE VILLAGE AT THE EDGE
OF THE FOREST

'SMALL THINGS and tiny parishes slipping more easily through the nooks and crannies of time sink deeper into oblivion,' wrote Reginald Hine, historian of Hertfordshire; and indeed to piece together the sequence of phases that makes up the story of a small remote village like ours we have to dig deep. The clues exist in three sets of evidence: the first of national fame, of kings, great nobles, their charters, decrees, state papers, laws, commissions, taxations, the whole accumulation of the archives of the past; the second of spiritual powers, of prelates, clergy, their instructions, visitations, orders; and the third so much smaller and more insignificant but easier to lay hands on, that of our own village matters, parish registers, township and poor-rate books, ledgers, old newspapers, deeds of property, and not least the memory of men and women:

all three are essential to our project. Yet when written evidence begins, not in the annals of Roman historians or the chronicles of the Anglo-Saxons, but for us in 1086 in Domesday Book, only the first exists.

It is as though English history lies like an amorphous vapour stretched up the centre of the country, filling the Plain of York—symbol here of the outer world—from which wraiths float sinuously up the western dales of north Yorkshire, thinning out and thinning out until the merest wisps link us with the main body. We cannot pick here and there from the central mass to illustrate our theme, though it is true we can infer from the general evidence. Every wisp that reaches us is invaluable. That we were joined closest in that vivid, cruel, beautiful, barbaric time of medieval England is the more tantalizing, for it is when documents were rare that the clues would have been most rich. So the shreds have to be supplemented by what is seen, or sometimes sensed, in the meadows and pastures, lanes, roads, and buildings, wherever there are traces of the work of man.

Walking the footpaths in the fields of the village is for us a winter pleasure; our enjoyment is attuned to a different mood from that which craves the exhilaration or the solace of the moor. In all directions there are ways that if followed lead to a hamlet fast on a hillside, or to a farm with its back to rough pastures, or merely to barns in outlying meadows. Some are trodden deep, the ground bare and hard, whilst others, faint and overgrown, are not easy to find. Leading from stile to stile in the walls, across steep hillsides or over undulating meadows, they meander in a series of twists and curves as if plotted by a small animal running nose to ground. Only here and there in the low-lying land a much-used path paved with flags follows a straight line. How seldom country people take an idle walk along them! Nor are they fashioned for lovers, for where all is grass land single file is the rule. They are made over countless years by the tread of man pursuing an easy course over hummocky land, man often carrying heavy loads, a back-can filled with milk, a burden of hay, a bundle of sticks.   They are for use rather than a purposeless stroll.

The fields are companionable.   Perhaps in the distance a farmer unloading muck from the trailer of his tractor leaves small heaps to dot the side of a hillock.   These, and a larger conical mound outside a barn telling of cows snug beyond the closed door, are the darkest notes in a dun landscape.   Sheep, brought from the moor because snow threatens, nuzzle at the white covering, and press down to minute green tufts of grass between the withered shoots.   The land is tamed, settled, breathing assurance that nature is under man's dominion, harnessed to fulfill his wants.   The warmth of humanity enfolds us: fields, houses, and people—blood, bone, and muscle, integral parts of a living organism.

Some years ago one clear sparkling Sunday when the snow-drops blossoming under the tall sycamores had drawn us to Nappa Hall, we returned through the East Field on a foot-path that leads directly to the village.   As we approached habitation where the meadows swept onwards to lap up against the backs of houses and the walls of crofts and gardens, a sense of great age rising like a swift current encompassed us, and after a faint brief ecstasy faded away.   Such a feeling can assail the mind amongst the debris of Iron Age huts and their square, walled fields high up on the hills, and it teases the imagination by its dim apprehension of circumstances far removed from present experience.   Small or great ruins may be thus haunted, perhaps sensed by a beholder sympathetic to their character.

A few years later we became conscious of and mapped out the terraces that formed the arable strips of early cultivation, and that, grassed over now, cover the East Field.   Then with a new awareness we saw the meadows peopled as they were once with folk bent over their ploughs, toiling with a stony soil, and battling against an inclement climate.   Somewhere at this east end of the village man made his first clearing that came to be called Askrigg.

Lest we be thought too unscientific there is other evidence. The level stretch of main road that runs towards the houses is called The Gate, and the sheltering hillock near by is Seata, both Norse words meaning respectively road and shieling; and in this nook alongside The Gate at the foot of Seata runs a quiet stream.   Here too are Cross Well and Kirk Close.   The wishing-well, telling of early superstition, is now overgrown, but its waters within living memory were thought to have healing properties for sore eyes; and that a preaching cross or a Saxon church stood in Kirk Close may be more than tradition, for there was once a building at this end of the village called St Oswald's Cross.

It is disconcerting to us who incline to set apart the dales as purely pastoral country, almost biblical in antiquity, to picture patches of arable land where now all is grass.   But so it was, that men with primitive ploughs pulled by oxen scratched furrows in a black soil.   They pursued their own form of agriculture that divided two or three large fields into narrow strips allotted to each man, a system that was common to many parts of England from the seventh until the end of the eighteenth century.   Both men and oxen dwelt in wooden cruck-built houses with ling-thatched roofs.   As time went by these dwellings, set in crofts, spread along what we now know as the main street, and more ground, hedged about with wooden fences, was cleared to support a slowly increasing population.   The East Field, the High Field, and the West Field came into being; yet they were small in extent compared with the pastures for sheep and cattle that stretched far and wide over the hillsides.

Here, in 1066 when yet another invader had stormed the country, five or six tough hard-headed Anglo-Norse families were living in the midst of a wolf-haunted forest.   They dwelt not in isolation but with other small villages near by, and not as unknown pioneers, for their territory was a part of the scattered and extensive lands of an English thane named Archil in the wapontake of Hang West.   Thirty or forty miles away in

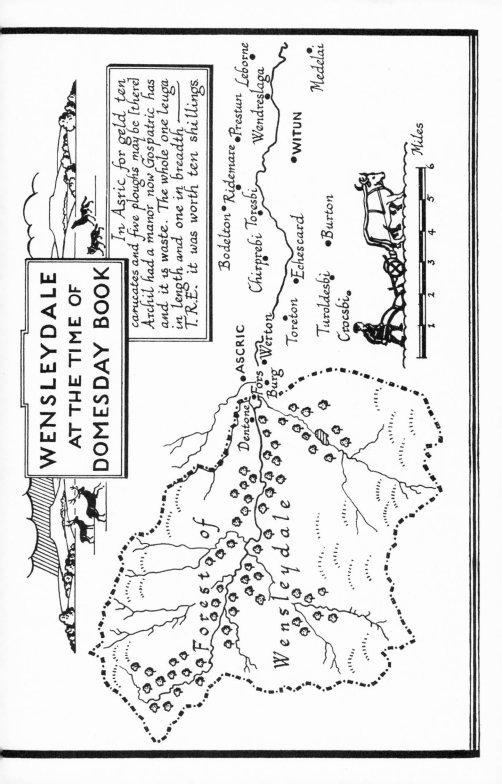

WENSLEYDALE
AT THE TIME OF
DOMESDAY BOOK

In Asric for geld ten carucates and five ploughs may be [there] Archil had a manor now Gospatric has and it is waste. The whole one leuga in length and one in breadth T.R.E. it was worth ten shillings.

Forest of

Wensleydale

Dentone
Fors
Burg
Werton
• ASCRIC

Bodelton • Ridemare • Prestun • Leborne
Chirprebi Toresbi • Wendreslaga
Toreton • Echescard • WITUN
Turoldesbi • Burton
Crocsbi

Medelai

Miles

1 2 3 4 5 6

the Plain complete and terrible devastation was soon to be wreaked by the armies of William the Conqueror. Archil with the northern earls led attacks on York, and gave his son Gospatric as hostage to the Normans. The army penetrated into the dale, and with burnings and slaughter destroyed crops and cattle. Much was laid waste, and the defenders vanquished; life faltered in the valley, and families for long struggled for survival.

Twenty years later the men of Askrigg journeyed to a centre near Northallerton, to render an account of their village to William's officials; and eventually his clerks set down an entry in the survey that, because it was as mysterious and over-whelming as its name implies, became known as Domesday Book. From it we learn that Askrigg was part of the 'Land of Earl Alan' and that Archil's son, Gospatric, held the manor as tenant. For purposes of taxation the land was rated at ten carucates (a thousand acres) most of which was rough pasture. Five ploughs were mentioned, though since the burning and pillage it was unlikely that there were any oxen to draw them. The manor was described as a leuga (a mile and a half) in length and breadth, and in the time of King Edward the Confessor it had been worth ten shillings.

Apart from three small places, Burg, Fors, and Dentone (a lost settlement in the meadows called Ingleby Leas), all a little farther up the dale, we were the last outpost in Wensley-dale, as Reeth was the last in Swaledale and Hubberholme, half a carucate, the last in Wharfedale. Only the Norse seters lay beyond. Bainbridge did not exist, nor did Hawes, that is first mentioned as 'le Thouse' in a monastic agreement of 1307. In comparison with other dales villages whose average number of carucates at a rough estimate was six, Askrigg was large, though of less monetary value than some. East Witton, with four berewicks, Thoresby, West Witton, and two Wensleys, was the most important place in the dale, its former valuation of four pounds reduced to twenty shillings.

Parcelling out the country amongst his nobles William the

Conqueror had given these dales, together with other extensive lands in far-apart counties, to Earl Alan, Alan Rufus as he is named, member of the ducal house of Brittany, son of Count Eudo de Ponthiévre.   He in turn granted property to relatives: Ribald, a bastard brother, was established at Middleham, and Bodin, another bastard brother, besides other lands, was given Worton and Fors near Askrigg.   In time the whole estate became known as the Honour of Richmond or the Honour of Brittany, so closely were its owners bound to foreign soil.   We were indeed in the lands of the Normans with Richmond in Swaledale the headquarters, its castle and all that it stood for a bulwark in the turbulent north.   From a charter it is known that by 1130 these parts were called Richmondshire.   The first designs in a new pattern of life were being laid down.

That some of these great men, Earl Alan and Earl Conan, who built Richmond Castle, came to Wensleydale, there is no doubt.   They came for two purposes, to encourage the founding of a religious house and to hunt in the forest; and though both forest and abbey are outside the main theme of our story, they are a very close background and need to be painted in.

It was Bodin who, in his old age retiring to St Mary's Abbey, York, 'desirous to serve God and quit the world,' left his property to Bardulf, whose son Acaris gave his land at Fors, Worton, and Brough to Peter de Quinciaco and other monks, foreigners from Savigny.   In 1145 Earl Alan with his knights was present when the first wooden building, Fors Abbey, was erected near the river a mile west of Askrigg.   That the site was here is proved in the Byland cartulary that says 'where now is Dale Grange': and Dale Grange it is still called.

The story of the monks' losing struggle in this too friendless place is well known.   Eleven years later they moved to Jervaulx, but not before their abbey had been added to the list of Cistercian houses under its Latin name Jorvallis.   Further lavish grants were made them: common of pasture, liberty to

D

fell timber for houses, to mine lead and iron, to take the flesh
of deer worried by wolves. Their properties, eventually
scattered over the whole of the upper dale, became by arrangement with succeeding lords concentrated on the north side of
the river, 'the abbot's side of Yore'—Abbotside that adjoins
Askrigg township on the west.

Not only were the monks by this ardent medieval piety
given a footing in the upper dale but the Normans' love of
hunting set it apart as a forest for the preservation of deer.
Unlike Galtres and Pickering elsewhere in Yorkshire, that
were royal forests, this was a free chase of the lords of Richmond, though because of their uneasy loyalties to the kings of
England and France it often came into the possession of the
Crown. Forest land was gradually settled into parks round
Middleham, Bishopdale Chase with West Burton as headquarters, Woodhall Park in Askrigg township, and the Forest
of Bainbridge or Wensleydale. The latter concerns us most.
It stretched from Meerbeck, less than a mile from our western
boundary, on the other side of the river from the Bain,
and so up the whole of the dale on both sides of the Ure as
far as the borders of Westmorland, a length of thirteen miles.
So we became a village at the edge of the forest.

Then, in the second half of the twelfth century, after the
monks had left for Jervaulx, another innovation startled the
men of Askrigg. Robert, son of Ralph, the reputed builder
of Middleham Castle, received the forestry of Wensleydale
from Earl Conan, and established a village a mile away at the
other side of the Ure, not far from the Roman fort and near
'Bein bridge.' Bainbridge became the home of twelve foresters,
and was developed as the centre for a vast farm with as many
as two thousand cattle going out to feed in the forest. In the
Barons' War in John's reign some of the houses were burnt
down, probably by one of the lawless bands that were only
too common at the time; and because this new village
threatened their privileges, in 1218 the monks bargained that
only those destroyed should be rebuilt. But ten years later

there were twenty-nine houses, described as houses with chimneys (doubtless merely holes in the roofs), to distinguish them as fit for human beings.

When the lands of Peter of Savoy, who had been granted the Honour of Richmond by Henry III, were valued in 1280 some years after his death, Bainbridge with thirteen farms in the forest was a valuable property worth £213 7s. 4d. compared with the 'Borough of Rychemunde with the demesnes' worth £44 4s. It is described as having a capital messuage, thirty-four acres of arable land, two hundred acres of meadow, a water mill, an oven, and a brewery—an early picture of a dales' village.

How beautiful Wensleydale must have looked from the scars of Ellerkin in the springs and autumns of the thirteenth century!

> The painted flowres, the trees upshooting hye,
> The dales for shade, the hills for breathing space,
> The trembling groves, the christall running bye.

Spenser evokes an era before man had felled and burned and wrenched and levelled. It is a true picture if we think of the forest in this high dale with the beech, oak, and ash not as trees large enough to furnish beams for a castle but of medium size and gnarled growth, with alder and willow in the swamps, scrub of juniper, thorn, and holly spreading over bracken-covered knolls, rock-strewn greensward, heaths, and furzy commons: the barren lands and the woodlands intermingled.

Forest land, lost to us, was ever present to medieval men. In many Yorkshire valleys it was said of those times that squirrels could spring from dale head to dale foot without touching ground. Butterflies and moths fluttered and sank to rest in sunlit glades, thousands of birds nested in their green cradles, eagles soared over their eyries on the scars, and when the grass was 'high and well waxen,' the deer and cattle roamed the high pastures of the mountains. But there were the dark days when snow eased the burden of heavy amber skies, or spears of rain pierced every secret dell, until the paths became blurred and misshapen and the glades by the river treacherous bogs; and crops failed, men and beasts starved, and wolves, made bold by hunger, howled near the villages.

Sometimes the abbot and the monks on their ambling mares, following the road along the northern hillside of Wensleydale, rode from Jervaulx to their walled-round vaccaries, now modern farms and villages: Simonstone, Forsdale, Thwaite Bridge, and Lunds. Their men built temporary wooden folds for horses, put up enclosures and sheds where they smelted iron, fished in the river, made hay in the meadows, and drove their thousands of sheep on to the mountains. Farmers from 'neighbouring towns,' such as Askrigg, rented agistment, pasturage for cattle in the summer, and pannage, the feed of acorns and beech-mast for their swine, in the autumn. Men acted as guides for travellers who paid toll to journey through the forest.

All these activities were lawful; but courts that levied fines for theft of game and wood were held at Bainbridge, and in early days offenders were taken to Richmond Castle. There were the Master Forester, as time went on a position often granted to members of prominent families in the dale, the Bow-bearer or Riding Forester, and the twelve walking foresters. Though a king never came here, the lords of Richmond and Middleham rode out with their followers, lances, horns, and dogs to hunt the deer, the wild boar, and sometimes the otter. As late as 1538–9 six hundred and ten fallow and sixty red deer roamed the Forest of Wensleydale. In 1296 Peter de Thoresby, parson of Aysgarth, who lived at Bainbridge, was licensed to chase 'the hare, fox, and cat with his own dogs.' On these days the dale rang with the music of horns, the shouts of men, the crackle of branches, the thud of plunging hoofs; and in the afterglow silence fell as the last rays of sunlight gleamed on the waters of the Ure.

Meanwhile our old-established village, wholly claimed neither by monks nor by great lords, suffered a period of barter and transference of land. After Gospatric's death, when most of his manors were granted to a Norman, Wimar the Steward, there was a division on which the development of the character of the village is based.   Part appears to have been given to Wimar, and part remained in the possession of the Englishman's descendants, of whom Peter, a great-grandson of Gospatric, was later living in Askrigg.   Wimar's bailiff and Peter lived in larger houses than the rest of the villagers, probably the one on the site of the Old Hall and the other on the West End.   Fountains Abbey held lands here, but by 1228 had exchanged them for others elsewhere.

In the hamlets benefactors with pious intentions made gifts of land to the abbeys.   At Newbiggin Adam Barn of Askrigg gave half a carucate to Jervaulx, and two acres of arable land and a toft and croft held by Ranulf the carpenter to Easby. At Woodhall, resembling on a small scale the upper dale shared by laymen and monks, there were Woodhall Park, a preserve for game, and Scall (Shalcoate), the territory of the canons of Easby.   Thomas de la Wodehalle (literally the Wood Hall) gave them pasturage for five hundred sheep and four cows, a sheep-fold for the stock to rise and lie in, a meadow, four acres near the river, and fishing rights.   In these trans-actions we read of woods at Askrigg called Langhout, Slehout, and Scalested, and of ox-drawn wagons, and pack-horses being driven on the common way along the northern slopes of the valley, and we sense the activities of monks and dalesmen busily engaged in sheep-farming.

Probably a little before Bainbridge had sprung up we had built a church.   In a charter of 1175–1204, connected with distant property, Uctred priest of Askrigg is named, and in 1218 an agreement defines 'the road that leads towards the church of Askeric.'   The road followed a route through the Roman fort, and, crossing the river south of the village, took a direct line to the site of the present church.   It remains now as a footpath between church and river, in part raised arti-ficially, and recently, until they were washed away, led to stepping-stones.

Land had been given by whom we do not know, perhaps Wimar or Peter; and the men of Askrigg had raised a small aisleless church for which a mason fashioned a tympanum [1] surrounded by dog-tooth carving. For three centuries the building was to stand overlooking the forest, and during that time it and the mother church of the parish of Aysgarth, that does not seem much more ancient than ours, were the only

Carved relief at Old Yorebridge School.
Overall size: 21 inches by 25 inches

churches in the upper dale. No greater event in our annals had taken place before nor has taken place since.

These were times of action and change when the village was growing and the church was being built. Domesday Book had recorded for the first time names both of places and people;

[1] It is likely that the carved relief, now preserved at Old Yorebridge School, came from Askrigg Church. Because of its character the stone was no part of the buildings at Fors Abbey. It crudely depicts a fish-tailed woman holding a comb. Dr G. Zarnecki places it in the third quarter of the twelfth century, and describes the figure as a medieval confusion between the antique siren and certain sea divinities.

and although place-names had remained unaltered, the new overlords were foreign and bore names strange and unreal: Ribald, Bodin, Bardulf, Wimar, sound grotesque to us even now, fit for the wicked barons in the folklore of fairy-tale. To the inhabitants of the countryside speaking their blend of Old English and Scandinavian tongues, the voices, habits, and manners of the Frenchmen must have seemed even more unfamiliar. No doubt they were little affected and referred to newcomers, as we do to-day, as 'foreigners' or 'they come from away.' When in 1951 dark-skinned men in turbans passed through, we stared and explained the phenomenon by remarking: 'The Festival of Britain's begun!'

Then, as now, war drew men abroad. About 1188 Ralph of Scall, living at Carperby, decided to join the crusade. Before leaving this cool Yorkshire valley he planned the disposal of his worldly goods by making an agreement with the canons of Easby Abbey for the provision of his family. He arranged for them to farm his lands in Carperby for three years on the understanding that they should supply his wife, Petronilla, with three household loaves a day and half a quarter of flour a year. If after that time he had not returned from his journey to Jerusalem they were to give his wife her dower, and hold the remainder for the maintenance of his only daughter until his return. Ralph never came back, and Petronilla probably married again; for later she relinquished all her rights to the canons.

In 1269, John, Duke of Brittany, obtained permission from Henry III to let Bainbridge and other lands in Richmondshire, because he required to raise a great sum to go to the Holy Land. Eight hundred years seem to shrink. To-day only the cause and the manner of combat are different.

Picture ourselves poised in time at the turn of the century in the year 1301. War with France observed a temporary truce. Five years ago it had begun with Scotland and was to continue. We were near enough to the borders to be affected. Richmond Castle was ordered to be kept safely 'so that no peril shall arise to the king or to the castle for lack of custody.' Men of Richmondshire armed with long-bows, or sometimes only with slings, were constantly called on to fight; knights followed the king, and men by condition of their tenure followed their lords. Murderers were pardoned if they would 'go with the king on his service at his wages.' Rape was common. Tithes newly valued in the Archdeaconry of Richmond had to be revised because they could not be paid. 'In the year 1315 the Scots renewing their rage againe plundered Cumberland, Westmorland, Tyndale, and Swaldale.' Swaledale and the villages in the Plain suffered far more than we did; the tithes of upper Wensleydale were reduced by almost half, but others had to be reassessed at a quarter of their value. The scourge, diminishing in strength, went on—Falkirk, Bannockburn, Flodden Field—until the union of the kingdoms in 1603.

In 1287 all lands were valued for Edward I by one John Kirkby, from whom the inquiry is named Kirkby's Inquest. At Askrigg five carucates had come to Sybil of Thornton Steward, a descendant of Wimar, and one carucate to the FitzHughs of Ravensworth. Amongst the five tenants holding land under Sybil, who held it of the Earl of Richmond, was Thomas Thornton. In 1316 Stephen Thornton was chief tenant of Askrigg. This family, connected with Thornton Rust, remained important in the neighbourhood, and in course of time, as a new form of society evolved, they step into our story again as the leading yeomen of Askrigg.

A few years later personal goods suffered a form of capital levy, a ninth part being taken from them in 1297 and a fifteenth in 1301, both to finance war. Small owners as well as large, of whom the abbeys were by far the most wealthy, paid; and remembering the comparison of Aysgarth and Halifax parishes the West Riding was the poorest part of the county.

The 1301 Lay Subsidy, as for centuries taxes were guilelessly called, is as satisfying to the curiosity as a nineteenth-century directory, and because of its age infinitely more valuable. In the two hundred years from the time of Domesday Book, Askrigg with sixteen taxpayers had grown, but not rapidly; and Nappa, to-day a hamlet of six houses, was almost as large with fifteen. New vigorous Bainbridge, the valuable property of rich landlords, claiming all the upper dale as far as Helbeck-lunds, has a list of forty-seven people who paid £19 13*s.* compared with Askrigg's £3 0*s.* 2*d.* Our most important inhabitant was Elya (Ellis), the reeve who organized the agriculture and paid the largest sum, 6*s.* 4*d.* There were two carpenters, a smith, a weaver, and a shepherd. The parson, Robert the Chaplain, living at Nappa, was taxed 13*s.* 4*d.* on his property and the tithes of Askrigg and Nappa, whilst John, his garcione (servant) at Askrigg, paid 4*s.* Others take their surnames from places, Kragg, Wayte, Haustewyk, though no one has a nickname such as the gem from Helperby near York, Galfrido Liggebiyefyre, unless it be Elya Fraunceys, the Frenchman.

So, if we add a mill, and picture the activities that the occupations conjure up, we may see this little band of perhaps sixty or eighty people living close to the land, treasuring their beasts, guiding their affairs by custom, paying their few pence of rent from the sale of their wool clips, men, women, and children, ignorant but pious, stubborn and amoral, happy, alarmed, frightened, loving, or hard-hearted.

At this East End of the village

IV

THE MARKET-TOWN

IT IS mid-afternoon of 13th February 1952. Snow streaks the fells under a frigid sky, and the lengthening daylight of winter's slow release still wears a relentless gaze. Assembled in the market-place people gather for shelter beside the church-yard wall; the grammar school children arrange themselves alongside in orderly ranks, and the smaller scholars of the elementary school take their places in front of the crowd. We look towards the cross as the chairmen of the Rural District and Parish Councils mount the steps, and listen in silence whilst the former reads the proclamation of the accession to the throne. A singer stands forward and strikes up 'God save the Queen.' There are no onlookers, no insignia of office. A small community, moved by loyalty and the passage of events, attends its own ceremony, performed because Askrigg was once a market-town.

The rise and decline of villages resemble in differing degrees

46

the tides of the fortunes of families, nations, and empires, and are no less often at the mercy of forces beyond either their knowledge or control. In a dale bounded by fells that breed a similarity of life these fluctuations seem emphasized and at first inexplicable. Yet a dale is not a single unit; each village in it is subject to change and stands alone. Necessity, a leading family, convenience, common sense, dissatisfaction, and rivalry dictate that first one and then another shall become the centre of trading.

Long ago, our only market, granted in 1202 when one Hugh Malebiche gave King John a palfrey, was eleven miles away at Wensley; but markets and fairs were established in 1305 at Carperby and two years later at the Abbot of Jervaulx's manor of East Witton. Not quite three centuries passed before Askrigg rose to a similar status; and Leyburn and Hawes, the present market-towns of Wensleydale, are the most recently chartered, the one in 1684, and the other in 1700.

At the beginning of the fourteenth century Askrigg was of no importance, and might well have been called 'litle' and 'poore' as Leland was to describe Wensley's market two hundred years later. Our village was overshadowed by Bainbridge, rivalled by Carperby, and no resident family brought either glory or fame. Yet general poverty in the north marked the times; Bainbridge's value was reduced by almost a half between 1280 and 1341. Tenants were beginning to farm the lords' demesnes; the era of the small men who were to grow into the yeomen approached. At Askrigg the ownership of land was becoming settled, and the village, centred round the church, pursued a slowly stabilizing course.

In this pastoral countryside wool was the only source of ready money. The huge flocks of the Cistercians and the small flocks of the villagers of the dales advanced the power of England; and the taxation of wool provided kings with funds for wars in France and Scotland. When in 1193–4 the whole year's clip of the Cistercians had been taken to help in freeing Richard Cœur de Lion from imprisonment, it is

stirring to think that fleeces from flocks grazing on Abbotside
went to pay for a king's ransom. Compared with the wool
of sheep in lowland country, ours was almost as valuable.
Yet the riches that made fair the houses of the Cotswolds and
raised up the soaring splendour of East Anglian churches did
not flow into the Yorkshire Dales, whence the monks drew
wealth to build abbeys of a mystic beauty, now in ruins, and
where a sturdy people, wrenching a hard livelihood from the
rough pastures of bleak hills, could afford only simple homes
and plain buildings for the worship of God.

Then the export trade was all important. For marketing
their wool the monks of Jervaulx had connections with
Flemings and Italians, and journeyed to the great fair at
Boston in Lincolnshire attended by foreign merchants, whilst
woolmen came up Wensleydale to buy the clips of the owners
of small flocks.   In 1338 at Leyburn and Richmond there were
merchants who shipped wool from Hartlepool to Flanders;
and later it was compulsorily taken to Newcastle or York
whose port was Hull. By the middle of the century came the
beginning of the turn-round from export to the making of cloth
in England; and though no more than a faint tremor borne
on the air, a far-distant knell sounded from the West Riding.

We view the fourteenth and fifteenth centuries in the north
as a frenzied drama seen at a distance.   There are a multitude
of angry faces, raised arms that brandish weapons, a tumult
of sound and movement.   The arts of war flourish, rather than
the arts of peace that blossom only in the seclusion of monastic
or clerical life.   Dominant in the northern scene during this
period that spanned the Hundred Years War, the Black Death,
and the Wars of the Roses, stride the figures of the feudal lords
who as Wardens of the Marches defended the borders, led men
to fight on foreign soil, endowed churches and abbeys, and
lived in great castles that to-day lie ruined in sequestered
dales.

From about 1300 until 1571 the FitzHughs of Ravensworth
between Richmond and Barnard Castle and the Scropes of

Bolton in Wensleydale shared the division of the village. Both families were less important than the Nevilles of Middleham, whose strength was sensed and patronage sought throughout the dale, and who for a time possessed the Forest of Bainbridge and Woodhall Park. Yet they were leaders of major stature: the FitzHughs, pious and chivalrous, numbering amongst their ranks men who attained high positions in church and state, and the Scropes building their castle at Bolton, still a memorial to those days, and rising by intellectual prowess to be judges, lawyers, and leading statesmen and soldiers.

Connected with the dale through their Norman ancestors, Bardulf and his brother Bodin, the FitzHughs held the larger portion of the village that included the corn mill, no doubt the lands of Sybil of Thornton Steward. The Scropes' share, granted to them in 1312 by a descendant of Gospatric, William of Hebden, in 1421 consisted of eight houses and fifty acres of land, and in 1546 the rents, described as outside the lordship of Bolton, amounted to £6 6s.

The bailiff of the FitzHughs perhaps occupied a house on the same site as that of Wimar's bailiff where the Old Hall stood in the market-place, and the Scropes' chief house was possibly on the West End where now, since the Hall was burnt down, stands the oldest house in Askrigg, distinguishable by its steeply pitched roof, once thatched. The FitzHughs' demesne lands lay south-east of the village, and they were leased in 1465 to Abraham Metcalf who followed Thomas Person as chief tenant.

Only poor copies of the records of the manor courts of Henry FitzHugh and Alice, his wife, dating from the middle of the fifteenth century, have survived. They give incomplete lists of names of the free tenants, such as Metcalf, Thornton, Ketilwell, Pickeryng, Clerkson, Robynson, Tuke, Lambert, Terry, Mason, Wilson, and Grysthwaite. From them nothing can be learned of the terms of tenure. No doubt the Askrigg men once performed boon-works in hay-time and harvest, duties that were gradually commuted by a money payment, and 'upon lawful warning' the chief tenants followed their lords in time of war.

Nor have we any details of the recreations of these people, some of them fore-elders of men living here to-day. There would be shooting with long-bows at the butts, church ales, and games and sports on the feast day, St Oswald's Day, 5th August, the people 'at those times mutually entertayninge one another with arguments of love, freedom, and hospitality.' They no doubt moved about the country freely, and some joined monastic orders; John of Askrigg was Abbot of Coverham in 1428.

In these early years when the daily occurrences of life go unrecorded, the violence of evildoers is better known. Four murders in one century are known because the criminals received pardon. In 1326 Lambert of Askrigg, having slain William Holebag of Newby, was pardoned 'on condition that he go against the King's enemies'; in 1375 Robert Addison, horseman of Bainbridge, in self-defence killed John Mees of Askrigg; three years later John, son of Nelson of Askrigg, slew John Dakson of Rygton; and again, at the supplication of Queen Anne, 'Adam Lyghfote of Wenselaydale' was pardoned for the death of James Chery, killed in the village on the second Sunday in Lent 1389.

Bands of ruffians, driving stolen cattle, wreaking damage to crops, and assaulting those who opposed them, came from afar to plunder game in the forest, fell trees, and fish in the river. Other marauders were local men, such as Elias of Gunnerside and Simon Bradderig of Swaledale, Robert Hunter of Woodhall and John Tyok of Nappa, who killed and stole deer, pheasants, partridges, rabbits, and hares in the chase and Woodhall Park. Bainbridge suffered a severe raid in 1375, when men 'who came armed' slew seven inhabitants and burned the houses of Geoffrey of Linton and Amand of Routhe.

Two later happenings illustrate the lawlessness and unbridled passions of the times. In 1474 Thomas Wyn, a yeoman of Askrigg, his brother Christopher, and four relatives from the parish of Sedbergh planned an attack on William Halmonde, 'a lawful man of St Wilfrid's,' Ripon, against whom they evidently bore a grudge. The conspirators, armed with lances, bows and arrows, swords, and Welsh bills, stole to the town by devious routes—one by Pateley Bridge and Nidderdale, the others by the village of Norton—and converging at the north bridge of Ripon, they waylaid their victim. Brought before the Chapter Court there, they were charged with doing bodily harm with malice aforethought to Halmonde.

The second occurred near Semerwater in 1554. 'Minian, late of Kidstaynes in the township of Thoralbye, "yoman," on 21 April made an assault upon Augustine Metcalfe of Countersett in the township of Bainbridge, and whilst George Fawcet of Thoralby, Minian's brother, was holding Metcalfe in his arms, Minian came furiously on him and Metcalfe in self-defence with a jestorne (gestro) of the value of 12d. which he had in his hand struck him in the stomach and gave him a mortal wound of which Minian languished and died on 24 April at Thoralby.'

These happenings were to diminish; and proof of the growing prosperity of the upper reaches of Wensleydale was the rise of the family of Metcalfe. There was an Adam Medecalf at Bainbridge in 1294; but our concern is with a later James Metcalfe of Worton. When Sir Richard le Scrope fought at Agincourt with fifteen men-at-arms and forty-five archers from Wensleydale, James, a captain in the army, appears to have incurred expenses on his leader's behalf; for on his return Sir Richard granted him the estate of Nappa. James lived to a great age, and in his seventieth year saw the completion of Nappa Hall in 1459. Leland accredited Thomas, James's son, with the building, but he was only a young man at the time.

The Metcalfes were not a great family; yet fame clings about them, and romantic legends elevate them beyond their deserts. Mary Queen of Scots, King James the First, Sir Walter Raleigh—none of these famous personages was likely to have visited Nappa as tradition relates, and even the three hundred white horses that bore the kinsmen who accompanied Sir Christopher, High Sheriff of the County, to meet the judges at York were not necessarily that colour. But whereas far more important figures, such as the Scropes, have become dim shades, the Metcalfes live in the annals of Wensleydale. Their fame rests on the flamboyant personalities of Sir Christopher and Sir Thomas, on the tremendous clan of men of their name, and on the romance of the ancient house that still remains not as a hollow ruin but as a habitable dwelling.

A mile from Askrigg, Nappa Hall stands below the rocks of the cliff against which it is wedged, and like the walls and fields that sweep down to the river below it and the scars of Ellerkin that fringe the sky-line behind, the weathered building reflects the changing moods of winter and summer skies. It is not large; the west tower, its corner-stones and the mullions of the windows of millstone hewn from the Greets, rises four-storeyed in the manner of a miniature Norman keep, and the great hall that joins the two towers measures only forty-four feet by twenty-three. Defence and comfort are here inter-mingled in an evolutionary style fitting to the times. The ambition of James is embodied in its walls, but the extrava-gances of Sir Christopher and the blusterings of Sir Thomas have long ago faded away. Instead of a minstrels' gallery, panelling, and vast open fire-places, there is now the necessary and inevitable equipment of a large, busy, dales farmer's household.

Four generations of Metcalfes, Thomas the first James's son, Sir James, Sir Christopher born in 1513, and Sir Thomas born in 1579, all married into important Yorkshire families: the Hertlingtons, the Pigotts, the Cliffords, and the Slingsbys; and in accordance with the ambitions of the men of their day they accumulated wealth derived from the dowries of their wives. Thomas held the position of Chancellor of the Duchy of Lancaster, and both Sir James and Sir Christopher became High Sheriffs of Yorkshire. They were rewarded for supporting Richard III's claim to the throne; they fought on the borders.

The West Tower of Nappa Hall

Many of the offices attached to the lordship of Middleham were granted them: they held leases for life of Raydale and Woodhall Park, and were supervisors of the castle and lordship, Master Foresters and Pinders of the Forest of Wensleydale. They were appointed Justices of the Peace. They leased lead and coal mines, and rented the tithes of the rectory of Aysgarth. The Metcalfes were a power in the dale.

In the year 1466 the stones of the hall at Nappa are beginning to be filmed with the mould of time. Men till the Haverlands at Newbiggin, and the fields of Askrigg year by year yield crops of corn and hay, food for man, and fodder for beast. Woods and rough ground shrink in extent, and habitation in the forest is more secure. The ring of hammer on iron peals over the village street. Small children, wild as the countryside they live in, chase each other, or run for comfort to the womenfolk who spin, cook, and stitch, make cheese and butter, fetch and carry, and labour on the land. The church is old; its ling thatch has been repaired many times. On Sundays in the dark nave there is the stir of rushes as men and women kneel and rise in obedience to the clerk who intones the unintelligible but familiar Latin phrases. Only here do the aspirations of men spring above mere existence.

At this time a project, doubtless bruited for many years, was afoot to enlarge the church; and James Metcalfe, in his latter days, wished to found a chantry in which prayers should be offered for the king and queen, his family, and their souls after death. The wall facing the river was pulled down, stones were dressed for pillars, arcades, and windows, and a south aisle was built. A little later, after foundations had been laid, a tower rose, to be topped with a battlemented parapet; and when another half-century had passed, the north aisle and the clerestory completed the church as we see it to-day. For the interior carpenters pinned together fine oak beams to support a lead roof, and carved a rood-loft to span the chancel. There were painted images of the Virgin and saints, and perhaps for the first time a bell tolled from the tower over the valley.

James founded his chantry chapel, dedicated to St Anne, in 1467 in the south aisle, and he set apart land in several places for its support. During the next eighty years Askrigg had a priest and a chantry chaplain, and according to a record dated 1524 as many as six other chaplains. They were simple men drawn from the neighbourhood, and the last chantry priest, Roger Kendall, was described as 'of a meane lerning, beyng of honest conversacon and qualities.' The Metcalfes were buried in the chapel, and perhaps it was James and his wife who were commemorated by the brasses of which only the matrices remain.

Askrigg Church was now large, nearer to the upper dale than Aysgarth; and although a chapel-of-ease was built at the growing village of Hawes about 1483, it served a small area. The new aisles seemed spread like sheltering wings drawing the people of the forest beneath them. Here families from Lunds, Cotterdale, Hardraw, Raydale, and Bainbridge gathered in what was a communal building for both spiritual and secular matters. Askrigg grew as a natural centre.

In the sixteenth century those figures with raised arms and angry faces still massed near the borders and out on the Plain. The tenants of Wensleydale had all their horses requisitioned in 1513, and rallying under Lord Scrope, joined battle with the Scots at Flodden Field. After the victory the horses and mares taken off the field of combat were claimed 'upon there book oaths' by the owners. Six geldings, three greys, a bay, a black, and one white ambling gelding were returned to Sir James Metcalfe. Of Askrigg men Thomas Roger claimed a red trotting nag with a white face, and John Robynson a bridled grey trotting horse and a white grey ambling nag. But many never saw their horses again, and for long remembered the catastrophe of that year.

At times the tumult was heard almost at our very doors. The men of the north, hastening to and fro, flung themselves into furious clashes, as, united by a common purpose, they sought to preserve old ways of life. When Henry VIII turned his covetous eye on the wealth of the monks, opposition crystallized in the Pilgrimage of Grace. Notices nailed to church doors warned the villages of Wensleydale of what was afoot. Abbot Sedbar of Jervaulx Abbey, an unpopular and weak man, was compelled to support the rebellion and was hanged for his participation. In 1538 the abbey was forfeited to the Crown; Easby Abbey had already been suppressed. The monks of Jervaulx and the canons of Easby were no longer seen in the dale. Though it heralded a time of unsettlement, this first great change of ownership since the twelfth century was to have far-reaching effects on our village and the upper dale.

Thirty-one years later came the Rising of the North, the upsurging of feudal lords and commoners in a last bid to retain the Roman Catholic faith and to defy economic change. The insurgents were quelled. Of eight men of Askrigg and Askrigg Common arrested, two were hanged, but Leonard Metcalfe of Bear Park near Aysgarth, condemned to be hanged, drawn, and quartered, was released. The downfall of feudal power and of families such as the Nevilles was complete. Henceforward the Council of the North ruled the countryside, and positions on it and the Wardenship of the Marches were held by men of unquestionable loyalty to the Crown. At long last the turmoil in the north was subsiding.

About the time of the Pilgrimage of Grace Sir Christopher Metcalfe was facing troubles of his own. The Scropes successfully opposed his appointment to the office of Master Forester, and far more disastrously challenged his legal title to Nappa. These disputes were only resolved by his parting with another estate. When the chantries were dissolved and their endowments claimed by Edward VI, this time, with some right on his side but partly by means of false evidence, he kept the property that James had apportioned for the support of the chantry in Askrigg Church. With diminished wealth Sir Christopher, especially when he was High Sheriff, continued his extravagant course, and mortgaging his lands, he left little but Nappa to his son James and his grandson Thomas, a baby at the time of James's death.

The reign of Elizabeth I with its plots and risings, its encouragement of trade, its passing of laws, and religious settlement following the Reformation, marks an epoch in our story. It was indeed appropriate that the proclamation should be read here in February of 1952; for the first Queen Elizabeth granted a market to the town. But before reaching this event, we may catch two glimpses of the times.

The first concerns a result of Protestantism, the edict to abolish 'monuments of superstition in churches' issued in 1547. Because of the influence of the Metcalfes who conformed to the Established Church, there were few Catholics in the upper dale. Yet the parishioners of Askrigg resented the order to destroy rood-lofts and images, later enforced from York by Archbishop Grindal, and they connived to pretend ignorance. But either information was divulged or officials visiting the church found them out. In 1571 at the Archbishop's Court the curate and churchwardens 'whos circumspection ought to have been such as they should know what is in ther church' were fined, the one 13s. 4d., and the others 10s. each, and under supervision they were compelled to burn the images on specified market-days at Middleham and Richmond, and to 'put the fyer with their owne hands to them till the imags be consumed.' In addition 'the vestements and other trumpery' had to be defaced, and the timber of the rood-loft sold for the use of the church.

The second glimpse is of the corn mill, a building either near or on the site of the present West Mill. For fifty years its vicissitudes can be pieced together from the leases granted to men and women of Askrigg who sublet to the millers. Following Ninian Metcalfe, in 1555 Lucy Kettlewell rented the mill for 'a terme of 21 yeres if she lyve so longe,' and accounted responsible for repairs she paid the accustomed yearly rent of 53s. 4d. When it was next let to Peter Thornton for thirty years, it was said that the watercourse was obstructed by rocks

falling into it from the cliff under which it ran, and that the
stream could not be 'removed or brought anny other waye
because the ground nexte adjoyninge belongeth unto the Lord
Scroope.'

Again in 1607 a surveyor stated that 'the same Mylle is in
greate decaie and of little valewe, by reason that it is dryven
by a small water cominge from the moors which in Somer
tyme is cleane dryed up, and the current runneth neere a
greate rockie hill, parte of which often falleth into the same
current and stoppeth the passage thereof.'   Evidently repairs
were carried out; for Edmund Pratt taking a new lease paid,
besides the old rent, a lamb valued at 6s. 8d., and a fine, that
was usually demanded with a new lease, amounting to £13 6s. 8d.

The mill was then Crown property; for the FitzHughs had
vanished as landlords after a descendant, the Marquess of
Northampton, was involved in the plot to set Lady Jane Grey
on the throne.   In 1553 the marquess forfeited his estates,
then had them returned to him; but on his death in 1571 they
reverted to the Crown.

The industries of dyeing and hand-knitting were being
developed in the neighbourhood, and probably, though we
have no evidence, the lead mines on Askrigg Moor and the
rich mine at Woodhall were being exploited.   In whatever
way their wealth was being earned a number of families were
rising in affluence.   Chief amongst them were the Thorntons,
whose pedigree and coat of arms, three hammers, are given in
Glover's Visitation of 1584.   Peter Thornton, no doubt the
same Peter who rented the corn mill, was foremost in furthering
the rising prosperity of the town.

For at least nine years prior to 1587 'a concourse of men for
the buying and selling of victuals, wares and other necessary
things' had gathered at a customary market in Askrigg on
Thursday of each week.   But certain neighbours, 'prompted
by desire of gain and labouring to draw to themselves the
tolls,' had complained of this unlawful trading; and in consequence Peter Thornton had appealed to the Queen, and

probably pleaded at the inquisition that followed similar petitions. He was successful. On 3rd October 1587 Elizabeth
granted a charter for a weekly market to be held on Thursdays
and two fairs to last three days in April and October of each
year. By this time Wensley had the nearest market, Carperby's
seeming to have fallen into disuse, and the grant expresses a
wish 'to lighten the grievous journeys and labours which the
inhabitants would be compelled to undergo.' For his trouble
and great expenses Peter was given the profits of the tolls,
fairs, and the Court of Piepowder for a term of twenty-one
years, after which the people themselves were to take charge.
So in time the Four Men, anciently regarded as a representative
body, came to govern the town.

We may picture the first legal market, perhaps after the
trading was over, celebrated by rejoicings in the form of sports
and games. Labourers have been employed to dig holes in
which poles to support the booths have been fixed. Men and
women of Askrigg, 'poor country people dwelling around,'
merchants with knitting yarn brought from Richmond, laden
chapmen, and ragged vagrants mingle under the shadow of
the church; and for the first time the crier is calling the tolls
and giving public notice of the market. The crowd surges
forward, the women to search for their wants amongst the
tempting goods: shoes, apples, herrings, cloth, honey, salt,
and onions, and the men to bargain for hides, iron, nails,
butter, cheese, and for corn.

On all sides in the town fields a tremendous change is taking
place about this time. Due to the increase in the price of wool,
and following similar developments that have transformed
some parts of England during the century, the arable land is
being enclosed and put down to grass, and the growing of corn
is ceasing. Askrigg, no longer self-supporting, is a centre for
the buying and selling of 'all manner of merchandise wares
and chattels.'

Worton Hall. Anthony Besson's house

V

CENTURY OF THE YEOMEN

1. ESTABLISHMENT

IN THE seventeenth century, as the written word extends in
volume and accumulates locally, the figures that pass
through our small world loom out of the haze of the past
more clearly than in former days. From deeds of property,
records of lawsuits, occasional wills, parish registers, and rare
lists of inhabitants we grow familiar with many names, and
adding one fragment of knowledge to another, warm towards
the individuals that evolve. They gather in the market-place,
weave in and about the town; some press forward, hold the

attention for a while, then leaving, make way for others. The imagination gives them thoughts and aspirations, pictures them with features not so different from the dalesmen's of to-day, and clothes them in varieties of contemporary dress. Each, immured in the armour of personality, contributes to the nature of the community that, reflecting the climate of the times, presents to view a distinctive facet; and of them all amongst the few gentry and the many poor, the yeomen play the main parts.

The name yeoman, meaning countryman, has already been applied to the free tenants whose customary rights secured their farms from father to son; and at the beginning of the century this was still the rule. In Askrigg the yeomen paid rents and fines to the Crown, the Scropes, Sir Thomas Metcalfe, and other landlords. On Abbotside the descendants of tenants of the abbey held their estates under the new owner, the Duke of Lennox, and the Manor of Bainbridge that included Woodhall Manor and the forest south of the river was Crown property. During the next forty years rapid change took place, and by the time of the Civil War many Askrigg men had become owners of their own farms.

Though the population had increased, the yeomen at first were not numerous. There were, to choose a few, the Thorntons, Bessons, Metcalfes, Wetheralds, Beezons, Clarksons, Pratts, Masons, Forsters, and Pearsons of Askrigg, Metcalfes at Countersett and at most of the hamlets along Abbotside, Lamberts in Raydale, and Fawcetts at Ballowfield, a farm on the eastern margin of the township. Many of these ancient families have since vanished, and even the names of some are forgotten, the Barwickes and Tukes at Nappa Scar, Lobleys in Raydale, and Nelsons of Camshouse; for, as W. G. Collingwood says of the Lake District, old stocks survived over fewer centuries than is often supposed. A number, of whom the Thorntons, the Bessons, and the Robinsons of Worton, newcomers to the dale, were the most outstanding, merged into the gentry, whilst others were younger sons of landowners. Eventually some of the craftsmen and tradesmen, dyers, stockiners, shoemakers, carpenters, and saddlers, all farming plots of land, amassed capital enough to be called yeomen.

We visualize them as stalwart figures surveying the valley from their hillside farms or stepping out of those carved doorways into the main street. Proud men, they relied on strength not only of body but of character; full-blooded personalities, jealous of their rights, given to feuds and fights with neighbours, they were only now emerging from the stresses of past times. Theirs was a background of long independence and the satisfaction of a full life rooted in the land.

Families intermarried and christened their children with old names. There were Elizabeth, Mary, Alice, Dorothy, Anne, Isabel, Ellinor, Margaret, and Jane for the girls; and besides similar well-known ones for the boys, Ninian, Augustine, Alexander, Gandrian, Tristram, and Adam breathed the spirit of this and a previous age. They prospered as land appreciated in value and good prices for produce prevailed, and sent their younger sons to York and London to become attorneys and merchants. They lent and borrowed money, paid infinitesimal sums in wages to servants, had few expenses, and in the latter half of the century many built houses of as sturdy a mould as the characters of their owners. Ever improving their farms, living in comfort rather than ease, breeding a sound stock, the yeomen were, in the words of a contemporary local deed, 'persons of good sort and qualitie.'

Only brief glimpses are allowed us of a family that was one of the few benefactors in a neighbourhood where slender means had precluded generosity, and where, whatever consideration the monks may have had for the spiritual welfare and education of the dalesmen, this was no concern of the speculators in land who followed them. It remained for the son of a yeoman, Anthony Besson, to respond to an urgent need by founding a grammar school at Yore's Bridge End in 1601. Most probably he and his relative, Richard, were descendants of the

Richard Bessons senior and junior who in 1535 attended the musters [1] on Middleham Moor, the one as billman, the other as archer, and whereas Richard farmed at Litherskew on Abbotside, Anthony was trained in law. Described as of the City of York, he was admitted to Gray's Inn on 11th February 1595, and was one of the attorneys to the Star Chamber. We find him and his wife Jane involved in transactions in land, or picture him at his chambers in London mingling with his fellow members of the Inn, yet not forgetful of his native dale.

In 1607 he, Richard Besson, and Peter Metcalfe of Dale Grange, 'Peter of the Bowebrigge,' spurred the tenants to challenge the Duke of Lennox's title to Abbotside, the Manor of Wensleydale; and the incidents that led up to a lawsuit unfold from the depositions of witnesses. Anthony, seeing one of the Lamberts in London, boasted: '. . . for an Askrigg shott I will discharge them by law against the Duke for his title of the lands in variance.' Perhaps the expression meant a share paid for ale on the feast day, or a rate that was notably small. The scene shifts to a Sunday at Hawes, when, impatiently leaving the chapel half-way through the sermon, the yeomen and the Bessons held a large and private conference. Next day Richard came into the house at Dale Grange where the duke's deputy steward sat, and addressed him 'verie con-temptuouslie "Howe nowe my maisters for whom doe youe keep a Courte here?"' 'For the Duke's grace' was the answer, to which Richard retorted: '. . . they are fooles that doe appeare here at this tyme.' At a third meeting in Askrigg Church, the tenants guaranteed funds to their attorney, who by then was less assured of the outcome; and the case coming before the Court of Exchequer was decided against them.

When Anthony Besson built a house at Worton in 1600, for he is said to be of that place in a general pardon granted him when James I came to the throne, he left his home, the White Swan in Coney Street, York, and transferred it and a smaller house adjoining to trustees in order that the rents, amounting

[1] See Appendix B, page 299.

to twenty pounds a year, should provide the schoolmaster's salary. The name of the White Swan was changed at this date to the Black Swan, and the second house was occupied by an armourer. In the foundation deed he stated as reasons for his gift 'the good and benefitt of the Parish of Askrigg' which was his native place, and 'in that regard both by the lawes of nature and his proper inclination more deare unto him'; and that he had observed a grievous want of men 'to instruct the children of the inhabitants there in civill manners, good letters, and other necessary, wholesome rudiments, and points of knowledge, and art.'

It had been agreed that the people of the neighbourhood should build and equip a school suitable for a master to live in, and that the Askrigg parish clerk should teach the 'pettie schollers' and be paid £6 13s. 4d. for his two occupations. But the foundation deed caused disappointment by stipulating that whilst the twenty-four trustees (thirteen of them Metcalfes) were to have charge of the funds, the heirs-at-law of Anthony Besson were to appoint the masters; the founder was childless but had four sisters. Largely in consequence of this division the fortunes of the school were to endure many vicissitudes.

The first master chosen by Anthony Besson was Richard Leake, curate of Hawes, who remained there until his patron's death in 1614. The appearance of the first building is unknown, and four reconstructions were to follow before the present Yorebridge Grammar School was built in the twentieth century; but at Worton the charming Elizabethan house remains with the inscription in small lettering on the lintel of the doorway, ANNO DOMINE 1600 A.B.

Two families were at this time faring ill, the Thorntons of Askrigg and the Metcalfes of Nappa Hall. The career of Peter Thornton, grandson of Peter who obtained the market charter, must have been the talk of the town as well as its concern. In his early years he was dismissed the post of bailiff of the Manor of Wensleydale. He married Jane Fawcett, the eldest

daughter of Giles and Isobel Fawcett of Kidstones at the head
of Bishopdale. Jane inherited the lease of the larger of the
two farms there. Peter was brought before Quarter Sessions
for refusing to watch in the night (a compulsory duty for the
detection of strangers) and in 1608, at the age of twenty-five,
he was indicted for felony and homicide, outlawed at York
Castle, and forfeited his estate. Shortly afterwards the town
of Askrigg was charged to answer for 'certain transgressions
against evasions and escapes.' Six years later, because they
had illegally retained some property, his wife and James Med-
calf, probably a relative, were outlawed (waived is the term
used for a woman).

In 1619 Peter was accused at Quarter Sessions of extortion
and bribery, and abusing the Bishop of Chester's commission
by altering replies to queries; and again the same year the
maintenance of his three children, in particular an infant son
whom he could not support, was in question. Jane's inheritance had been made over to the Robinsons of Worton who
had charge of the older children. At this time the family was
living at Brown Moor, perhaps Browna Parrocks, a lonely farm
on Abbotside. By 1620, when inquisitions were being taken
to ascertain particulars of his property, Jane had died. It is
an unhappy story that with few records available has to be
filled in by the imagination.

Meanwhile, Sir Thomas Metcalfe, a childishly passionate
man, not content with a small heritage, hampered himself on
all hands by mortgages. Blundering from one disaster to
another, he resorted to bribery, force that caused bloodshed,
and smooth pleadings in courts of law in vain efforts to
extricate himself.

If we had been living in Askrigg on 4th June 1617, we
should have known that a serious brawl had begun over beyond
Semerwater. The story of the Raydale Riot is well known; of
how William Robinson, with both interest and capital of a
mortgage at stake, claimed Raydale House, a prized Metcalfe
acquisition; of how whilst he was away from home, Sir Thomas,

drunk and insolent, with a company of sixty armed men for four days laid siege to it; and how Mrs Robinson having fled barefoot, apparently disturbed as she was retiring to bed, eventually brought help from York, but not before one of the attackers had been killed by a chance shot. Sir Thomas, narrowly avoiding imprisonment, parted with his last distant estate to settle the prosecutions that ensued.

Almost more disastrous was the lawsuit in 1609 that the yeomen of the forest brought against him, when, as farmer of the tithes of the rectory of Aysgarth, he demanded hay tithe that had not previously been paid in the upper dale. Though he won, Sir Thomas said that the case, costing him £2,000, was the ruin and overthrow of his estate, and that through it he lost to his great prejudice 'the love and affection of most of the inhabitants within the rectory the greatest number of them being of his own name and kindred.' In 1618 Trinity College Cambridge, the tithe impropriators, averring that the lawsuit had been no concern of theirs but brought by Sir Thomas for his own profit, prosecuted him for not paying several years' rents. By now Nappa Hall was mortgaged to some of the speculators who had bought Abbotside from the Duke of Lennox, and one of them, John Colby, actually lived there for several years, whilst Sir Thomas dwelt 'in obscure and unknown places.' At length friends and relatives of his wife, the Slingsbys, rallied to his aid, and paid off his debts. He returned to Nappa, and dying there in 1655 was buried in the Metcalfe chapel in Askrigg Church. But the family was a power no more.

Apart from the manorial rights, Crown property at Askrigg appears to have been sold off to private individuals at the beginning of the century. In 1628 Charles I sold the Manor of Bainbridge to the citizens of London, who in turn sold to the yeomen in 1663. The early years of the seventeenth century indeed marked a period of important change.

In the disturbed times of the Civil War the Scropes, Sir Thomas Metcalfe, William Robinson, and Francis Boulton of

Mowton near Richmond, probably a speculator, were all selling
land at Askrigg for long terms of years, sometimes three
thousand, often two, and sometimes one, with the ancient rents
commuted to a peppercorn or a few shillings 'if demanded.'
Even Drunken Barnaby, 'Richard Braithwaite of Burntheade
in the County of Westmorland,' owned several closes from
1616 to 1638; and Dr John Bathurst, physician to Oliver
Cromwell, seeking profitable investments, bought the Old
Hall property in 1641 from Christopher Peacock of Easby,
who had it of Brian Willance of Clints in Swaledale, who may
have purchased from the Crown. Transferences were to continue. In 1787 a tithe farmer said of Askrigg '. . . the lands
in this town have been very fluctuating and seldom been in
one person's possession twenty years together.'

The outbreak of Civil War interrupted ordered life. In the
summer of 1644 after Marston Moor Prince Rupert's defeated
troops may have passed through Wensleydale from Richmond
on their way to Lancashire. Six miles from Askrigg Bolton
Castle was besieged, and its defenders starved into surrender.
When in 1647 an attempt was made to quarter Parliamentary
troops in the dales, probably both in Swaledale and Wensleydale, the army was attacked by the 'clubmen' who fought
with anything to hand, stones included, and drove them out
'sorely bruised.'

The same year the inhabitants of Bainbridge were brought
up at the Quarter Sessions for refusing to pay 'the late Constable' their proportion of an assessment made for 'the satisfaction of four horses' bridles and saddles bought by him for
the service of the Parliament,' and ten years later an Askrigg
man was bound to good behaviour 'for not prosecuting evidence on behalf of the Commonwealth.' As might be expected the Metcalfes took the king's side, and one son of Sir
Thomas, Scrope Metcalfe, died from wounds received at a
skirmish near Oxford.

Meanwhile the forest was fast disappearing, though deer still
roamed the lonely valleys of Raydale and Cotterdale, and

Master Foresters with their sonorous titles were appointed. Bow-bearer and Forester of Wensleydale, Park-keeper of the Park of Woodhall, Forester of Raydale, of Cotterdale, of Worton, reads the grant to a Maior (Mauger) Norton in 1630. Roads from village to village, though they might be called the highway or the king's high street, were circuitous rocky lanes or narrow ill-kept causeways, and the Roman roads over the hills and the common way of the monks were the most easily negotiated.   A witness in Sir Thomas's hay tithe lawsuit laid stress on the primitive state of life in the upper dale: 'The said forest is mountainous and bare and barren ground as annie in the world in his thinkinge and that the inhabitants most of them are verie poore and do live hardlie and barelie.'   But prosperous times lay ahead; there were new chapels-of-ease at Hardraw, Stalling Busk, and Lunds, and Hawes, naturally placed where many tracks from the side valleys crossed, was a growing place.

At Askrigg a craft was the mainstay of the inhabitants. 'Here poor people live by Knitting to their Trading, breeding fitting,' wrote Drunken Barnaby in 1638.   Stockings to wear with breeches or under top-boots were the demand of a well-organized industry; and all day men, women, and children strove at their monotonous task.   The dyers, increasing in number, built dye-houses by the becks, and sold knitted goods, yarn, thimbles, needles, and pins in shops that were rooms in their houses.   Stockiners, the middlemen, carrying yarn and buying knitted goods, travelled up and down the dale.   Housewives carded and spun, and the men wove cloth for home use.

Each day boys were taught their lessons by masters, often new men, for they were continually being appointed afresh, at the school near Yore Bridge.   Only twenty-five years after it was founded the school was in difficulties.   The heirs-at-law, descendants of three sisters of Anthony Besson, headed by William Turbatts, brought a case against Anthony Metcalfe, the son of a fourth sister, who was allied with the twelve remaining trustees, before the Archbishop's Court at York.   The depositions reveal a sorry tale.   Four masters had followed the first in rapid succession, some appointed by Leake. The school and the walls round it were in ruin, and the Black Swan in York in no better a state. Anthony Metcalfe was accused of allowing 'insufficient and illiterate schoolmasters' to be appointed, and of intending the overthrow of the school and the sharing out of its endowment. The then master, Adam Foster, who was approved in the parish, and who had himself laid out money to repair the school building, had paid Metcalfe twenty pounds for his appointment. Eventually the heirs-at-law appealed to the Council of the North. The verdict is unknown; but the school continued.

In the town the setting as yet had 'no handsomeness about it'; many of the houses were crude wooden structures, and squalor prevailed in the street. Week by week the market drew the people of the neighbourhood, attorneys to meet their clients there, buyers and sellers, and some to visit Daniell Tetlaw, the local wise man, who practised 'devillish artes called charmes and sorceries.' In the summer of 1621 gipsies perhaps told fortunes, for there were at Bainbridge 'wandering Egiptians troubling the countrie by filching and stealing.' Occasionally the press was so great that booths were set up in the churchyard, and the churchwardens fined in consequence.

At the time of the spring and autumn fairs children kept watch on The Gate for the packmen from Richmond to descend the hill with laden ponies; and later, crowds milled round the stalls to finger lengths of silk and flannel, to covet seeing-glasses, buckles and buttons, hat-bands and neckerchiefs, or to buy farming and household necessities from amongst the copper kettles, iron chafing dishes, frying-pans, wicker-baskets, knives, wooden trenchers, piggins, skeels,[1] and churns. They found customers for their horses, cattle, and wethers, vied with each other at sports and games, and perhaps engaged in bull-baiting or cock-fights, or watched the performances of jugglers, acrobats, or players of interludes who might have passed through on their rounds.

[1] Piggins and skeels are small and large wooden tubs or pails.

F

If we could return to join these people in the market-place, we should find ourselves hampered and confined by many of the ills that exist to-day: rising rates and prices, shortages of food, controls of wages and labour, restrictions, regulations, form-filling—all were there. This neighbour, William Baitman, a thatcher, had been fined for 'taking wages contrary to the statute,' and that yeoman for using 'the trade of a joyner' without his seven years' apprenticeship. The differences lay in religious intolerance and the often cruel form and degrees of punishment. A drunkard might be sitting in the stocks below the cross, and a fornicator reciting a declaration as a penance. George Metcalfe, convicted of forgery, had been seen standing in Bedale, Richmond, and Middleham market-places on three days with his crime written on a paper 'in his hatt,' whilst another bore the scars of branding on his hands for stealing a sheep. For besides the civil there were the Church Courts enforcing penances for moral transgressions; and if we had lived on the south side of the valley there would have been the Bainbridge Manor Court imposing fines on men and sometimes women 'for makeing an affraie and drawinge blood.'

From the minutes and orders of the North Riding Quarter Sessions a picture may be formed of the unruly side of the town's life in the seventeenth century. By ancient custom the inhabitants had served the town as constables, and for at least three hundred years elected churchwardens as trustees of the parish; then, after the passing of the Highway Acts, and later the Poor Laws of Elizabeth's reign, they furnished surveyors of the highway and overseers of the poor; but of their work no early records have survived. On the Justices of the Peace, the gentry, fell the upholding of the law and the conduct of local affairs, and under them the chief constables and the petty constables carried out the orders. Besides these, the overseers of the poor and the churchwardens were responsible for that thankless task, the assessment and collection of the poor-rate. There was a House of Correction at Richmond where offenders from 'lewd women' to rogues and lunatics were imprisoned. That times were rough, punishments cruel, and local men not always worthy of the positions entrusted to them is shown by many cases.

The Highway Act of 1555 had laid the responsibility of the upkeep of a main road on the parish; and bridges, mostly for foot passengers, heavy wagons having to use fords, were a constant drain on money and labour. In July 1611 the people of Askrigg were in trouble for 'not repairing a hie waie lying at the west end of Askrigg Holmes' (a boggy stretch between the town and Paddock Beck), and soon afterwards were threatened that if 'it be not sufficiently repaired by Lammas next, a forfeit of 10s. be imposed upon them.' Men were fined for throwing out rubbish and stones in the street and lanes, and for piling up 'dungehills' in the market-place. Yore Bridge, Bain Bridge, and Bow Bridge ranked as county bridges kept up by public rate, not by the parish as were the smaller ones. In 1607 'a bridge over the water of Yoore a litle from Bainbridge' was reported to be in 'great ruyne and decaie' and was ordered later to be repaired at a cost of twenty pounds borne by all the Wapontakes of the North Riding.

In 1673 an Askrigg yeoman, using the practice of assessment and rate collection to his own advantage, received money 'under colour' of collecting a rate; and in the middle of the century when the expenses of the Askrigg constable had not been refunded for two years, the inhabitants of the common were ordered forthwith to pay what was due. In 1654 the parish officers failed to make any assessments at all; and two years later eight men assaulted George Frear, the chief constable, in the execution of his office, and attacked and imprisoned the rate collectors.

Besides the constable's rate, there was the heavy strain of poor-relief, a cause of much misery; for no one wanted to support illegitimate children or the poor of other parishes who might have obtained a footing. In 1650 not only had money been collected and not distributed 'to the great prejudice of the poore,' but the old churchwardens and overseers of Askrigg had five years' rates still in their hands. In July the following year the overseers were fined twenty pounds each; yet three months later a man was petitioning the court that they had 'contemned severall Orders' and failed to give him relief for a bastard child that he kept.

Thefts were frequent, and often mean and vexatious. In 1615 Daniel alias Barnabas Scott of Askrigg stole a black stott (a young ox) from the common fields of Kettlewell in Wharfedale; later a Woodhall yeoman broke into a close and took away hay, and another was suspected of stealing a mare. Of two Hawes men accused of stealing a spade, one was whipped. Shoes, stockings, ewes, tups, and geese, even buildings, were not safe. In 1622 a Shawcoate labourer took a door, valued at sixpence, perhaps the same man who two years before had stolen 'one sheeps skynn, valued 16d.,' and 'two shoulders and two hinder legges of mutton.'

In 1608, owing to an acute food shortage, the constables of the North Riding had to report on whether maltsters and badgers (corn dealers) sell their grain 'in markettes or hoord it up in chambers.' The following year nine men from the township were all 'buying corne to thintent to sell the same again.' Irregular trading, as that of George Atkinson of Askrigg who used the art or mystery of a badger without licence, was common; and time after time people, including the parson, seeking to supplement their incomes, brewed ale without permission. In 1620 nineteen ale-house keepers of Askrigg were summonsed for keeping unlicensed ale-houses.

Bastard children were usually bound as apprentices; and one original order of 1682, signed by the local justices, one of them Thomas Metcalfe, son of Sir Thomas, of Nappa Hall, has survived. George Metcalfe of Thornton Rust, the reputed father, was to pay sevenpence a week until the child reached the age of eight, and then give the overseers eight pounds towards putting it out as an apprentice; and lastly there was the terrible order to the constable that the mother, Mary

Walker ('having several times before offended in the same kinde') shall on a specified day 'between the hours of nine and twelve be stripped naked from the midle upwards, and tyde to the taile of a Carte, And shall be openly whipped from the one end of Thornton Rust to the other until her Body bee bloody.'

There are few cases of women's misdeeds, and only one person from the town, committed in 1657 to the House of Correction, was described as 'a woman of lewd and evill behaviour.' In 1614 an Askrigg labourer was brought up for 'common assault on two females in the churchyard,' and in 1668 a Bainbridge ale-house keeper was ordered 'to suffer no man's wife to drink disorderly, against their husband mind.'

In spite of their illegality games like football were surreptitiously enjoyed, and there were 'common plaiers of cardes' within the township. Poaching was indulged in, even by the yeomen; Richard Besson shot two hares in the Forest of Wensleydale with a 'fowling piece charged with powder and lead shot.' As a result of information supplied by James Render of Burton in Bishopdale, a common informer, in 1699 several Askrigg yeomen were brought before the justices: James Hollyday who kept nets and had 'destroyed 100 fish called trouts in a certain river called Youre,' John Metcalfe, John Foster, and Christopher Walker who, being unqualified to do so, kept 'setting' dogs and had destroyed moor game, Christopher Alderson, accused of tracking hares in the snow, and George Smith who having a greyhound 'by that means destroyed 10 hares.' In 1621 two labourers in Bishopdale Chase killed 'a doe younge with fawne with an arrow shot out of a crossbow (arrabalista).'

People broke into houses smashing doors and windows, and once a man was assaulted and his house thrown down. Bands of men, occasionally as many as a hundred, took the law into their own hands and, obstructing officers in the course of their duties, rescued prisoners. There were repercussions from cases brought before higher courts, such as the disputed lease of

Kitlades Farm in Askrigg parish, when Matthew Metcalfe threatened to kill Sir Thomas Metcalfe and to blow up William Robinson's house with gunpowder. For this he was whipped and put in the stocks. It is plain that the Metcalfes favoured their adherents, as, besides other pointers, in later years two men were presented for saying false and scandalous words '. . . if a dog or a cat went to Mr Metcalfe for a warrant they might have it granted.'

The poorer folk were as always at the mercy of those in authority. On 11th June 1699, whilst Thomas Nellson, a brazier of Newbiggin, was away at Boroughbridge Fair, his son 'goeing for recreation with other young men to the River of Yore to bathe themselves—was unfortunately drowned.' William Shaw of Bedale, the coroner, for three days 'obstinately refused' to come and view the corpse. Later he demanded ten shillings from Nellson's wife, and 'impudently swore' that if he took less 'the rest of the children would infallibly be drowned.'

Lastly, we learn of the 'evill example' of John Metcalfe of Low Inn, Askrigg, who one Sunday in September 1614 with others shot at the butts, drank in his house at time of divine service, and assisted 'James Mason being the same day druncke and put in the stocks.' For these crimes Metcalfe was discharged from keeping an ale-house; and we may picture the scene when the constable went to pull down the sign.

2. PROSPERITY

'Askrigg is a great Markett Towne' was proudly stated in a letter, pleading for an increase in the curate's stipend, written to the master of Trinity College Cambridge, about 1655. Some thirty years later when a curate was leaving a second letter, appealing again, was sent. The writer of this was William Thornton, who was either a great-grandson of Peter who obtained the market charter, or a member of a branch of the family. Like his fore-elder the affairs of the town revolved round him: the church, the grammar school, farming, money, and market matters, all were his concern; and an upright progressive man emerges from the strands left us to plait together. Described as an innkeeper in 1662, a not unusual occupation for a prosperous yeoman, he had married Bridget

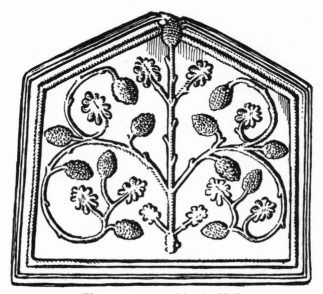

Plaster overmantel in the Hall

Barwick of Nappa Scar, and, living in one of the houses at the West End, they had two sons and a daughter, Simon, William, and Ellin.

In 1670 William bought the Old Hall property, including land, for £650 from the widow of Richard Atkinson of Dandro-garth, Garsdale, who had purchased it from Dr John Bathurst, and eight years later, prospering in lead-mining ventures, he added on to the existing building a magnificent four-storeyed façade. The ancient house of the bailiff of the FitzHughs took on the aspect we knew until fire destroyed it.

It may be that from early days the building was two houses —a Henry Smyth and a Thomas Person lived in the lord's chief house in 1465—and it had two outer doors and two spiral staircases.   Many reconstructions must have been carried out;

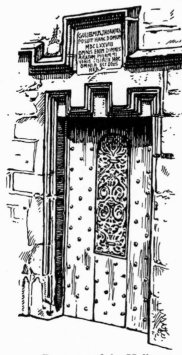

Doorway of the Hall

there was a carved lintel, dated 1616, at the back of the northern half.   Under the dripstone of the new doorway on the left side William caused to be placed a square stone with his name and a text from Hebrews in Latin carved on it, 'For every house is builded by some man; but he that built all things is God,' and he adorned the interior with fine oak panelling and plaster work.   He no doubt occupied the whole, for he paid hearth tax [1] for five hearths.

Amongst all the building and alteration that took place during the century, especially that of the yeomen in the Restoration years, the handsome hall, built by John Colby in 1655, proved the most ambitious.   In its setting of spacious meadows and pastures that fall steeply behind it to Grange Gill Beck, Colby Hall, as it is now called, still graces the hillside behind Dale Grange.   Three arched fire-places chiselled with masons' marks, and the entrance porch in the central gable, are its most arresting features.   Though it has witnessed many changes, and been divided into two, the house has attained the peacefulness of old age.   It is lovable rather than grand, and as the home of a twentieth-century yeoman, the Hall lives on.

[1] See Appendix B, page 300.

Askrigg was granted a market charter in 1587, but as roads improved Hawes obtained a charter in 1700 and in time Askrigg's market declined and disappeared. The water colour of market stalls in front of the Old Hall is dated 1871, a time when an attempt to revive the market was made as the railway was about to arrive.

Main Street, Askrigg, in the early years of the century. John Gill is the grocer, and on the left is the antique shop of Skidmore and Sons. The Old Hall was then a private house.

The Colbys, who came from Suffolk, were of sufficient status for their pedigree to be included by Dugdale in his Visitation of Yorkshire, and in 1666, like the Metcalfes, they entertained that historic personage Lady Anne Clifford, Countess of Pembroke, Dorset, and Montgomery on one of her journeys from Wharfedale to Westmorland. John Colby, father of the builder, in 1614 acquired a lease of a third of the Manor of Wensleydale, and he it was who lived for a time at Nappa Hall. He married Mary, a sister of the notorious Walter Calverley who murdered two of his sons, and leaving two boys, Francis and John, he died at an early age, in 1616.

Francis did not survive childhood, and John was only forty-one when the hall was built; probably his mother, a capable woman who after her husband's death bought a share of the manor, organized the work. Lawsuits continually beset the family, that at times did not occupy Bowbridge Hall but Heaning, a house in Askrigg parish. There were disputes with the co-purchasers of Abbotside and with the tenants; the estate, sold in 1678, three years before John Colby died, after prolonged litigation was restored to Alexander, his eldest son; and after Alexander's death, Simon Thornton, who had married a daughter, Margaret Colby, sought unsuccessfully to claim the property from a mortgagee. It is the story of the fall of a family. Though another daughter Anne married James Metcalfe of Nappa Hall, and a son Christopher became a dean of Middleham, when Alexander's three boys all died, the Colbys ceased to exist in the neighbourhood.

From 1655 James and Thomas Metcalfe, sons of Sir Thomas, lived in separate halves of Nappa Hall, and after James's death, in 1671, Thomas occupied the whole until he died thirteen years later. He was a Justice of the Peace, and with lead- and coal-mining projects in view leased from the Crown the royalties of the Manor of Askrigg.

Perhaps James, who practised as a barrister, was away when Lady Anne Clifford stayed the night at Nappa on 7th October 1663; for she only speaks of 'my cousin Mr Thomas Metcalfe's house.' We could wish for an eye-witness account of the sparkling sight of coaches, horsemen, and followers passing alongside Cragdale down the Stake Pass, of the halt for the fording of the river either at Yorebridge or Worton, and of the roasting and baking in the kitchen at Nappa, the adornment of the best bedroom, and the allotting of rooms for members of the retinue. But only the imagination may picture this fleeting yet stirring event, tales of which must have enlivened many a winter's evening.

In the meantime several new families settled in the surrounding hamlets, that, as if in keeping with Askrigg's status as an industrial town, were developing in the manner of suburbs for the wealthier inhabitants, the yeomen-gentry. Some of these sojourners, as for example the Dodsworths of Woodhall Park and the Nortons of Worton, made little mark, whilst others left permanent memorials. Abraham Fothergill of Burgh Hill near Bainbridge in 1683 gave a field, Blades Intack, worth three pounds a year, for the upkeep of the grammar school building, and his brother, Anthony, took a leading part in land purchases at the time. But of them all the Smiths at Camshouse, a scattered group of farms on Abbotside two miles west of Askrigg, enter our story most fully, for they remained. Bernard Smith and his numerous descendants built up prosperous estates, and marrying into dales' families of similar rank laid the foundation for a new development, the growth of a middle class.

Picture Camshouse on an April day in the year 1660. A narrow lane bordered by thorns and hollies leads down from the common way to four homesteads spaced well apart on billowing land. Here and there the sunlit branches of ash trees glisten against a background of brushwood that clothes the sides of hillocks. Bernard Smith's farm is the most westerly of the four, and is as often as not called Cannonhouse. The low grey building faces south, tucked at the back of a ridge of hill before descending ground reaches the river, and opposite to it, like the limbs and loins of a beast stretched full length,

Wether Fell fills the horizon. The old house basks in the calm of a golden day, and though its meagre windows let in little of the sun's bright glow the stones are warm to the touch.

A stallion neighs from a paddock. A man and a maid-servant, the one dangling a lamb in either hand, the other carrying a pail of milk, pass each other in the paved yard between the thatched barn and the turf house. On either side, the doors of laithes stand open. The cows in their cramped booses need no longer be imprisoned in fetid air, every inlet sealed against the blasts of winter, and soon the heifers will be out in Sargill Park where the monks' cattle grazed before them. Through the open door of the house a savoury smell floats from the kitchen; and a peal of laughter rings out as two children skip down the steps into the cool depths of the dairy, where freshly churned butter stands in wooden bowls and a few of last year's cheeses lie on stone shelves overhead. At this time of year the house is seldom silent. Bernard goes to bed late and rises early to see to his ewes, cows, and mares, for he keeps three hundred and eighty sheep, fifty-one head of cattle, and twelve horses and rears some sixty lambs, thirteen or fourteen calves, and four foals each year.

There are nine acres sown with barley and oats, and forty acres of meadow land, part of which, Yoken Garth and Faw, slope towards the river. Westwards spreads a great pasture, a territory to itself full of little dales and brows of hills, and crossed by tracks, one that leads over a ford, Coolwath, across the pebbly bed of the river to Burtersett and Hawes. Curlews soar and trill above Hocket Dale, plovers swoop on flashing wings, wheatears flit from rocks to hummocks of turf; and lambs like blobs of spilt milk sprinkle the pasture. Not until May will the mares that graze it drop their foals that, as they grow, will be given appropriate names, Longlegs, Mad Brains, Thick Knee, or Black Lock. The stillness of waiting hovers over Camshouse this spring day. Man and beast and earth are held rapt by the ancient sense of renewal.

In 1652 Bernard Smith had bought the property consisting of two houses and 333 acres of land for £1,125 from one of the Abbotside speculators, Sir Robert Bindloss. He had three sons, Thomas, Alexander, and John the youngest, of whom we know little, and three daughters who all married Wensleydale yeomen. He was chief constable of Hang West in 1665, and the year before contracted a second marriage that was unhappy; for he was sued for alimony both at the Consistory Court and the Quarter Sessions. He died in 1672, and by his will apportioned his estate to Thomas and Alexander, household goods to his daughters, horses to his sons-in-law, and money to his grandchildren.

Door-head at Old Camshouse

Five years before Bernard's death a new house was built in place of the old, and Thomas and his wife Elizabeth had their initials carved on both the door-head and a second stone that displayed their coat of arms. This house too has gone, and a modern one standing on a different site has incorporated into it the dated inscribed stones that drawings can best show. The Latin sentence reads 'God with us who can be against us,' and the arrangement of the English 'O man remember death' obviously puzzled the mason, who designed it badly, but carved it well.

In 1678 when he was twenty-five, Alexander Smith, together with Anthony Fothergill and Thomas Lambert, bought John Colby's share of the Manor of Wensleydale, and he took his wife Sarah, daughter of William Haward of Wakefield, and their three-year-old child Grace to live at Colby Hall. Here three more of their eleven children were born, and here they remained seven years, until, as the result of the lawsuit brought by John Colby's son, the purchase was found to be invalid, and the Smiths perforce had to seek a new home.   There was

Part of Alexander Smith's house, Low Camshouse, drawn from a photograph taken about forty years ago, before it became ruinous

no difficulty, as in 1679 Alexander had for £525 bought Bainbridge Hall and Gill Edge Farm near Countersett, the latter for his wife's marriage portion.   They remained in Bainbridge either at the Hall or at Cravenholme Farm, whence their eighth daughter was taken to be christened at Askrigg Church, until 1692–3, when they returned to live at Low Camshouse, the second of the two farms bought originally by Bernard.

The Smiths did not move again.   Alexander settled to cultivating his land, the Taw, the Hill, the three Water Ings, the

Huntkeldings. Then, doubtless finding the house too small
for his growing family of girls, he set about enlarging and
beautifying it, and ordered the mason to carve on the door-
head the initials A S S and the date 1695. A year later, on
25th March, at one o'clock in the morning, an only son,
William, was born. Their happiness was brief; for the following April the boy died, and they had only one more child,
another girl, Jane. During the rest of his life the support of his
family was Alexander's concern, and in 1724 nine daughters,
six of them married by then, 'followed their father to his grave.'
It was they and their descendants who, as attorneys, parsons,
surgeons, and apothecaries, were an influential group in Askrigg throughout the next two centuries.

To-day Low Camshouse is a ruin, a fit place for the roosting
of hens and the storage of farm implements. When the
foundations gave way and a wall cracked some fifty years ago
it was deemed unsafe for habitation, and the land was farmed
by a Kettlewell whose family had outlasted the Smiths, for
their fore-elders had lived at Camshouse in 1613. All the
adornments, including the carved door-head, were later sold.
The masonry crumbles; and it is plain that Alexander's alterations to an earlier building were ill-constructed. Over the
fire-place of the main room and under the beams of the bedroom floor is a compartment measuring 6 feet by 4 feet by
4 feet 9 inches, which was a beef loft used for hanging beef
for winter food. But for all its sorry condition the ruin, like
that of a castle, evokes memories, not of feudal lords and armed
sallies, but of yeomen, the raising of stock, and the reaping
of crops.

During the Restoration period numerous Acts of Parliament
affected both Catholics and Nonconformists. As in the previous
century there were few Recusants in Askrigg chapelry, at the
most sixteen in 1685. Whether the remoteness of the dale was
taken advantage of for the safe seclusion of priests, as perhaps
at Camshouse when the Thwaites, who were Catholics, lived
there before the Smiths, or at Bear Park that has a priest's

hiding hole, or in Cotterdale where an extraordinary number of titled men owned property, we cannot be sure.

On the other hand George Fox, who visited Wensleydale in 1652 and again twenty-five years later, persuaded many of the yeomen to adopt the new faith of the Quakers, as they came to be called. The ground had already been prepared by the Seekers, who, held together by itinerant preachers, existed in the western dales of north Yorkshire; and due to unsettlement during the Commonwealth, and a lack of endowments for ministers' stipends, church-going had fallen into neglect. Frequently at this time the chapels-of-ease in the forest, and even Askrigg Church, had no curates. We may imagine the excitement when the news of George Fox's coming spread abroad, the enthusiasm and the hostility with which he was greeted, and the power of his eloquence over the many to whom so individual a faith appealed. No doubt when, the day over, he entered Richard Robinson's home at Countersett he spoke of the reception on his second visit with thankfulness.

On Sunday, 31st August 1662, when a meeting was held at James Wetherilt's at Askrigg, James Metcalfe of Nappa Hall, a Justice of the Peace, came to the house. In consequence nineteen people were imprisoned at York Castle and four sent to the House of Correction. During this crucial year as many as a thousand Church of England clergy who could not accept the doctrines gave up their livings, and two years later a further Act brought severe punishment on those taking part in Quaker meetings. But the people of the district obstinately continued to worship as they pleased, despite being fined at the Archbishop's Court at York and the Consistory Court at Richmond for being 'negligent comers to church' and not paying church rates; and many, including John Lambert of Askrigg and Alexander Fothergill of Carr End near Semerwater, were imprisoned for their beliefs or for the non-payment of tithes. Looked upon as 'contentious' and 'disaffected persons to all Government,' they were persecuted as much by suspicion as by punishment.

Dissent in religion and dissatisfaction with the monarchy, interwoven as they were, gave rise to many expressions of unrest at this time. Askrigg was linked by the participation of a townsman, John Atkinson, with the conspiracy known as the Yorkshire Plot, a Nonconformist reaction to the series of Acts called the Clarendon Code. It sprang up in 1663 in several counties, chiefly Yorkshire, Durham, and Westmorland, and was doomed from the start by the number of informers and the successful spy system set up by Sir Thomas Gower, High Sheriff of Yorkshire. Their moves known in advance, the plotters were outmanœuvred time after time: an attempt to seize York Castle in assize week was frustrated, and an effort to rise on 12th October at Farnley Wood in the West Riding and at Kaber Rigg near Kirkby Stephen met with similar failure.

John Atkinson, member of 'a secret junto,' acted as envoy between the north and London, and, in spite of his occupation as a stockiner that normally took him abroad in the country, he became a marked man. So urgent were the rumours of unrest that even Richard Robinson, who took no part, was followed when he was in London on private business, and he and a drover whom he had met by chance on the way were questioned. In September the king's agents found that Atkinson with others, on pretence of seeing the armoury, planned to take the Tower of London. A week later a spy reported that he was 'a little man' with 'sad browne haire something thin with a light coulered stuff cloake seems to bee about 40 years old grey stocking browne shoes hee who takes him must plante himselfe in ye black greyhounde over against Worcester Court.' 'The fugitive of Askrigg' was not caught until the following March, and when examined he said that he was engaged by 'Baptists of desperate fortune, but grew wearied of their selfish designs, and looked for an opportunity to discover them.' We do not know his fate. He was not amongst the eighteen condemned to death at York, nor was he hanged with three of the Westmorland plotters at Appleby, in 1664;

for the following year he was writing a 'discourse on the reasons why England has to reject the Stuarts.'

On his way through Wensleydale in the autumn of 1687 the traveller crossing Yore Bridge would pass the grammar school close to the river, a new building, or the old one altered, with the date 1660 on a door-head, and, stopping at Askrigg, he might put up for the night at the sign of the King's Head in the main street, a little above Pudding Lane. He would see his horses bedded down in the stables that flanked the long

Door-head of Thomas Forster's house

narrow yard behind the inn, and after a meal of trout, mutton, and ale, he might stroll out to see the town.

Most of the buildings are of stone now, several newly erected on the cleared sites of ruins, and many, including the old house of the Scropes on the West End, still thatched. Yeomen's farmsteads lie unevenly up either side of the street, barns and yards interspersed between them. Some have orchards at the back, and all have gardens planted with raspberry canes and gooseberry bushes, cabbages, leeks, parsnips,[1] carrots, and herbs. Cottages, each with a small garth and occasionally a garden, straggle down wynds or up the moor road. Near the church and below the cross is the Toll Booth filled with market gear. Opposite it the fresh-hewn stone of Thomas Forster's house with its fine doorway, T A F 1687 carved on the lintel,

---

[1] In 1659 'one parcell of parsnippe ground' 14 by 7 yards was sold.

G

catches the eye; but here in the market-place William Thornton's house, the new Hall, dominates the rest.

In the dusk there is the glow of candles from mullioned
windows and the open front of a shop near the church.
Grovers carrying lanthorns are returning from drawing lead
ore at the mines on the moor, and the men, who all day have
wrought at dressing stone roofing-slates in the wharrell at the
top of the Cow Close, straggle home.   More people are to be
seen than to-day, for the population was probably greater
than now.   They pass purposefully to and fro: a yeoman to
look before nightfall to the township bulls for the present in
his keeping in the field called Bull Farmer, a labourer to
'sarra' his swine, a widow to exchange butter of her own
making for yarn at a shop.

In the Hall the family sit in the parlour where firelight
illumines the panelling and flickers on the adzed oak of cup-
board, table, and stools.   Bridget has set the maids to scour
pewter in the kitchen, and begun her knitting of thick stockings
against the coming winter, whilst William enters up his
memorandum book that contains particulars of sales of stock,
and calf and sheep skins, repairs to buildings, servants' yearly
wages, the purchase and the barter of goods, and perhaps
records of the marriages of his son William to Grace, daughter
of Alexander Smith, and Ellin to the former curate, Cuthbert
Allen, and, a recent entry, the death of Simon.   (We know
that such a book was kept, but it has not survived.)   Perhaps
he is interrupted in his task by a visit from Mr Peter Alcock,
the parson, who from being deacon at Ely, priest at Peter-
borough, and now parson of Askrigg, is soon to leave the dale
for a better cure.

The talk may well turn on the successful outcome of William's
letter whereby the college has agreed to augment the curate's
stipend, or the perfidy of Hawes people, who, in the lately
concluded lawsuit, brought in false witnesses, and purchased
freedom, the separation of their parish from Askrigg chapelry,
'at a very dear rate.'   Mention may be made of the Quakers

and of one of their number, John Ogden, who makes clocks and who has recently come to live at Bowbridge. They perhaps compare the differences between the speech of the Fen men and that of the dalesmen, a speech that here is losing many a turn of phrase and innumerable ancient words. William may speak of his son's death and deplore the sore feud between himself and the Metcalfes, who are inveterate against him since the Woodhall Mines dispute. There was no lack of stirring topics in the latter half of the century.

The mines of which William spoke were at Woodhall on the hillside under the Coombs, the easternmost edge of Ellerkin, and judging from the jealousies they aroused and the lawsuits that ensued, they yielded fortunes. Thomas Metcalfe, William Thornton, Thomas Smith, Anthony Fothergill, George and Adam Fawcett of Ballowfield, and others were involved. In 1670 three of them, representing the rest, bought the royalties of the Manor of Woodhall for £41 from the Bainbridge yeomen; and two years later trouble had begun. They quarrelled amongst themselves; the Fawcetts, owing money, were ejected from their house, and Thomas Metcalfe and William Thornton became enemies for life.

These disasters were due to the debts incurred by the suit instigated by the heir of the Scropes, Lord St John, the Marquess of Winchester. He, owning the estate adjoining the manor on the east, claimed that the mines lay in his territory, and he was supported by the Woodhall yeomen whose land was affected. On a summer's day in 1673 news doubtless travelled swiftly to the town of the fight that was taking place between the rival parties on the disputed ground; later, on 5th November, the Askrigg men and their sons rode the bounds from the river Yore up Ellerbeck, past Goose Caw, Nettle Hull, to Bellfield behind the Greets on Ellerkin, and then down to Cranehow Knot Nick, Askrigg Gate, and Elveshawes to the river. In 1677 they were surveying the points of the 'water called Ellerbecke' with two dials (a mine surveying instrument resembling a mariner's compass).

The prize at stake was such that the marquess to win his case resorted to forgery. In the June of 1673 his agent, Peter Atkinson, searched in vain for documents relating to the title of the land amongst the public records in the Tower of London, and at length promising £50 as reward he induced the apprentice to the Deputy Keeper, William Thompson, to forge the necessary deed. Eighteen months later the clerk, remorseful and ashamed, confessed. He told that he was asked to take the document 'to one Wilkinson that lived in an alley near the Queenes head in Chancery Laine whoe ingrossed the same,' that afterwards he 'blacked the parchment with a water,' and laying it for a time on a shelf in the office, later put it in a trunk. Twice he was taken to see Lord St John at his house in Lincoln's Inn Fields, and he was even brought to Atkinson's house at Temple Dowskar in Wensleydale. There were four trials, and at each of them the verdict was given against the marquess.

When William Thornton died in July 1698, his only surviving son was executor to the will that after a pious preamble reads: 'I give and bequeath to my son William Thornton all my real and Personal Estate paying after my Death to his Mother Bridgett my Wife thirty pounds per annum during her life and likewise to keep her two Cows as long as she lives.' To his daughter Ellin he left six pounds a year and a house to dwell in during her lifetime.

At the end of the century the forest could no longer be called by that name; green fields stretched from river to moor round the yeomen's houses, innumerable flocks and herds pastured where long ago wolves had lurked and deer once grazed, and thriving villages and hamlets covered the sites of seters and abbey farms.

For some time a gathering of people had met at Hawes each Tuesday to buy and sell 'as if the public and common market were there lawfully established.' In January 1699 twelve of them, accused of illegal assemblage, were brought before Quarter Sessions with the common informer, James Render, as testifying witness. No definite judgment was given. Their trade threatened, the townspeople of Askrigg, led by William Thornton, spent the proceeds of the market tolls on prosecutions, probably on the Quarter Sessions indictments. In the first half of that year first one group of men and then another, from Hawes, Gayle, Thoralby, and other places, even including Askrigg, were charged with holding an illegal market. But it was in vain.

In September the inhabitants of Hawes petitioned for a market and fairs, and at an inquisition taken at York Castle it was found that a grant would not damage neighbouring markets (although Askrigg was little over five miles from Hawes). On 20th February 1700 a weekly market and two annual fairs were granted to Matthew Wetherald, gentleman of Gayle, in trust for the town of Hawes. The yeomen of Askrigg had to meet a new challenge.

Thomas Smith's coat of arms
at Old Camshouse

The church tower, raised like an admonishing finger

VI

EIGHTEENTH-CENTURY HEYDAY

1. THE SETTLED YEARS

VIEWING ASKRIGG from across the valley in the pale sun-shine of a late autumn afternoon, we might be looking at an eighteenth-century scene. The town lies against a wide-flung hillside, its buildings packed into the shape of a narrow ellipse, the focal point of the church tower raised like an admonishing finger held stiffly upright. Behind it a shallow dip in the fells lifts on the right to Ellerkin, and farther off on the left to Whitfield Crag. There is no disharmony either of sight or sound. The wan hues of dying vegetation match the umbers of roofs and walls, and the shadow thrown by the western cliff of a solitary gill is little darker than the russet of sparse groups of trees. Rooks fly down the dale, their leisurely squawking floating across to us.

Apart from the absence of thatched roofs, the town's appearance is much as it was two hundred years ago. This was the peak of its prosperity, and no wealth flowed in later to enlarge it or alter its character. Without effort we visualize those days. The place looks busy, crowded, industrial. Many activities are in progress there. It houses dyers, hosiers, knitters, weavers, lead-miners, blacksmiths, masons, glaziers, and plasterers. There are many shoemakers, a cooper, glover, slater, gardener, greengrocer, and a baker. You may hire that precursor of the taxi, a post-chaise, at the sign of the George, or buy a supply of candles from the chandler, or a buttock of beef to pickle for the winter from the butcher; see patterns of cloth at the haberdasher's, ask the tailor to come and make up a suit of clothes, or order a grandfather's clock if you are thinking of getting married. Thomas Metcalfe, the parson, may be visiting his parishioners, Anthony Fearon, the attorney, and his clerk drawing up a deed, James Lightfoot, the apothecary, mixing physic, the surgeon, Francis Wilson, bleeding a patient, the barber, Thomas Forsyth, dressing a wig; or John Pratt is inspecting his racehorses, and Alexander Fothergill giving orders for the next day's statute work on the turnpike, whilst perhaps an innkeeper is adding two gallons of brandy to twelve gallons of ale in readiness for an auction sale when many will be 'full of liquor.'

The town revolves in its own orbit. In county rates for 1747 Askrigg pays far more than Leyburn or Middleham, and though outstripped by Bainbridge, West Burton, and Thoralby, with these villages are included Hawes, as part of the Manor of Bainbridge, and the hamlets and farms of wide areas of side valley. Askrigg is the centre of the dale in men's minds.

At that date the town is on the threshold of great change, with the appearance of improvements, some of which may be called modern. A drainage system is completed, the street paved with cobbles, and, joining up with the roads of England, the Richmond to Lancaster turnpike, passing through Askrigg, is made. Houses are built to shelter the rapidly increasing

population. The vicar's stipend is augmented by a local subscription, a legacy, and Queen Anne's Bounty. The church
is beautified with a new font, a new clock, a singing gallery,
and many box-like pews.

But even now the importance of the town is imperceptibly
slipping away. The chapels-of-ease one by one become separated from the parish; and in time, as better roads link up with
the head of the dale, Hawes creeps into prominence. Already
the population of centres of industry in the West Riding
numbers thousands as against the hundreds in Askrigg, and
unbeknown to those busily employed dalesmen, inventors are
soon to perfect machines that will affect them more than they
can dream. From our vantage point across the valley we now
see shadows thrown by a few small clouds move along the side
of Ellerkin, and as we look, like a portent of the future, a black
goods train, smelling of far different towns from the one we
contemplate, comes up the valley.

Picture Askrigg Beast Fair during the town's heyday. On
18th October 1733 bells jingle as pack-horse trains laden with
wares plod into the town, and the market-place is filled with
the monotonous rise and fall of the bleating of sheep. Cattle,
driven from upper Wensleydale and Swaledale, mix with
flocks from far-away Scotland. The animals plunge and bunch
together with eyes rolling and heaving flanks; men and boys
shout and whistle; and the drovers stand in small groups, the
Scotsmen apart, their plaids thrown over their shoulders. On
the stalls lie woollen cloth, pewter, and millinery. Part of the
market-place has been paved, and the booth where the toll
farmer sits ready to receive 1d. for each loaded horse, 2d. for
every beast bought and sold, 2d. from each butcher, and various
sums, 3d. to 2s. 6d., from other vendors, is freshly flagged.
Amongst the throng walk the constable holding his staff, and
two men bearing halberds. There too is Mark Metcalfe, the
clock-maker, who for the sum of 5s. has just made the town
seal of brass.[1] It depicts a cross with three steps enclosed by

[1] Depicted on the title-page.

circles with the inscription *Sigillum commune inhabitantium de Askrigg*, the common seal for the town of Askrigg.

That year, three days before the fair, four gentlemen had assembled at the house of Widow Lawson in Askrigg to examine witnesses in a lawsuit that had come before the Exchequer Bar. It was a case that must have injured the market. Nine inhabitants who had held the same office as the Four Men in the previous years were accused of misuse of public funds and of jobbery at elections. These dignitaries were in charge of the toll money of markets and fairs, the income by which the town's amenities were maintained. Amongst the fifteen people interviewed were a yeoman, a whitesmith, a blacksmith, a widow aged ninety, 'one of the people called Quakers,' and James Watson, bellman of the town. James, born in Askrigg seventy-five years before, had 'frequently given public notice to the inhabitants to meet in the Toll Booth to choose four persons for the ensuing year for the managing and letting of the tolls.'

We learn that two fairs were held, the first on 30th April and 1st May and the second on 18th October, and that several recent Four Men had distributed the toll money by 'house-row,' each householder receiving a shilling, instead of using it to better purpose, though it was stated that this method had been practised at irregular intervals for eighty years. Others said that in the past gifts were made from it to the poor, and any surplus, when not shared among the inhabitants, 'put out at interest.' One man remembered that forty shillings used to be given to the vicar, and 'seventy shillings yearly for several years to Samuel Garnett for ringing the Eight of the Clock Bell in the winter in the church of Askrigg.'

The Four Men's account-book produced at the examination has been lost, but a later one has survived. The book is craftsman made, bound with leather, embossed with lines and corner motives, and containing pages of the beautiful cream-coloured paper of the time—no dull binding and machine-made ruled paper such as we use nowadays. It begins in 1731, and with gaps of ten and thirty-five years contains accounts, and, after 1839, the minutes of the activities of the rulers of Askrigg, until 1894; when, after the passing of the Local Government Act, most of the duties were taken over by the newly formed Parish Council.

As we read the entries, there emerges a picture of the yearly round of town affairs. Time passes and it seems that only the names of the people change. William Thornton and later John Pratt, of whom we shall hear more, acted in the capacity of bankers, lending money if receipts fell short of expenditure, or keeping any surplus in hand. The tolls were let in 1731 for £16, and £11 or £12 and often £9 up to 1770.

Every October, a fortnight before St Luke's Day, the inhabitants met to elect the Four Men, and 'according to custom' the holders of the office declared themselves willing to nominate their successors provided they were reimbursed any losses by the persons chosen. Blacksmith, innkeeper, hosier, joiner, butcher, woolcomber, dyer, and attorney all took their turn. For carrying out their duties each received 2s. 6d. a year, and responsibilities included the annual letting of the tolls by public auction, advertising and crying the fairs, organizing the sports, and maintaining the Toll Booth, stalls, streets, cross, and the three pumps. They spent money on rejoicings on November the Fifth. They settled the Fee Farm or 'King's Rent' that originated in the market charter, due on Lady Day and at Michaelmas, discharged the land tax quarterly, and paid church, constable, poor, and highway rates.

Held in August, probably on St Oswald's Day, the ancient feast day, the sports required a special meeting. At this, accompanied by the drinking of the usual quota of ale, the Four Men proceeded to decide questions of advertisement (proclamations both at Askrigg and that other neighbouring market-town, Reeth in Swaledale), the mending of the race ground, and the prizes. The latter, doubtless for horse and foot races, were handsome: a saddle costing 12s. 6d., a bridle

1745 Disbursments this Year

	Paid the four men	0:	10:	0
	To the Cryer	0:	1:	6
	To Ino Thompson for mending Stall Gear	0:	2:	0
	To Wood for Tressell foot	0:	1:	6
	Paid for cleaning the streets	0:	3:	4
	To Antho: Metcalfe for Horses Man and Cart 7 Days	0:	12:	0
nov'r 5	To the Publick Rejoycings	0:	10:	6
	Candles in the Toll Booth	0:	0:	6
	To five Floaks	0:	1:	6
	Poor Sess	0:	3:	10
Febr 21	Constable Sess	0:	1:	2
Aprl 12	Fee Farm Rent & Carrage	0:	11:	8
15	Poor Sess	0:	0:	3½
18	2 Payments Land Sax	0:	5:	0
19	Man & horse cleaning ye streets 4 Days	0:	6:	8
29	To Rejoicings of the Victory over the Rebells	0:	10:	0
	Church Sess	0:	0:	11
	2 men 2 Days raking the streets	0:	2:	8
May 11	To Ino Thompson for 13 Tressles	0:	4:	0
22	To Poor Sess	0:	6:	8½
June 2	Paid about application of Rent	0:	1:	0
	To Poor Sess	0:	1:	11
July 4	Land Sax	0:	2:	6
31	To a Boys Hatt 3/8 Ditto mans 5/6	0:	9:	2
	Bridle 2/6 Whip 3/6 for fetching them from Galek	0:	6:	4
	Expended in agreeing about the Sports	0:	1:	0
5	Paid Prize moneys for the Horses	0:	12:	6
	To Proclaming the Sports at Askrigg and Reeth	0:	0:	10
Sept 18	Expended about bargain with Workmen about Cross	0:	3:	6
Octr 2	To 4 Load of Lime & Carrage	0:	2:	8
9	Land Sax	0:	2:	6
13	To 4 Load more Lime and Carrage	0:	2:	0
	To Francis Sidgeswick and Geo Scarr for } reparing the Markett Cross }	1:	10:	0
	For leading 21 Cartful of Stones at ye ff Cartfull	0:	15:	4
	Ino Garnett for work at the Pump	0:	8:	6
	Spent when the Stall Gear were reviewd	0:	2:	0
	Ino Metcalfe for giving Notice	0:	0:	6
		£ 9:	18:	2

Page from the book of the Four Men

2s. 6d., a whip 3s. 6d., a hat 6s., cloth for a smock and 'ribband' 5s. 6d., and 1s. 2d. worth of tobacco. Besides these half a guinea was usually given as a purse, probably for wrestling, a man was paid 1s. 9d. to drag a dead cat for a dog trail (the 'catt' cost 3d.), and once 5s. was offered as a 'Prize for Asses to Run for.' The races are mentioned for the last time in 1783, though because of the gap in the accounts from 1786 to 1821 we cannot be sure when they ceased.

Before Fair Day came the 'viewing' of the stalls. Sorting out the gear stacked in the Toll Booth, the Four Men made an inventory, checked the weights and measures, and examined the booth itself. In 1731 and 1732 three trees were bought for £3 2s., and the felling and leading, the making of twenty new stalls, and mending other tackle, carried out by the Thompsons, father and son, amounted to £3 14s. 9d. Boards, trestles, stowars (posts), two cowling rakes to scrape the streets, a marking iron to brand the gear A. T., Askrigg Town, and a shovel were the equipment. In the early half of the century the pumps were kept in order by John Garnett, the blacksmith, for 2s. a year, but in 1759 the plumber, William Terry, repaired all three, the high, middle, and low, and allowed £1 1s. 3d. for seventeen stones of lead taken from one of them. Sometimes the Toll Booth needed improvements, such as a new 'flower,' or a new window, or moss to fill in cracks in the roof. Regular disbursements were made for cleaning the streets and dressing the market-place, before it was paved with cobbles a muddy morass; and occasionally the 'paveior,' an important personage, was employed and encouraged like the rest of the workmen with ale, the equivalent of the present-day cups of tea.

Little is reflected in the book of events in the outside world. In 1743 travelling players passed through, and paid 6d. for 'acting one night.' They came again the following year, and this time performed on two nights. In 1740 we read 'Spent concerning Carthagena 5s.,' perhaps a commemoration of the attack on the place of that name in South America during the war with Spain. Six years later the accounts include an entry dated 29th April: 'To rejoycings of the Victory over the Rebels 10s.' The victory was Culloden fought thirteen days earlier; but what form the celebrations took we can only surmise, perhaps the lighting of a bonfire, the holding of sports, and the ringing of church bells.

Though the army of the Young Pretender passed on the other side of the Pennines, the '45 Rebellion naturally excited the dalesmen. In the previous year the arms of Papists in the township had been confiscated by the constable. John Dupont, vicar of Aysgarth, who as 'the son of a French Protestant' was bitterly opposed to the Catholics, printed a pamphlet addressed 'to all true Englishmen,' preached three sermons on the rebellion, and was reviled by 'a sturdy fellow' sent by local Jacobites to his home. Then, the retreat of the Scots from Derby and the advance of the English army were regarded as sights worth travelling some distance to see.

One who embarked on such an expedition was Alexander Fothergill of Carr End, near Semerwater, member of the Quaker family. We shall hear more of Alexander, for he kept a voluminous diary, once thought to be lost, but of which a fragment remains. On 17th December 1745 he set out with several neighbours for Westmorland, and caught up with the army at Orton, south of Penrith. Here his horse was seized by a constable and a dragoon who, hearing how far he was from home, lent him a galloway too small for an armed man. 'I mounted,' he says, 'and went cheerfully along with them'; but by this delay he lost his party. Singled out by his dress as a Quaker, Alexander drew the attention of both officers and men, and he conversed with General Oglethorpe, 'which made the time agreeably spent.' Later the Duke of Cumberland and other important personages were pointed out to him.

At length near Clifton he found himself in the thick of the skirmish, that included volleys shot over walls 'followed by a Highland hurrah.' Then, whilst the English army remained in the open during a cold wet night, he sought shelter in a cottage, to which some local men brought plundered arms. He ordered them to surrender these, and next day, reporting the incident, he was returned his horse. With a soldier he chased an armed rebel at full gallop, and claimed the man's pistol as a memento. Obviously Alexander enjoyed himself hugely, and he ended his account with a lengthy and severe criticism of the generalship.

Alexander Fothergill was a grandson of the Alexander imprisoned for non-payment of tithes, and a son of John Fothergill who spent a large part of his life on preaching missions. Settled at Carr End, near Semerwater, this Quaker family was outstanding in Wensleydale. John had five children : Alexander, the eldest, remained in the dale, Dr John Fothergill was the founder of Ackworth School and a famous physician in London, where his sister Anne kept house for him, and Samuel followed his father as a preacher in America.

Alexander was married twice, to Jane Blakey who bore him two daughters, and to Margaret Thistlethwaite who had six children. His profession of attorney took him abroad in the country, and when appointed surveyor of the turnpike road he threw himself wholeheartedly into the work. Farming at Carr End was in the nature of a hobby that, had he pursued it more diligently, might have spared him the bankruptcy that overtook him in later life. He was admonished by the Quakers of the neighbourhood for drinking in ale-houses, and reprimanded for keeping company with women of ill repute, a charge he denied. He championed the poor, wrote letters for public causes, and was involved in most of the local affairs of the day. He was a snob, a seeker of excitements, yet, touchingly at times, was only too conscious of his failings, vowing, albeit not always very convincingly, to mend his ways. He was, in fact, a mixture, a member of a strict religious sect and a man of his time.

In local society Alexander Fothergill was a yeoman, or in the terms of the eighteenth century a member of the middle class. When Thomas Metcalfe, a grandson of Sir Thomas and a bachelor, died in 1756, that 'hierarchy made up of country gentlemen, clergy, yeomen, and labourers, what might be called the standard equipment of an English village,' was shaken; for those who inherited Nappa Hall owned other estates and lived elsewhere.

In 1789 the vicar of Askrigg stated that there were no families with more than £300 a year in his parish; and at the same time it was said in a tithe dispute: 'The property in the rectory of Aisgarth, exclusive of eight or nine estates and only two or three of these above £500 per annum, is generally occupied by the owners whose estates run from £10 to £100 a year.' Amongst the middle class were members of branches of the Metcalfe family, whose sons, educated at Cambridge colleges, became parsons at Askrigg, the descendants of Alexander Smith's daughters who inclined to turn to a profession for a living, and the dyers and hosiers. Together with the labourers and servants, by far the largest body, they comprised the society of the town. It was more diffuse and sprawling than the close-knit growing one of the preceding century.

During the reign of Queen Anne these middle-class people enjoyed the leisurely life of those settled years. Thorntons, Pratts, Metcalfes, Smiths, Whaleys, Harrisons, Rouths, and Lightfoots, living up and down the dale, engaged in farming their own land, invested capital in lead mines, and pursued professions. Most had small libraries of books, and some perhaps took lessons from John Johnson, the 'musician.' Mary, daughter of Alexander Smith, and her husband Thomas Pratt, living at Low Camshouse, kept a coach; and when Thomas died, Mistress Mary Pratt was plainly a person of consequence, heading subscription lists for charities.

The Thorntons put out two doorways that led to an outside gallery between the gables of the Hall, and from it, as tradition relates, they watched the sport of bull-baiting in the market-place below. Following the current fashion, they built a summer-house on Croft Hill. It was two-storeyed, with a flight of outside steps to the upper floor, the corners of the roof surmounted by stone balls; and on the map that pictures it a flag is shown flying from the pinnacle. From its windows there was a fine view up and down the dale. The barn that

The Old Hall, with the eighteenth-century additions of the balcony and upper doors

has replaced it retains one of the balls on a gable-end. In a garden at the back of the Hall they had a second smaller building similar in style that remains in a ruinous condition, and near it a large walled orchard. It was indeed the era of callous sports and outdoor extravaganzas; the ring to which the bull was tethered still remains, and though most of the summer-houses have gone, seven gardens surrounded by lofty walls, some in parts twenty feet high, are still a feature of Askrigg.

When on 26th November 1746 Grace Thornton, who had outlived her husband by six years, died, she was the last of that name. After four hundred years one more ancient family had passed away, and as leaders of the town they were never wholly replaced. The Hall then reverted to its old division,

Bull-ring

for John Addison, a dyer, lived in one half. Grace left an unsigned indenture, whereby her house and several closes of land were to be transferred to her nephew, James Lightfoot; and Sarah Killinghall, her only child, who had married well, carried out the wishes of her mother.

James, born at Yarm in 1719, was the son of Margaret, another daughter of Alexander Smith, and James Lightfoot, originally of Redmire. He was a bachelor, and as trustee for many of his relatives, much of his time was spent in resolving their affairs. He had set up in business at Askrigg as apothecary, a profession that was then approaching in scope the work of its direct descendant, the general practitioner. We may picture his shop in the house that he built about 1756, the shelves filled with a picturesque array of bottles and jars, and we may imagine his prescriptions made up from the crude substances available in those days, and the journeys in his chaise driven by a servant to visit his patients.

Dying in 1807 at the age of eighty-eight, James lived throughout the town's heyday. A benevolent honourable man, foremost in promoting the union of parishes for the building of a workhouse for the poor, a glimpse of his character may be had

H

from a dedicatory prayer headed 'Dr James Lightfoot, Askrigg, Declaration on beginning business':

Most gracious God who alone has the power to give success to my undertakings. I Thy most unworthy servant, whom Thou has appointed to administer Physick, to be a help and comfort to all those who are afflicted with sickness, and in extremity of Pain; do with all Humility prostrate myself before Thee, beseeching Thee to grant me Thy Divine assistance in these my performances, have mercy upon and bless me, guide me and govern me in all my actions, prosper all my undertakings; and grant that I may be as careful of the poor, as of the Rich, that I may do good and not harm, save life and not destroy it: Help my infirmities and imperfections O Lord! and grant that I may neither be too rash nor too timorous in the performances of my Duty, but grant me Art and Judgement in the happy finishing of all my Operations, work in me a tender heart and whatever else is necessary for me to Thy glory and my own credit and whensoever my duty calls me either by night or by day I may be always prepared. Preserve and defend me from the infection of all contagious diseases, and grant me a prosperous success, that whatsoever I do or undertake may add to Thy Glory and comfort and help of all those committed to my charge, and my own credit, through Jesus Christ my blessed Saviour and Redeemer Amen.

The prosperity of the town depended on industries, that of dyeing combined with the manufacture of knitted garments taking precedence. Forty people, about half the total number who paid poor-rates in 1756, were assessed on trade as well as land, and there were other smaller tradesmen. Many had a varying amount of meadow and grazing rights on the Cow Pasture, where they kept stock to supply their families with milk, butter, and cheese. The farms mostly lay in the hamlets, as they still do. Clock-making was a specialized work that employed a few craftsmen. The mines at Woodhall seldom remained idle up to the decline of lead-mining in the next century, and ground on Askrigg Moor was frequently leased to partnerships of local and Swaledale men to make trials for ore or to dig for coal.

During the century eleven families of dyers are recorded in the parish registers and deeds of property. The trade carried on from father to son; a few of the same names recur throughout

Hanoverian times and into Victorian. The dye-houses, some by the becks, some making use of wells, were often situated near the bridges. Vats of liquid, steaming kettles, and the smell of wet yarn and dye permeating dark rooms with paved floors were a feature of the town. Hosiers, weavers, and knitters of stockings for their own wear from all parts of the upper dale and from Swaledale brought their goods to the Askrigg dyers.

This trade and the manufacture of knitted goods were inextricably linked. More numerous than those employed in dyeing were the knitters, men, women, and children, stockings draped round their waists, pursuing other tasks, or sitting at their doors, and always rhythmically plying their needles. Then there were pack-horses, and later carriers' carts, setting out laden with neatly packed bundles of the finished articles. We have found no Askrigg records of marketing, but from what was happening in neighbouring dales we may infer that through wholesale merchants in London goods were sent to Holland and the West Indies, and thousands of pairs of stockings supplied to the army and smaller quantities to drapers' shops.

As yet banks did not exist to tide people over emergencies, so that mortgages on property abounded. The case of Christopher Alderson, a dyer and a considerable landowner, who became bankrupt early in the century, was an unhappy affair that needed two commissions to satisfy the creditors. Several fields are known to this day as Alderson Lands. In 1755 Peter Brougham, a hosier, dealer, and chapman, connected by marriage with the Smiths, was declared a bankrupt; and, as we shall see, there were other pointers later in the century to the recession of trade from small towns such as Askrigg.

One or two account-books of yeomen of the locality record the hiring of servants. The God's Penny, a shilling, was first given in earnest of the agreed wage, in the middle of the century about £2 10s. for a maidservant and £3 10s. for a man, paid at the end of the year. Meanwhile small sums were loaned by the master or mistress as required for clothes or amusement, and finally deducted from the wage.   Items bought in this way by the maids include 'a pair of prod pattens' 9*d*., 'one shamey [chamois] skinn to cover her stays' 1*s*., 'a new twilt [quilt] and cardinal [hood]' a guinea, buckles 1*s*., 'shiftin cloth' at 1*s*. a yard; whilst the men bought shoes, clogs, 'handchurchifs,' and buckskin for breeches. Clothes must have lasted long and, handed on, have seen service on many people's backs. Most money was spent at those great events the fairs, Askrigg, Hawes, and sometimes Kettlewell in Wharfedale, and once a man was loaned 5*s*. to attend the cock-fighting at Hawes on Shrove Tuesday. But in spite of these expenditures there was usually more than half the wage to draw at the end of the year.

These sums seem pitiably small; but wages were rising. In 1757 those of a manservant in the same employ for some years rose to £6, and in 1776 an experienced maidservant received £3 15*s*. a year. Arthur Young in his *Tour to the North* gives £4 as the latter's wages. The same authority records that lead miners earned at an average about 1*s*. 3*d*. a day, women workers in the mines 1*s*., and boys and girls from 4*d*. to 9*d*., and continues: 'But the day's work finished by twelve or one o'clock, after which no bribes are sufficient to tempt them into the farmer's service, in the busiest times, not even for an hour.'

The price of food, in keeping with the value of money in those days, also seems low, but it can hardly have allowed a varied diet for labourers' families.   In 1787 a pound of butter cost 6½*d*. at Bainbridge, and a 15-lb. cheese 3*s*. 5½*d*. Alexander Fothergill paid 3*s*. 2*d*. a stone for beef, and 5*s*. for half a stone of green tea. A pint and a half of milk cost 1*d*., potatoes from between 2½*d*. and 5*d*. a peck, hams were sold at 4*d*. a pound, and mutton at 3*d*.

The miller at Nappa in 1781 was selling oatmeal at 1*s*. 3*d*. a peck, malt at 1*s*. 2*d*. a peck, the same quantity of flour at

1*s*. 8*d*., and peas at 1*s*. 6*d*. His accounts and those of a Bain-bridge miller of a similar date reveal that oatmeal was bought in far larger quantities than any other meal. This, eaten as porridge and oatcake, was the basis of diet. Yet people were tall and big-boned, and as one of the eighteenth-century tourists remarked, lived to a great age in their health-giving surroundings.

2. THE TURNPIKE ROAD AND THE SURVEYOR

IN 1751 the Act of Parliament for the raising of money to be spent on the making of a turnpike road from Richmond to Lancaster was passed; and at a meeting of the trustees held at the Red Lion at Askrigg on 19th June Alexander Fothergill was unanimously elected surveyor with a salary of £30 a year, raised eventually to £40. The road was divided into two, his province being from Brompton near Richmond to Ingleton Bridge. It was an undertaking that affected the whole dale. When disagreement on the expenditure of money arose later, a lawyer of Richmond said that Wensleydale should be grateful in any circumstances, and implied that it had never before possessed a road worthy of the name.

The route followed was in parts ancient, for instance down Scarth Nick, but instead of continuing along the old common way of the monks, through Castle Bolton and above Carperby, it linked village to village, passing through Redmire, Carperby, Woodhall, Nappa, and Askrigg. Then proceeding across Yore Bridge to Bainbridge, it ascended Wether Fell up the Roman road over 'the high Mountain called Camm,' and so from Ribblehead to Ingleton. For almost another half-century this route was adhered to.

In the Act of Parliament the usual twenty-one years were allowed for the completion of the road and a hundred and ninety-eight trustees were appointed, though any nine formed a quorum. John Dupont of Aysgarth, George Metcalfe of Askrigg, George Metcalfe of Shawcoat, and James Allen of Snaizholme represented the locality. Heavy tolls were fixed, for example 4s. 6d. 'for every Coach, Chariot, Landau, Berlin, Chaise, Calash, or Hearse drawn by Six or more Horses,

Elm Hill and Ellerkin

Mares, Geldings, and Mules,' and so on in decreasing scale to 'every Drove of Calves, Hogs, Sheep, or Lambs, the sum of 10d. a score.'

A clause exempting carts carrying coals was taken advantage of to the extent that in 1756 a second Act was passed to impose a toll of such vehicles, and at the same time the rest were drastically reduced. Evidently a tremendous traffic in coal from Durham had started up, so much so that the finishing of the turnpike was 'greatly obstructed and retarded.' To present the case before Parliament Alexander Fothergill was in London, and later he stayed there nine weeks to assist in pleading for a turnpike planned from Manchester to Newcastle via Burnley, Colne, Settle, and Ingleton to join up with the Richmond road on Cam, a project that failed.

During the first years Alexander was daily riding up and down the valley on turnpike business, and often staying over-night at the inns. With Mr Dixon, the clerk and treasurer, a Richmond attorney, he attended the meetings held about eight times a year at Richmond, Lancaster, Askrigg, Ingleton, and occasionally at Leyburn. At these meetings methods of raising public loans were considered, new trustees appointed, toll-gate matters arranged, and Alexander was given his orders and his reports and accounts were examined. Once, staying at Forrests in Richmond, he says that the gentlemen were 'in such hurry and confusion about their cock-fighting which hath been all this week' that it was not until after late dinner that they got to discussing turnpike affairs; and another time he found the house 'harryed with gentlemen about entering horses for the races.' He himself was eventually in a muddle when in 1774 he records '. . . my turnpike accounts now 7 years undigested.'

Alexander controlled the local surveyors, who, appointed by the justices at Highway Sessions, assessed the inhabitants on the labour they should provide for repairing the road through their parishes. A footnote to one of his notices to the three Askrigg surveyors reads: 'Each person must come at eight o'clock in the morning each day, and bring proper tools for working with, or I shall reject them. Of this you must give immediate notice from house to house, and return me this paper on Monday morning when I call for it.' Labour could be avoided by the payment of composition money. An Askrigg Statute List for 1768 gives a hundred and fifteen people assessed to pay sums ranging from 5s. 4d. to 8d. and twenty-four of them due to provide a horse and cart.

Money was much preferred to labour; as Alexander said, people were unskilled, often 'in liquor,' they sent women and children, and wasted his time. He wrote of the Askrigg workers who were called out from each side of the street on separate days: 'They wrought very idly and little could have been done if I had not provided skuttles [containers, probably baskets]

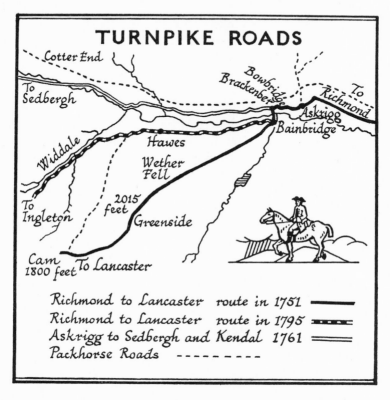

TURNPIKE ROADS

Cotter End
To Sedbergh
Bowbridge
Brackenber
To Richmond
Askrigg
Bainbridge
Widdale
Hawes
Wether Fell
To Ingleton
2015 feet
Greenside
Cam 1800 feet
To Lancaster

Richmond to Lancaster route in 1751 ——————
Richmond to Lancaster route in 1795 ▰▰▰▰▰▰
Askrigg to Sedbergh and Kendal 1761 ══════
Packhorse Roads ----------

in their carts at which they were so greeved that they often threw them away over into the fields.' Another time the western half of the town 'appeared pretty generally but brought ill carts and behaved with their usual perverseness. Richard Woodward burst a scuttle with sitting upon it.' As for Askrigg Common, Francis Robinson 'was very saucy and went from work at three o'clock tho' he began but after nine and was above one hour at noon.'

The real construction was carried out by 'undertakers,' partnerships of men who put in tenders. Alexander met them on the ground, selected the most reasonable offers, and contracted with the men to make 'parcels of road turn-pike wise' at between 5s. and 7s. 6d. a rood. They had 'to beat in fill and levell all the wheel rutts.' An agreement of June 1754 for a stretch over Greenside reads:

> The road is to be casten six yards broad within the trenches, to be well formed and as near as can be levell taking down ridges and filling up hollows. To be stoned four yards broad and ten inches thick. To be very small brocken and well covered with the best gravill and earth, conduits to be made where necessary. Three fourths of the price to be paid at the end of each sixty rood made and the residue to remain as a security for keeping the said road 12 months in repair. The said road to be completed on or before the last of Septr. next.

One of Alexander's first actions was to erect the toll gates at Redmire, Askrigg, Brackenber, and Bainbridge. As they were fixed before the road was in repair, passengers were 'very riotous and unwilling to pay tolls,' and evaded them by riding round, for which they were fined. The collectors had to be assured of protection, 'they being discouraged by the continual rudeness of passengers.' Farmed out like the market tolls, Askrigg Gate was worth about £50, the largest sum taken there up to 1773 being £61 13s. 3¾d. in 1762; and the gatekeeper's salary amounted to £16.

In 1756 it was decided to move the gate at Brackenber into the north part of Askrigg Town Head, and the gate now in Askrigg to 'the Cross House Lane Ends.' An old building was converted into a toll house at Town Head, a common practice, though Alexander would never buy 'an old rotten house at a great price.' For the Lane Ends he bargained for the building of a new house. Very good stones were supplied and led at 10d. a yard; the mason-work cost 6d. a yard, and the woodwork £13 10s. Although the old turnpike house had been thatched, the roof of the new one was to be slated at 12s. a rood by James Metcalfe. This man caused much vexation, for one day having neglected to dress the slate he went to work in Swaledale.

Taking with him an old sword to slash the hedges, Alexander rode about the countryside, saw that rubbish was swept up, and drains kept clear. He paid the workmen, gave them ale for overtime, and examined their work, such as the new paved causeway, eleven feet broad, costing £3 6s. 8d., at the low end of Askrigg, and the repair of the battlements of Scarr End Bridge at the top of Howgate, east of Askrigg. He purchased tools and implements; hammers often needed renewing, as people disliking stonebreaking deliberately broke them. He fined defaulters or distrained their goods, sometimes at Buckden in Wharfedale, and he settled differences at Horton-in-Ribblesdale, through both of which parishes the road on Cam passed. He helped local surveyors with their accounts, collected the gate money, and occasionally escorted important visitors or friends of the trustees travelling in post-chaises along dangerous stretches, as over Wether Fell and Cam to Ingleton.

On 15th March 1774, meeting several trustees in Askrigg, he took two of them on to the hillock, Seata, to view the roads and gates near the town, and in June accompanied them on a tour of inspection through the township. The road from Ballowfield to Bow Bridge, ordered to be widened, was measured by Alexander and the local surveyors. Carrying a chain to take the lengths and a rod eight yards long marked to links to check the breadth, he set down in a book some nineteen places where the road, being less than seven yards broad, needed widening. He notes 'close at work till even.'

In September of the same year he rode from Askrigg with Justice Chaytor and two trustees, one in a chaise with two spare led horses, up the dale to view the Mossdale and Cotter roads. Travelling by horseback over Cotter Rigg and to Hell Gill Bridge, the route that Lady Anne Clifford traversed in a coach, he showed them 'the impracticality of ever making a road over the mountain and the advantageous track of the

new road.' This, a turnpike dating from 1761 leading from
Brackenber Gate near Askrigg to Sedbergh and Kendal,
pursued something of its modern course up to the Moorcock
Inn. Then, having dined at 'Bell Parkins on beefe, wine,
brandy etc. returned in the chaise along the new road.' The
vague tracks in the farthest reaches of the
almost forgotten forest were being defined. But at times travellers still found
them hazardous; two highwaymen were
apprehended at Hawes Fair in 1798.

The turnpike meetings could be ill-
humoured affairs; and there was from the
beginning a difference of opinion between
the 'Richmondites,' represented by a Mr
Hartley, and Wensleydale, supported by
Justice Chaytor of Spennithorne near
Leyburn. Alexander's relationship with
the trustees, always a carefully balanced
one, fraught with jealousy and suspicion,

Milestone on Abbotside on
the Askrigg to Sedbergh
turnpike road

gradually deteriorated. At a meeting held in 1774 to appoint
thirty-three new trustees, they took his provisional list of names
and 'dashed out one, introduced another as suited each gentleman's caprice.' But the real trouble had begun in 1755 when
disagreement arose about a gate to be erected east of Richmond. The project was shelved, for the time being.

Then in July 1774 at Askrigg the decision to have the gate
was confirmed, and the trustees hurrying off, not waiting to
sign the minute book, the blame fell on Alexander's shoulders.
Next the 'Richmondites,' realizing that the only way to avoid
the gate was the dismissal of the surveyor, came in force,
the mayor and many aldermen, to a meeting at Leyburn.
Alexander was accused of procuring a clause to prohibit the
erection of the gate to be repealed by Parliament, of not paying
bills, and told to set £130 10s. 'immediately upon the table,'
which he could not do. They had, he said, already squeezed
£600 out of him. Finally the trustees declared the meeting

at Askrigg in July void; Alexander was dismissed; and 'a shabby fellow picked up in County Durham' was set in his place.

He attended his last turnpike meeting in December. 'Hartley stormed,' and read out the accounts, 'making remarks thereon with his usuall malicious accrimony and frequent falsities'; items were 'struck out furiously.' But, 'the most arbitrary nay vilainous part was' that when a gatekeeper said he had not been paid any wages the sum was deducted from Alexander's account, at which he told them they were 'picking my pocket wilfully.'

Three days later he sorted his papers, burnt any that were useless, and handed over his tools—three hammers, a hack, a rake, a hedge-bill, and a scuttle—to the new surveyor. But Alexander had left a permanent memorial. The road was made, and a new epoch opened up for Wensleydale.

Meanwhile, no doubt influenced by the turnpike in the one case and perhaps by an epidemic that had broken out in 1754 in the other, the people of Askrigg planned to pave the main street and Pudding Lane with cobble-stones and to drain the town by driving a common shore. In 1758 the Four Men and Alexander, as surveyor, made an agreement to cause 'the Town Street of Askrigg from the high end of the present pavement upwards to the end of the turnpike road to be well and sufficiently new paved and laid out in a proper and regular manner from the whole breadth of the street with drains and channels where necessary'; and the owners and occupiers of the houses on each side promised to pay the share of the cost of paving their frontages. For his part Alexander was to be responsible for a fifteen-foot-broad stretch up the centre of the street.

The paving seems to have been finished in the following year, for Alexander noted in his diary: '25th June 1759. I then attended John Charlton, who had now finished the paving in Askrigg, and measured the whole 1,233 square yards broad up the middle, and 102 yards long at the turnpike

Pudding Lane

expense, viz. 510 yards at 2*d*. a yard: for levelling the street
is £5 to the fronts £7.'

John Charlton also undertook the making of the common
shore and was paid £17 for carrying it up the length of the
main street.   It had to be driven six feet deep, flagged at the
bottom, well walled up at each side as high as was necessary;
and leave was given to get stones in the township.   A further
£24 10*s*. 9*d*. was paid him the next year for 'levelling and
cutting the cross drains into the common shore and paving
the street.'

The whole affair, including labourers' wages for leading
stones and the hire of horses and carts, cost £90 5*s*. 7*d*.   Money
was borrowed from John Pratt, and the cost of paving Pudding
Lane, £14 17*s*. 8*d*., from Jeffery Wood.   At the time of John
Pratt's death twenty-four years later interest was still being
paid on the loans out of the market tolls.   The drain serves
the town to this day, but the cobbled paving only survives
here and there from the invasion of tar macadam.

July 30th 1754.   I went down to Nappa and dined . . . acquainted
Mr Metcalfe with my intentions of offering myself as candidate for
Bridge Master for the North Riding of Yorkshire.   He was pleased
to approve my design and advised me how to proceed.

I beg Mr Fothergills acceptance of them [some books] as an
acknowledgment of my gratitude for many and friendly offices I
have received from him for several years.

These two entries, the one from Alexander Fothergill's
diary, the other from the will of Thomas Metcalfe of Nappa
Hall, sum up the relationship that had existed between the two
men.   The former as agent, lawyer, and family friend had
looked upon the latter not only as an employer but as a
benevolent patron.   When Thomas Metcalfe died in April
1756, Alexander lost a staunch supporter; and it must have
been with a heavy heart that he settled up the Metcalfe affairs,
carried a picture of Thomas's brother, Henry Metcalfe, and
a diamond ring of great value to John Hutton of Marske in
Swaledale, and found Susan Paget, the faithful housekeeper, a
cottage in Askrigg.   Nappa, let to George Dinsdale, was

inherited by Richard Weddell, and Alexander continued as agent. Serving Sir William Robinson in the same capacity, he also managed an estate at Marsett.

As we read the diary, we see him from time to time as a family man going with his wife to Dentdale to visit his children at school at Harbourgill. Before his brother Samuel, the Quaker missionary, went to America, Alexander rode to Marsden Heights General Meeting to say good-bye and give him a gold watch and letters to deliver to a Friend in Virginia. To his brother, Dr John, he sent ham, beef, and oatmeal purchased in Askrigg.

When his right eye is exceedingly inflamed by an angry boil, we sympathize; if he is decked in new fustian gamashers or smart woollen spatterdashes, we admire. In consternation we gaze on the body of Mr Pickering of Helm found drowned in the Ure, and attend the coroner next day; in anxiety we await the outcome of the five-day search for Richard Trotter who disappeared a week ago. We ride beside Alexander, as on a borrowed horse he travels as far as Masham, by which time the old galloway and he are sufficiently tired of each other. With him we return from a visit to London, taking five days on the journey, or find ourselves in Richmond at seven o'clock in the morning to meet visitors off the Carlisle coach.

We learn of the difficulties of travelling in hay-time. His married daughter Ann arrives late from the south, having been disappointed with horses engaged at hay—none could be hired at Middleham and the Masham chaise has to take her on and stay at Carr End overnight. The following month we set her and her husband and a friend on their way back by chaise over Bishopdale, to Skipton, Leeds, and so to London.

As a member of the Society of Friends Alexander went to General Meeting at Bainbridge, and on 'First Days' to Meeting at Bainbridge, Hawes, or Countersett. In 1757, on 5th January, he attended Quarterly Meeting at Lancaster where reports were given of the sufferings in London; and at a similar gathering in Kendal he promised to help the Friends of Dent, Garsdale, Grisedale, and Sedbergh to mitigate their suffering on account of tithes being demanded. His religion took him or his family even farther afield. Early on 18th April 1774, fighting against a north wind and showers of hail and snow, his son William, accompanied by Francis Lambert who was to bring back the horse, rode to Otley, where he was to continue by chaise to London. There he purposed to visit relations and attend Yearly Meeting; but Alexander remained at home cutting willows and pease rods. Three days later he went to Askrigg to witness the auction of goods distrained from Friends for not paying tithes.

Work on the land takes shape, and local happenings spring to life: we learn that George Dinsdale, the lessee of Nappa Hall, is planning the propagation of a breed of rabbits to keep down the whins at Nappa, and asking permission to plough the West or Little Elveshaws; that Alexander is transplanting and dressing young trees at Carr End, and each April cutting the hedges round the house. He sells the sixteen-year-old cow, buys and later kills the swine, and one day goes to the fell to find a suitable stone for a swine trough. On 16th May 1774 he cuts peat, and next day finds it white with snow. He sells John Metcalfe, dish-turner of Woodhall, 'eleven small plain trees' for £4 10s. We watch him acting as auctioneer at a sale at the Swan Inn, Redmire, where the house is full of wild company, and at another at Bainbridge, which is very slow and only four bidders present who refuse and run off their bargains, and he, after a wrangle and some drinks, pays his shot and goes home. In severe weather, following the directions of old persons from Askrigg, he takes the young sons of Mr Weddell round the boundaries, and another day sets off to Richmond on business with the snow and wind in his face.

His relaxations were few. He bought 'a boat for Semer-water at the price of £2 7s. 6d. with a pair of good new oars and the boat to be well chaulked and painted in the said price.' In April 1774 he had built for him by an Askrigg joiner a pair of trows, a double boat made up of two long narrow ones fastened together. He says 'I put them on the River [Bain] and came home in them for breakfast.' Later in the year he was busy all day with some plans, 'save for a little excurtion onto Semerwater in the trows.'

Both Bainbridge and Nappa Mills needed repairs; and in August 1774 the river, 'wearing the land,' caused Alexander to lay stones to defend the dam of the latter. Turf-leading in June, hay-making in July, and bracken-cutting in October took their usual course. Rents were collected for Mr Weddell and Sir William Robinson; the Court Leet and Court Baron were held at Bainbridge; and tolls collected at Askrigg Beast Fair. He bought a grey horse for £10 'to be delivered at home new shoed and in a good bridle,' and failing to sell his mare at Hawes took her on to Brough Hill where she fetched six guineas.

One December day Alexander let the right to get coals on Blackstone Edge on Askrigg Moor; and to the same partnership the slate quarry there for £2 12s. 6d. for three years on condition that they took care to serve the township before strangers; and returning home noted that it was very cold and fresh with Northern Lights. Disputes often arose about mining and quarrying: when Alexander had sent Tom Blaids to dress stones required for Nappa, the lessees of the quarry complained that 'he did not take those before him but culled out the largest' which they wanted themselves; and when he surveyed Thomas Metcalfe's colliery on the moors, where, out of charity, the latter had allowed two men to get two hundred loads of coal, he found they had abused his kindness and destroyed too much ground. One year he himself with two others made trials for coal on Askrigg Moor, but they had difficulties owing to much water; and the results of his share in a venture for lead on Bearshead and Wether Fell we do not know.

Interested in everything, he dashed about from one place to another. At one moment he might be breakfasting by the bedside of one of the turnpike trustees and agreeing to procure

I

for him twenty gallons of stout and Jamaica rum, at the next
going to meet the children and relations of a dead friend and
client to read to them and explain the will.   Always ready to
give a helping hand, he championed old Betty Metcalfe, 'who
in a long course of years, with great care and industry and
pinching and starving herself,' had saved a little money, and
when she thought she was dying left it to James Walker, who
when she recovered tried to claim it.

In 1774, when, after the allegations of disorderly conduct
made against him at Preparative Meeting at Bainbridge, with
his position as surveyor of the turnpike threatened, and his
property mortgaged, he was feeling in a poor, distressed, and
almost alienated state, he had a pathetic meeting at Knares-
borough with Dr John and his sister.   Tenderly, affectionately,
not upbraidingly, they showed him the strongest concern
and gave him good advice.   After visiting their father's grave
together they parted; and riding homewards he was so buried
in thought that he missed his way, but reached Middleham
safely, 'it being a rainy dark evening.'

3. A LOSING STRUGGLE

IT TOOK TIME for the effects of the turnpike to become
evident.   Thirty-three years passed before a new industry invaded the town for a brief space.   Meanwhile goods passed
more freely to and fro, a mixed benefit to country tradesmen.
'Everything wears the face of dispatch,' declared a contemporary writer on the turnpike roads.   Askrigg appeared in
Cary's Traveller's Companion, and the tourists, the first visitors,
came to gaze not only at the scenery but at the inhabitants.
A multitude of local idiosyncrasies gradually died away, as,
their isolation broken, the people became conscious of other
habits and manners.   Strangers came in, but dalespeople left.
A few of the adventurous settled in the American colonies,

and one that we know of was drawn to the West Indies. Doubtless prosperity was taken for granted, for few see beyond the small compass of men's vision.

In the spring of 1753 the seeds of dissension sown in the foundation deed of the grammar school again sprang up. This was the third occasion; for in 1673 a commission had held an inquiry into alleged abuses at the Guildhall at York, and had stipulated amongst other clauses that the heirs-at-law of Anthony Besson appoint a master within six months of a vacancy occurring. The trouble was not peculiar to Yorebridge. Both Sedbergh and Skipton grammar schools, for example, suffered from a cleavage between governors or trustees who managed the funds and those who chose the masters. Whilst the latter were usually many miles away, the former lived near at hand and evinced a strong local opinion.

The Rev. Anthony Clapham, curate of Stalling Busk and master of Yorebridge School for thirty-two years, died on 5th November 1752; and the next month five trustees, most of them unaware that it was not their right, together with a Mr Wadeson of Sedbergh as examiner, met at the Red Lion at Askrigg to appoint a master. Three candidates presented themselves; and to the chagrin of Thomas Metcalfe of Nappa Hall, a trustee, his friend Charles Udale, curate of Hawes, withdrew his nomination, and a Robert Thistlethwaite of St John's College Cambridge, then living at Sedbergh, was chosen. Having possession of the school deeds, Thomas Metcalfe was well informed, and he sent Alexander Fothergill to notify the heirs-at-law, represented by four Harrison sisters living near York. Eventually, after advertising in the *London Gazette* and the *York Courant*, on 2nd May 1753, a few days before the six months allowed them to fill the vacancy expired, the heirs met in Askrigg Church and appointed the Rev. Thomas Morland, vicar of Askrigg, as master.

A lawsuit between the two nominees ensued. Acting as attorney to Robert Thistlethwaite, Samuel Lindsey of Camshouse, one of the Smith family by marriage, obtained the support of local people who subscribed considerable sums of money.   On the other hand the rivals had to persuade Thomas Morland not to leave to take up an appointment at Darlington Free School.   First there was a case of forcible ejectment at the school.   Then in 1754, the suit coming before the Court of Chancery, commissioners visited Askrigg.   Two years later Thomas Metcalfe died, and we find Alexander asking Richard Weddell, the new owner of Nappa, to assist.   When original nominations for the post were urgently required from the Diocesan Registry, Robert Thistlethwaite rode to Chester so furiously that he killed the mare that Mr Lindsey had lent him.   But in 1758 the verdict was given against him.   The costs amounting to £231 15s. 8d., including £7 7s. for the poor mare, might well have been put to better use.   The master's salary was then £33 10s., and the school never benefited from endowments for bursaries to Oxford or Cambridge colleges.

Whereas to-day no solicitor lives in the parish and the three firms who serve the dale have their offices at Hawes and Leyburn, during the eighteenth century there were six attorneys: Alexander Fothergill at Carr End, Samuel Lindsey at Camshouse, Thomas Lambert of Bainbridge, also connected with the Yorebridge case, Anthony Fearon of Askrigg, practising here for fifty-seven years, Miles Alderson of Bainbridge and Yorescot, whose tombstone dated 1746 in Askrigg churchyard records that he was an honest attorney, and towards the end John Driver of Askrigg.

Samuel Lindsey, who came of a Middleham family, married Sarah Lightfoot, James the apothecary's sister, and so was a near relation of Alexander Smith's daughters.   Evidently thought well of by his aunts, he was left High, Low, and Old Camshouse.   Though it is undated and without initials, he probably rebuilt High Camshouse three storeys high in accordance with the prevailing style in Askrigg.   The house is still approached between the elegant stone pillars of the original gateway, through an avenue of eight limes, and up a flight of broad steps; and though it is now a farmhouse and one storey has been taken down, with its small-paned sash windows, six-panelled doors, and well-proportioned rooms, it preserves the atmosphere of a residence of that century. Samuel, we fancy, was an ostentatious personage; and when he died in 1782, he left so many bequests and annuities that James Lightfoot and James Brougham, his son-in-law, appointed executors, refused to act, and a new group of trustees had to settle up the estate. His wife Sarah outlived him by thirty-six years and died in 1818 aged ninety-seven.

In company with many English towns, whether in the south or the north, this latter half of the century was at Askrigg an era of rebuilding. In the Plain, at Northallerton, Bedale, or Yarm, the medium was brick; here, in keeping with the material to hand, it was stone: stone surrounds for the windows and graceful if simple stone-carved doorways. All the craftsmen connected with building, including glaziers, plasterers, and a plumber, were present in the town. Land was valuable, the frontage to the street limited, and the lofty façade of the Hall there to give a lead, so that three-storeyed houses became the fashion.

Buildings now flanked the street on either side; one adjoining the Hall, built in 1770, was then probably a shop as it still is, and opposite to it a little higher up the street was the Metcalfes' house of a similar date. To reach the backs of those on the west side Robinson's Gateways were built before 1755. These great archways once had doors and a postern between them, and they may have been used as an approach to a warehouse for the wool clips of the farmers of the neighbourhood; for the building known as the Wool Room remains in the yard.

A small but charming house, Grenada Hall, situated near Askrigg Beck, was built about 1782. The name derived from the West Indies whence its owner, Matthew Terry, returned to his native place; but whether he was a sugar planter or a merchant we do not know. He soon mortgaged the house and its 'beautyful' garden, and went to live at Settle.

Nor do we know of his connection with the Terrys who were corn millers at the time. John Terry, miller of Askrigg, had five sons, of whom John became miller at Redmire, George at Bainbridge, James followed his father at Askrigg, and a sister married the miller of Horton-in-Ribblesdale. John Terry in the later years of his life was the largest landowner in the town, and, as the parish registers record, he died from an operation for the stone. About 1785 James Terry 'kept eight or more horses which were used for the purpose of carrying corn both from Richmond market and other markets to Askrigg, Hawes, and other places where the same was sold.'

Chief amongst the new houses was that built by John Pratt in 1767 in the main street above the Hall, the present Manor House and the Kings Arms Hotel, then all one. The story of John Pratt, racehorse breeder and prominent figure amongst the sporting gentry of the day, begins with the adventures of his father Simon Pratt of Low Abbotside. He and his brother set out to seek their fortunes in London where Simon found work as an ostler at an inn. By diligence and a pleasant manner he earned enough money to buy a hackney coach and a horse, and eventually adding others, and with his brother as partner, he established a large business that made what was then considered a handsome fortune. He returned to Askrigg where he bought property, married, and had one son.

John Pratt went to Yorebridge School, and from there to a Cambridge college where, from its proximity to Newmarket, he appears to have developed his passion for racing. He married Jane Hammond of Naburn, near York, who brought him a small fortune, but they had no children; and as nephew of Thomas Pratt, the husband of Mistress Mary Pratt, he inherited some of the Smith estates. His house was larger than it is now with a gallery at the back, and his coat of arms showing three elephants' heads (not registered at the College of Heralds) is still to be seen on a lead water-pipe head.

Like his father, John Pratt was lucky and a supremely good judge of a horse. When Simon died he bought the stud of

Painting by George Stubbs entitled *Gimcrack with John Pratt up on Newmarket Heath* in the Fitzwilliam Museum, Cambridge. The painting was commissioned by Lord Bollingbroke, one of the owners of the horse, from the artist in 1765. John Pratt was born on Low Abbotside, became a race-horse owner, and built the Manor House and King's Arms Hotel, than all one, in the main street.

William Calvert, blacksmith, about to shoe Old Rowly held by Joseph T Chapman at the smithy behind the Crown Hotel, Askrigg.

Mr Hammond of Cumberland, and from one of the mares, called Squirt Mare, he bred seventeen foals, twelve of which became valuable animals; on these his own stud was based.

Part of John Pratt's house

Living part of the time at Newmarket, he supported race meetings there and also those at York, Richmond, and Doncaster. Many of his horses were trained at Middleham, and he employed jockeys famous at the time. His filly Imperatrix won the St Leger in 1782, and Camden, later re-christened Rockingham, was sold for seven hundred guineas to Peregrine

Wentworth, who sold it to George IV, then Prince of Wales, for two thousand guineas. This error of judgment was said to have hastened John Pratt's death. One of his mares, Miss Nightingale, was 'killed by privately giving her hail shott the night before the race at Boroughbridge,' as is recorded in a foot-note to a doggerel rhyme on her, and another gave her name to an Askrigg inn that was called the Mare Phoenix.

It was a time of facetious verse-writing. John Pratt himself wrote a long poem that describes a great storm at Askrigg in December 1784, when the drifts were 'much deeper than oldest men know' and his boys were shovelling snow 'to turf and coal houses for lasses to go.' A punning epitaph, composed after his death at Newmarket a year later, was printed as a broad-sheet by J. Todd of Bedale, and in 1803 was issued from Doncaster headed with an engraving of the racecourse. It begins:

> A Character so excentric, so varible, so valuable,
>   Astonish'd the Age he liv'd in.
>   Tho' small his Patrimony,
> Yet, assisted by that, and his own Genius,
>   He, for upwards of thirty years,
>   Supported all the Hospitality
>   Of an ancient Baron.

In August of the year he died his stud was sold by auction at Askrigg, and later his property and the leases of lead mines on the moor and in the neighbourhood were sold. His had been a tempestuous career; for his estate was mortgaged, and as a sad end to this story, his nephew and heir, Thomas Pratt, died a debtor in York Castle.

In John Pratt's time Askrigg presented a lively noisy scene. On a summer's evening the street, especially outside the inns, must have been thronged with people, each and all quick to pursue any sport that might be afoot. A main of cocks was no doubt often fought between rival villages; and sometimes the gentlemen of neighbouring dales challenged Wensleydale in three-day events that, advertised in the *York Courant*, took place at an innkeeper's pit. As master of the Askrigg Harriers,

John Pratt kept hunters, a pack of hounds, a huntsman, and a whipper-in, and with his fellow townsfolk enjoyed long days of hunting and wild runs over the fells. Stable boys might have been seen riding horses in and out of Robinson's Gateways, that led to the back of his house. There, behind a

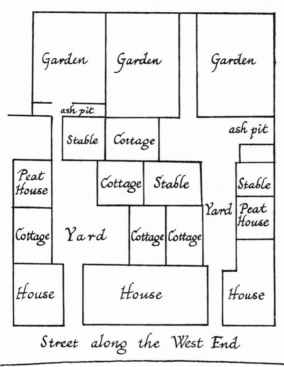

Plan of buildings behind houses at the West End, showing overcrowding. The cottages are now either incorporated into the houses or used as outbuildings

semicircular enclosure with kennels for the hounds, was a long range of stabling; and other archways in those high garden walls led on to Croft Hill. Filling the position of squire, he was generous to his neighbours, he entertained the local gentry, and his house, with a staff numbering at times as many as twenty, was the hub of the town.

At this time the population rose to its peak. For twenty years, from 1769 onwards, births show a preponderance over deaths in the parish registers; and up to 1800 there is no sign of a decrease. Probably twice as many inhabitants as to-day dwelt in the same area. All the buildings crowded at the backs of the houses in the main street, the West End, and Pudding Lane were occupied. Even so and in spite of the new building there was an acute shortage, so that most were occupied by two families and many let out in smaller divisions. Outside steps led to flats in upper storeys, and hovels with earth floors were desirable dwellings. An epidemic was followed by a more than usual number of marriages, for homes were thus tragically made available.

As in any town of the era, slums must have existed and morals in consequence have been lowered. Scandalous tongues wagged, reviling neighbours in bawdy language that, if the defamed ones resisted, came out in Church Court cases. Some contracted clandestine marriages. In 1768 the Quakers at Aysgarth resolved that the keys of the meeting-house be carefully kept to prevent such occurrences there. Drunken orgies often followed gatherings for public affairs held at the inns. Though his fellow Quakers accused him of drinking, Alexander frequently fled these scenes.

A piece of contemporary dialogue has survived. In 1766 Mary Sagar of Askrigg, spinster, went to a friend's house and cried 'Have you heard this news?' She said 'What news?' 'This kissing match between a geld wife [1] and a man of Mr Pratt's.' After hearing more details, a man present asked 'Was't my wife?' She said 'Nay.' 'Was't Richard Holme's wife?' and she answered 'Thou's guess'd it.' But they then 'stopped her discourse, for it was not the first scandal she had raised.'

There was no falling off in religious worship; and as we shall see in more detail in a later chapter the church was restored. A new Nonconformist movement was beginning. On 30th

[1] A barren married woman.

October 1743 John Wesley preached at Wensley Church, and in June of the following year at Redmire and Castle Bolton; thirty years later, crossing over the hills from Swaledale into Wensleydale, he came again. In 1789 the parson of Askrigg, in answer to questions put at a Bishop's Visitation, stated that there were 'some few Methodists' in the chapelry. By 1804 the sect had an unlicensed meeting-house and a teacher named Samuel Holgate, a weaver. It was the start of a movement that by missionary zeal reached the hearts of humble people, and that, beginning with assemblies in houses, was to grow and establish itself permanently—the aspirations of men still unchecked by the cold logic of later knowledge.

In 1757 the Seven Years War brought privation consequent on the high price of corn. Evidently it was usual to bring meal to Worton for collection by Langstrothdale farmers; and on 5th November of that year a mob, composed of miners, seized the better part of the consignment. As usual Alexander was involved. He remonstrated with the rioters, and that night was attacked and seriously injured on his way home. Then, on 27th November, the mob rose again, and demanded money from householders at Bainbridge and Raydale. Later they proceeded down the valley, and took all the meal and corn in Middleham market at their own price, returning at night to Askrigg, and again violently demanding money from the inhabitants. Several of the ringleaders were imprisoned in Richmond Jail; and on 5th December a rumour spread that a plan was afoot to release the men and destroy the town. A party from Askrigg hurried there to sound the alarm; patrols were posted; and several hundred armed horsemen assembled to keep order. On the 8th over a hundred met at Askrigg, and captured ten of the rioters, some escaping to the moors. Eleven of the ringleaders were tried at York Assizes: one was hanged, one transported for life, and the others were fined or sentenced to short terms of imprisonment. That December Alexander took an active part in calling a meeting at Bainbridge and raising funds to supply the needy with oatmeal and provisions at a low price.

The only surviving poor-rate book for Askrigg covers the years 1755–71. From it we learn that the churchwardens, overseers, constable, and varying numbers of the ablest inhabitants met either three, four, or five times a year to make a rate 'proportionably on the respective persons' according to the best of their judgments 'in order to defray and discharge the expense of household goods provisions and other necessary disbursements for the poor of the Township of Askrigg'; and that before the rate could be collected, the assessments were ratified by two local justices, and the Sunday following published in the church.

The assessments, that varied considerably even within the same year, were for periods of four months, three months, and after 1762 one month only; and up to this date, at each meeting an account was made, and a list of names given 'of poor persons commonly called pentioners,' old folk or young children, incapable of work, who received a monthly payment. Practically all lived in the township, though one or two residing elsewhere came under the Act of 1662, whereby they remained the responsibility of their original place of settlement.

Although there is no record of the fact, a large proportion of the money must have gone towards the upkeep of the poorhouses at Askrigg and Newbiggin, both referred to in the parish registers about 1740. A dispute between the town and the hamlets in 1709 had been settled by the justices who ordered each place to maintain its own poor, an arrangement common to many townships. The separation did not last, but the poorhouse at Newbiggin may have originated from it.

On 21st July 1756 Alexander Fothergill wrote in his diary: 'In the evening to Askrigg to attend and assist the inhabitants there to make a poors rate which we got thro'. Very late lodged at Askrigg.' Turning over the pages of the rate book, we find the appropriate entries. With the daylight fast dwindling, candles soon to be lit, and doubtless a tankard of

Land And Trade Totharll
The First Column - - - - 3 . 7 . 9¾
The Second Do - - - - 2 . 1 . 4½
The Third Do - - - 5 . 11 . 11
                                    11 . 1 . 1¼

THE several Sums mentioned on the Otherside are by our Approbation Rated
Proportionably on the Respective persons according to the best of our Judgments
in order to defray & discharge the necessary Expence of Relaveing & Maintaining
the Poor of the Township of Askrigg

Geo Metcalfe   Witness our hands

Geo Smith   Richard Wood Churchwardens

Aland. Tothanjill   William Thompson
                            John Beezon   Overseers

                            John Padison   Constable

_____

A List of the Names of the poor people Commonly Called pentioners belonging to the
Township or Villiage of Askrigg who Receive a monthly Portion out of the Same. Made
this Eighth day of October - 1756   s   d

        John Metcalfe Since the 30th of Aug. - - - -   5 . 0
        John Whaley (Speddy) - - - - - - - - -   2 . 0
        Chris: Whaley (Speddy) - - - - - -   2 . 0
        John Metcalfe's Wido - - - - - -   4 . 0
        Jane Metcalfe Gitt gate Since the 30th Aug' - - 5 . 0
        Jusson Metcalfe Since the 30th of Aug. - - -   4 . 0
        Margaret Clarkson - - - - - - - -   2 . 0
        Cathorine Reynolds - - - - - - - -   2 . 0
        Christian the wife of Aland Spence Since 30th Aug. 3 . 0
        Henry Robinson's Child being young - - -   10 . 0
Newbiggin Thomas Teesdale Since the 30th of Aug'. -   10 . 0
at Thornton Eden Chapman - - - - - -   3 . 0

Page from Askrigg poor-rate book

ale at each elbow, there sat round the table that summer's night Alexander, Richard Wood, one of the churchwardens, William Thompson and John Beezon, the overseers, John Addison, the constable, a member of a family of dyers, George Smith, a prominent dyer and hosier, and George Metcalfe from Nappa Scar.

First they wrote down all the names of the inhabitants under their places of abode: Askrigg, Newbiggin, Nappa and Nappa Scar, Shalcoat, and Woodhall. Next, on the right of the page they drew two columns headed 'Land' and 'Trade'; for everyone was rated as occupiers of houses, land, mills, shops, and on trade. The collectors of the tithes and the market tolls were also assessed. Of the hundred and nineteen persons listed, ninety-five lived in Askrigg, the rest in the hamlets, and forty paid infinitesimal additional sums as tradesmen. The total assessment, to last for three months from 6th July, amounted to £11 0s. 11d. On another page we read the names of twelve old persons or children who received monthly pensions, none over 10s.

Though the figures set down by Alexander, who often acted as clerk on these occasions, are typical, two years later the total for the year, £48 15s. 7½d., was the lowest recorded over the period covered by the book. The largest, collected in 1767, was £123 16s. 8d., after which the figure dropped to just under £100. Apart from the occupiers of Nappa Hall and the Hall in Askrigg, whose assessments were usually the highest, the yeomen paid the most as owners of land, and poorer folk subscribed a minute proportion: James Metcalfe (Long Jammy) paid ¾d., and Christopher Caygill (Jock Cit) 2d. In regard to trade the dyer, George Smith, and the hosier, George Burton, seem to have been the most prosperous, followed by Alexander Blyth, butcher, James Lightfoot, the apothecary, and other dyers and hosiers, all paying more than the smaller tradesmen and craftsmen. The latter, often owning no land, such as William Terry, glazier, or Mark Metcalfe, clock-maker, paid a shilling or sixpence on their trades.

The number of pensioners rose from eleven in March 1756 to twenty-two in February 1762, twenty residing in the township, one at Thornton Rust, and another in Kettlewell. Occasionally laconic notes were set against some of the names: 'Alexander Spence's wife for lying in 5s.,' 'Elliner Miller dead July 4th 8s.,' 'Henry Robinson wife sick 17s.,' and the pitiable sequel, 'Henry Robinson his child being very young 10s.,' 'Henry Robinson on account of his children,' 'Henry Robinson being gone his two elder children are boarded with Christian Wright at 3s. 6d. pr week till May Day next and 3s. per week so long as the Churchwardens and Overseers think proper,' and his youngest child 'boarded with Alice Nicholson at 2s. 6d. per week.'

One of the entries in Alexander's diary records in January 1775 that he 'executed a pair of parish indentures,' binding out two boys as apprentices, one for five years until he was nineteen and a half, the other at the age of eleven until he was twenty. The churchwardens and overseers were doubtless exercising their right to make provision for children whose parents were unable to maintain them.

As the century wore on additional resources were necessary to meet the needs of the growing population. The dyers' trade was rapidly dwindling as shop goods increased and home weaving ceased, and the hosiers', for long threatened by the stocking looms of Nottinghamshire, was losing ground. Already inventors had patented their flying-shuttles, spinning-jennies, and carding engines, and across the Pennines the factory system was developing in the West Riding and in Lancashire. In this changing scene of the Industrial Revolution, a new enterprise entered Wensleydale, an enterprise that from the beginning met with difficulties, and that eventually was to fail.

In the years 1784–5 cotton mills were built at Askrigg, Aysgarth, and Gayle. Although the projected Manchester road did not materialize, it was no great distance to Lancashire via Cam, Settle, and Colne, and these mills were only a

few of the many built at the time beside the becks of Yorkshire valleys, in particular Ribblesdale and Dentdale.   Spurred
on by the release of Arkwright's patents and the ambition to
grasp easy money, men from all walks of life plunged into the
cotton trade.   Very many failed in these years.   Here an
attempt was made to bring the industry to where there were
work-people, but as is now well known, the people had in the
end to go to the industry.

In Askrigg churchyard near the east window of the church
stands a headstone encrusted with lichen and mouldering with
age.   An interested passer-by might sense the unusual in the
double inscription, but could not tell that a name in the right-
hand column is the key to the puzzle: 'Agnes Hastwell who
died April 2nd 1835.   Aged 75 years.'   Agnes was a descendant of a family of tradesmen, her great-grandfather,
George Burton, a dyer in the seventeenth century, his son
Thomas a stockiner, and her father a hosier.   The latter,
George Burton, his wife, and two children, who died early in
life, are commemorated on the left side of the headstone.
Above Agnes's name are those of her two husbands, John
Driver, attorney, who died in 1787 aged thirty-six, and
Abraham Hastwell, who died in 1796 aged thirty-nine, and
below, her sister's, Martha Burton.

It was John Driver, his brother Joseph of Keighley, and
John Dinsdale of Nappa Hall who as partners ventured into
the cotton trade at Askrigg.   Leasing land from the Duke of
Bolton for twenty-one years, with the right to obtain wood,
they built a small mill and a dam near Paddock Beck just
below the corn mill.   Machinery was installed and work begun.
Their business did not prosper.   After only two years the
partners, having put up a capital of over £1,000 each, were
out of pocket by £2,567 5s. 2½d.   Perhaps due to their failure,
they quarrelled; and after several abortive attempts to come
to some agreement they met at an Askrigg inn on the night of
9th January 1787.   There in the bar parlour after much talk,
John Driver agreed to buy out both his partners, who were

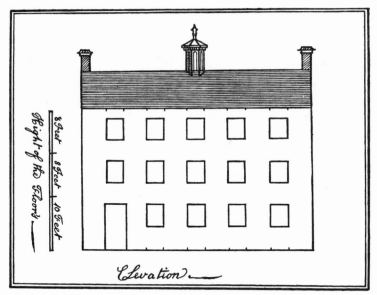

Plan of cotton mill

COTTON MILL.

To be Let or Sold,

(And may be entered upon immediately),

All that well-built

COTTON MILL,

Situate at Askrigg, in Wensleydale,

Three Stories high, 56 Feet in Length by 30 in Width; a capital Water Wheel with tumbling Shafts and Gears; also a *CLOSE of rich LAND*, by estimation 1¾A. wherein the Mill is erected, likewise containing a Reservoir by which the Mill is supplied with Water. The aforesaid Mill would answer for Woolen or Flax; is pleasantly situated near the Market Town of Askrigg, where a sufficient number of Work People may be had on very reasonable Terms.

Askrigg, April 20, 1814.

PRINTED BY M. BRANTHWAITE AND CO. KENDAL.

Sale bill

Reproduced by permission of the Yorkshire Archaeological Society

K

heard 'to acknowledge the articles and drink good luck to them many times.' Joseph delivered up his share to his brother, but Dinsdale, repenting his bargain, denied it; and the workmen were ordered to prevent his entering the mill.

Meanwhile in 1784 John Driver had married Agnes, who was then twenty-four. He was a widower with a daughter, Mary, by his previous wife, and a natural son John. They went to live eventually in the market-place in a house purchased by George Burton in November 1786, either the old King's Head or a house on its site. In December, on the death of their father, Agnes and Martha, known in the family as Patty, inherited the house, several others, some cottages, a dye-house adjoining to the High Bridge, and fields and cattle-gates.

Agnes was in these years haunted by death. A few months after the meeting at the inn John Driver died. The first child of the marriage had not survived infancy, and the second died an infant only two months after his father's death. In his will John left his daughter Mary £400 to be paid when she became twenty-one. But for this legacy we should know little about Agnes Hastwell and the cotton mill; for pleading John's insolvency, she withheld the payment of it to her stepdaughter, and was in consequence involved in cases at the Consistory Court at Richmond and in Chancery, from both of which suits the story can be pieced together.

John Dinsdale took immediate advantage of the tragic circumstances. He seized the mill, manned it with an armed force, and proceeded to collect all the outstanding debts. In 1788 the affair was handed over to arbitration, but shortly afterwards Dinsdale was declared a bankrupt. A public auction, in which Agnes joined with her share of the machinery and the remaining term of the lease, followed; and no other bidder coming forward, she bought the lease and stock for £318 in Joseph Driver's name, though she held back payment of a third of this to the assignees of Dinsdale as due to her husband. Then she herself carried on the business.

Once more, on 6th August 1793, Agnes was married in Askrigg Church, this time to Abraham Hastwell who came from the Eden valley in Westmorland, and once more, after less than three years of married life, she became a widow. There were two children of this marriage, who fortunately lived, John eventually to become a wine merchant in London, and Elizabeth to marry Richard Thornton of Cottingley, near Bradford. Meanwhile the family, including Mary, Agnes's stepdaughter, grew up. We fancy that poor Mary was not happy, and in 1798 at the age of seventeen she married a Thomas Moss.

In her home, graced with the elegant furniture of the period, Agnes possessed a varied collection of books. Perhaps some had belonged to her great-great-uncle James who was a parson, and others to her uncle Thomas, the stockiner, noted in the parish registers as 'skilful in learning.' There were books on divinity, logic, astronomy, and Roman antiquities; volumes of poetry, plays, and the novels of Goldsmith, Defoe, Smollett, and Fanny Burney; books on travel, cookery, husbandry, Egyptian hieroglyphics, and a Greek lexicon, a translation from Horace, and Seneca's works. Sometimes she lent out one of them or her copies of the *Lady's Magazine*, and wrote the borrower's name in her catalogue.

At the mill, with Joseph Driver acting as book-keeper and journeying to Manchester to buy cotton, wool, and twist, and supported by Patty, Agnes must at least have paid her way. The bell daily clanged out calling people to work. Men, probably one or two women, and perhaps children, who all could be had 'on very reasonable terms,' toiled as pickers or in the carding- and spinning-rooms in the manufacture of cottons and muslins.

The building, now called the Flax Mill, still remains as a farmhouse, and from an original plan of it that has survived it can be seen that a house was added on to it later, the bell-turret removed from the centre of the roof to one end, and eventually many of the windows blocked up.

In 1801 Lord and Lady Bolton sold their land in Askrigg
for the redemption of the land tax, and Patty Burton bought
the mill and the mill paddock for £348 15*s*. Two years later,
when a plot of ground lower down the beck and beside the
turnpike came up for resale, Agnes bought it, and shortly
afterwards built there a new mill. Leaving Patty, who leased
it in 1803 to a Miles Robinson Parke, in possession of the cotton

Cotton mill

mill, she turned to a new venture more nearly related to her
ancestors' trade, the spinning of yarn and the manufacture of
cloth.

The years passed uneventfully until in June 1813 a fresh
blow fell. Bent on securing the legacy, Thomas Moss, Mary's
husband, wrote: 'I had determined never to make another
application to you until I found myself enabled to enforce our
demand; the period I am happy to say has at length arrived.'
The lawsuit followed. Agnes's counsel told her that she had
acted very imprudently, and had had no right to purchase
John Driver's share of the mill. At the Consistory Court she
showed long lists of expenses. They included the crape hat-
bands and mourning gloves bought for her husband's funeral,
the household linen priced at its original value, though she
hastened to add that it was 'now wore out,' the gig that John
had possessed, but this, she said, was in fact lent and had been

broken afterwards by Joseph, and the law books sold to Mr Topham of Middleham for £14. After settling up the estate, she averred that the balance of her fortune was £547 6s. We do not know the result of the case, but clearly Thomas had right on his side. At this time the cotton mill was put up for sale, but was not sold.

In 1825, when she was sixty-five, Agnes sold the worsted mill, Low Mill, as it was called, to John Banks Robinson for £230. Ten years later she died. Patty, still owning the cotton mill, went to live at Cottingley House, near Bradford. She and John Hastwell, Agnes's son, mortgaged the mill, now called the Flax Mill, and three years after Patty's death in 1843 John sold it for £270 to the Rev. Richard Wood, when it became a house.

Marking the end of an era, the eighteenth century drew to a close. When Lord Bolton sold his land in Askrigg in 1801, he severed a connection with the town that through the Scropes had begun five hundred years before. It was a break that coincided with many happenings both national and local. The redemption of the land tax was to raise money for the war with France. The French Revolution took its stormy course, and the Napoleonic wars approached.

In 1770 the yearly value of the tolls of markets and fairs had dropped to £7 15s.; twenty-seven years later they were no more than £6 4s. and they were to diminish as time went on. At Hawes the market tolls held by shareholders, differently managed from those at Askrigg, slowly increased.

In 1795 a new Act of Parliament was passed to divert the turnpike road. Instead of following the Roman road across Wether Fell and over Cam, a way notorious as 'one of the longest, steepest, and most stoney in Great Britain,' it now was to proceed from Bainbridge up the valley to Hawes and so up Widdale, where in parts 'no road has ever yet been completely made,' to Gearstones and Ingleton. At the head of the valley local surveyors were engaged in repairing roads and building bridges. Hawes, better placed to serve the populous upper dale, was winning the long struggle for supremacy as a market town.

The dyers and hosiers were doomed. With insufficient capital to build large mills and install steam-power, their stocking trade irreparably damaged by a new fashion that dictated the wearing of long trousers instead of breeches, and an economy that was to concentrate manufactures in industrial towns, one by one they fell away. The cotton venture, as we have seen, failed; and the day of farming as the sole means of livelihood was at hand. Askrigg's heyday was slowly fading.

From a window of the Kings Arms Hotel

VII

NINETEENTH-CENTURY DECLINE

1. THE TURN OF FORTUNE

THROUGHOUT our story it has been evident that village life has continuously reflected that of the nation. In the nineteenth century this is apparent in every phase. More widespread in effect than any previous development, the social movements of the Industrial Revolution drew away our people, and changed the fabric of life in Askrigg. The far-distant knell that sounded long ago from the West Riding as the cloth trade grew now rang near at hand.

Many other national trends and events affected the village. During the first years, wars, as ever, increased poverty. Acts passed in Parliament concerned us: the first Reform Bill brought an election to our doors, poor laws enforced a new system for the maintenance of the destitute, Police, Highway, and Local Government Acts, and many other statutes directed and limited our powers with far-reaching consequences. An Act for enclosing the commons, coincident with a spate of similar ones in all parts of the land, caused the reorganization of farming custom. The railway, linked with main lines, crept slowly up the dale. Wesleyan Methodism rose to vie with the Church. The fortunes of the grammar school reflected current moral standards, and, as happened elsewhere, a national school was established. The Swaledale and Wensleydale Banking Company opened a branch at Hawes, and exhibitions of farming stock were promoted. That diffuse sprawling leisurely society of the eighteenth century was slowly beaten into a shape that began to take on the features of our own times.

The gradual shrinkage of population, observable throughout the land in village and country town as industry fled to great centres, was hastened in our case by the rise of Hawes. In 1801, the year of the first census, the inhabitants of Askrigg township numbered 761, and after a drop of a hundred during the 'hungry forties' they had dwindled to 624 in 1881, and twenty years later to 462. The graph of births and deaths plotted from the parish registers shows a similar slow fall. At the same time the population of Hawes increased in a hundred years from 1,223 to 1,586, and that of Leyburn, only 446 in 1801, almost doubled. The populations of Bainbridge, Carperby, West Witton, and Aysgarth remained steady until 1881, about the time when the waning of that ancient industry of the dales, lead-mining, was felt.

One by one, families, single men and women, young people in their teens, emigrated or left to seek employment in cities and towns. The sea and shipping attracted a few to Liverpool; or milk-houses were started there by those fitted by their background to take up this branch of town-farming, the indoor keeping of cows. Others became domestic servants, and by far the largest group found work in Lancashire cotton mills.

The adventurous sailed for America and Australia and went their different ways, some to the Californian gold-fields, others to clear land in new territories, especially in Wisconsin and Illinois.

In spite of this falling away more than forty occupations were pursued in the village throughout the century. If the dyers had vanished by 1860 and the hosiers diminished in numbers, the tailor, the clock-maker, the instructor of singers, the writing master, masons, carpenters, blacksmiths, corn badgers, a crowd of farmers, a group of shoemakers, and a host of labourers all found a living; and if the market had lapsed and the cotton and worsted mills failed, wealth enough remained to restore the church and to build large houses. There was no lack of an active self-contained life; yet it was a life some of whose roots were struck at by decay. The community was to reach for its livelihood to the land. Retrenchment and consolidation rather than enterprise were the key-notes.

The enclosure of Askrigg and Newbiggin Cow Pastures and Askrigg Common took place in 1819–20. (We shall describe the award and its effects on farming in a later chapter.) Before this time the land above the village was unenclosed except for the long meandering walls round the two cow closes, and the moor road above Low Straits Lane was not bounded by restricting walls as to-day. The four miles of hillside from Whitfield Crag to Ellerkin were strung with walls. It was a revolution in the scene. The green lanes, Low Straits, High Straits, the Heugh Lane, and others, came into being as occupation roads. The walls dividing up the land in the straight lines of allotments planned on paper, must have shone out with the brightness of fresh-hewn stone. To-day it is difficult to think of them as any less aged than the walls that enclosed the common fields in the sixteenth century, and mellowed and darkened by years of weathering they have long been absorbed into the scene.

The century was a time of unsettlement for many families.

John Fothergill, one of Alexander's sons, attempted to make a living in the town as a physician, but he left before 1821 to practise in Darlington; and James Lindsey Brougham, son of the surgeon who had married a grand-daughter of Alexander Smith, went to London, though his brother, Samuel Lindsey Brougham, was curate of Askrigg. A Thomas Parke, migrating by degrees from Swaledale to Newbiggin in the township, and from there to Liverpool, made a fortune as a merchant. There were, too, the indecisive and the faint-hearted. Some set out for Australia, and after encountering the gales of the Bay of Biscay, turned back. Eleazer Chapman in 1850 wrote to relatives in America: 'Your Aunt Betty has said a great deal about coming but I think she will let talking serve.' But he himself, while the gold rush was at its height, went to Australia and profited so largely by selling groceries to the miners that he returned to England within a twelve-month.

On the other hand James Lightfoot of Liverpool, a nephew of James the apothecary, came to live in the Old Hall. A John Lodge of Deepdale in Langstrothdale, an attorney, and a Joseph Lodge, perhaps a relative, were newcomers of means. George Winn was tenant of Nappa Hall in 1804, and his son George and grandson William followed a Richard Balderstone as the Askrigg solicitors. Miles Robinson Parke, doubtless connected with Thomas Parke, was captain of the Loyal Dales Volunteers and the lessee for a time of the cotton mill.

We could trace the story of some of our families farther afield. George Lightfoot, James's father, was a master mariner of Liverpool, who lost his life when for a second time he was washed overboard on a stormy voyage from Jamaica in the ship *Birch* on 2nd June 1815. Agnes Hastwell's grandson, Richard Thornton, was Livingstone's surveyor, and later joined Baron C. Von der Decken in the survey of Kilimanjaro. He died in Africa at the age of twenty-five. Thomas Parke's son, Judge Parke, was created Lord Wensleydale, and his daughter Alice married Sir Sitwell Sitwell—a romantic match mentioned in Sir Osbert Sitwell's *Left Hand, Right Hand*.

A few of these people left recognizable memorials of their sojourn in the village. In 1836 James Lindsey Brougham refaced the house below the Temperance Hotel—what was in fact the doctor's house, probably where James Lightfoot the apothecary lived. John Lodge in 1818 and George Winn in 1841 built adjoining three-storeyed houses, of which Winnville, distinguishable by its gateposts topped with stone lions, still dominates the main street. To make way for these and other new houses many cottages were pulled down; and modern Askrigg took shape.

Perpetuating his memory by a charity Christopher Alderson of Middlesex, a native of Askrigg, by his will allotted funds to build and endow the Dale Grange almshouses near the site of Fors Abbey in 1807. They then consisted of six one-roomed cottages for poor women of good character, but in 1880 they were reduced to three, thus improving the size and the individual incomes. They still benefit and make comfortable homes for elderly women.

Little is known of this Christopher Alderson. His great-nephew, Christopher Alderson Harker, changed his surname to Alderson to inherit a legacy from his uncle. With part of it he bought the old house, Woodhall Park, from the descendants of the Beezons, the Quaker yeomen who had lived there throughout the eighteenth century—a move symptomatic of the times, for the Beezons' property was heavily mortgaged—and in 1828 he altered the house, laid out drives and terraces, and probably built the large fishpond in the grounds. Woodhall Park was for long tenanted by the Rev. Richard Wood, vicar of Askrigg for forty-five years, who drove to church each Sunday in his carriage.

In that other part of Woodhall, once the property of Easby Abbey, John Rider Wood, a relative of Parson Wood, in 1802 purchased a house that had been converted into three cottages for miners, and probably it was he who built the present house called Wood Hall. Of all the mansions once occupied by the minor gentry of the township, this is the only one not lived in now as a farmhouse.

Lastly Joseph Lodge, whom we first hear of as an excise man and then as a brewer, about 1800 bought the larger part of John Pratt's property, including the Kings Arms Hotel.   It is said that Joseph, removing most of the lead-piping, received more for it than he paid for the whole.   South of the stable yard he built a new house, a brewery, and the first village hall, named grandiloquently the Assembly Rooms.   The primary use of the latter's long, narrow, upper room, with its musicians' gallery at one end and oak bench (now removed) round the walls, was to accommodate meetings of the Askrigg Equitable Benevolent and Friendly Society that Joseph was instrumental in re-founding on 4th March 1809.

Though partially superseded by modern insurance schemes and the National Health Act of 1948, the Friendly Society still has fifty ordinary and ten honorary members.   It began with sixty-three and soon rose to over a hundred.   From time to time the rules have been revised.   There are scales of quarterly payments, sickness benefits, and sums paid out on the deaths of members and their wives, and fines, for example for night poaching whilst receiving sick benefit, for swearing at meetings, and for interrupting other members when speaking.   Its merit may be judged from the fact that during the first eighty years of its existence about £10,000 was paid out in sick relief.

The date of the annual meeting coincided with that of Askrigg June Fair.   The celebrations began in the forenoon with a procession of members preceded by a band that paraded to Town Head and back to the market-place, and continued with a service in church, dinner at the Kings Arms Hotel, the meeting, and finally sports.   The colourful banner, carried by two men at the head of the procession, has a stencilled border and in the centre a hand-painted picture of angels, a lamb, a cornucopia, and an eye, presumably representing the eye of God looking down from the clouds, and 'Peace and Plenty' written on a scroll.   A photograph of the members grouped in front of the banner, dating from about 1890, shows the old men, and doubtless those not so old, wearing every

Askrigg Equitable Benevolent and Friendly Society was founded in the eighteenth century by James Lightfoot, and was re-founded by Joseph Lodge in 1809. It still flourishes. (1890).

A group of Askrigg ladies, date unknown.

conceivable variety of beard, and different fashions in head-gear from straw boaters to silk hats. Family resemblances are plain to see. 'That's a so-and-so,' people say as they look at the photograph.

The brewing of ale was one of Askrigg's trades that like

Banner of the Askrigg Friendly Society (breadth 8 feet 4 inches, length 7 feet 3 inches)

most of the rest eventually vanished. Besides Joseph Lodge's there was a second brewery whose large buildings, situated alongside Askrigg Beck near the High Bridge, still remain. Its history is obscure. In the early years of the century John Thompson, brewer and maltster, probably ran it, and in 1840 James Burton Wood was the owner.

As spirit merchants Joseph and his son James bought in

casks of liquor, and supplied gallons of gin at 14s. 6d. (purchased from Messrs Nicholson of London), rum at 15s., and brandy at 27s. to 32s. to private individuals and to local innkeepers. In the 1820's their customers included Alexander Pounder of Tan Hill Inn, David Calvert of the King's Head, Gunnerside, Robert Brunskill at Shaw Paddock, and the innkeepers of Muker, Keld, Horsehouse in Coverdale, Dent, Redmire, Aysgarth, Worton, and others. After Joseph's death James Lightfoot, a son of James at the Old Hall, who had married Joseph's daughter, continued the business, given in 1840 as a partnership, Lightfoot and Jacques. James went bankrupt, and in 1841 the premises, described as a large and commodious brewery with a maltkiln and spirit vaults, were up for sale. But presumably they were not sold; for James Lightfoot and a Jonathan Robinson are noted as brewers in an 1848 directory.

In these years the old and new industries continued on their often wayward courses.   As yet the ancient corn mills of the township, Askrigg, Woodhall, and Nappa, ground corn for the neighbourhood.   At Askrigg the Addisons had followed the Terrys as millers.   The tenant of the cotton mill in 1823 was Joseph Siddall, described as a flax manufacturer; in 1838 Low Mill, already mortgaged to the Blyths, warehousemen and hosiers of London and Hawes, passed into the hands of James Blyth who doubtless combined the knitting trade with the manufacture of coarse cloth.   In 1823 only two hosiers, Thomas Pratt and Jeffery Wood, remained to carry on that once important trade: perhaps one of them was a lessee of Low Mill.   Though records are few, speculators in leadmining leased ground on Askrigg Moor and at Woodhall. The better off, joining in partnerships and employing miners and smelters, ventured capital, and often miners themselves took the ground.

In the early years of the century three national events affected us closely. During the Napoleonic wars the Loyal Dales Volunteers, numbering 1,500 men, were raised by

Colonel M. Turner van Straubenzee, and under the then Lord Bolton a company was recruited in Wensleydale. In 1805 they became the first of six regiments of the Yorkshire North Riding Militia. Like the Home Guard of the last war they were mercifully spared active service; but in 1803 when a warden mistook a distant fire for one of the beacons appointed to be lit on the landing of the French, and set light to that on Penhill, alarm spread throughout every village in the dale. Hastily mustered by drums in the early hours of the morning, the Askrigg company, led by Miles Robinson Parke, marched to Richmond. The Volunteers were disbanded in 1815; but their colours still hang in Wensley Church.

At the end of May 1807 occurred that memorable event in the annals of Yorkshire, the poll for the election of knights of the shire, with William Wilberforce, Viscount Milton, and the Hon. Henry Lascelles as candidates for Parliament. It has been recorded that the large contingent of voters from Wensleydale who journeyed to York, the polling place for the whole county, was met on the road and asked 'For what parties do you come, gentlemen?' to which they replied 'Wilberforce to a man.' Thirty-seven freeholders from Askrigg township, representatives of many of the trades of the town—farmers, hosiers, yeomen, a butcher, tinner, glazier, mason, and a clock-maker—set out for York. They joined the multitude on the road, witnessed the spirited scenes in the castle yard, and heard the shouted slogans such as 'No Yorkshire votes bought with African blood.' Twenty plumped for Wilberforce, fifteen cast their votes for him and Lascelles, and two plumped for the latter.

In 1832, on the passing of the first Reform Bill, Askrigg was made one of the polling places for the North Riding, to serve upper Wensleydale and Swaledale; and the general election that took place on 20th and 21st December of that year was an event long remembered. Both Whigs and Tories, led by bands and carrying large banners, marched up and down the main street. By carriage or cart, on horseback or on foot, voters pressed into the town. A noisy throng filled the market-place; the inns were crowded; Askrigg ladies watched from upper windows; and attorneys inquiring their intentions followed voters to the booths. The tearing of a banner started a fight that developed into a pitched battle in which the Whigs' blue banner was torn to pieces, and some of the rougher elements of the crowd broke in the side of Lord Bolton's carriage. Order seems to have been restored fairly quickly, and the sound of drums, trumpets, and bassoons again rose above the babble of voices. A Whig, E. T. Cayley, and a Tory, the Hon. W. Duncombe, were the members returned. Many years later an Askrigg man might have been seen wearing a blue waistcoat. He was the Whig banner-bearer who had rescued enough shreds of his party's colours to have a garment made up from them.

Though gradually shorn of their reason for existence, throughout the century the Four Men continued to hold office and to enter their accounts in the leather-bound book. In 1822 they paid Mr Fidler £1 for translating the charter from the Latin, and thenceforward dropped their ancient title and called themselves the trustees. Save for a brief revival at the coming of the railway in 1877 the income from the market tolls diminished rapidly (it was 10s. in 1858), but the letting of the Toll Booth, now called the Town's House, provided some funds. The upper room was in demand at election times, for sales, and for public meetings, whilst the ground floor appears to have been leased to the churchwardens as a 'hearse standing' and to others as a cart-house, and another portion was used as a vagrant room.

As before, the pumps and the Town's House were repaired, and like his predecessors, James Pratt and Jeffery Wood, James Lightfoot lent money on which he received interest. In the autumn of 1830 the old cross was pulled down, and the following spring a new one, the present cross, was built by Leonard Hesletine, an Askrigg mason, who received about £21 2s. 5d. Numerous persons were paid for taking away stones, 'raising the pillar,' 'carting sand from Batt,' and 'leading flag from Penill [Penhill].' The total cost was under £30, towards which expense six inhabitants, including Agnes Hastwell and Patty Burton, gave small subscriptions. In 1849 the same mason erected a new substantial pump in a handsome stone case. Although later the pump was discarded for a time, it was replaced and still stands in the market-place. The last big undertaking of the trustees was carried out in 1842. Three Askrigg masons superintended the making of a road in the back lane at the West End, the extension of the common sewer in that direction, and the laying of fresh paving in Pudding Lane.

During the nineteenth century village administration, scarcely touched for over two hundred years, underwent complete reorganization. The calamitous increase of the poor due to economic disturbance and the rise in population necessitated many Acts of Parliament. These and others led by slow degrees to centralization and the extinction of the village as a self-governing unit. As paid men took over the work of the old parish officers, the vestry meetings of ratepayers held to conduct parish affairs were gradually stripped of their powers.

In 1782 Gilbert's Act, an adoptive, not a compulsory, measure for the union of parishes to maintain their poor in workhouses, and for the appointment of the first guardians, had been passed. In 1819 an Act allowed committees called Select Vestries to be formed for out-relief; and the great statute of 1834 removed the administration of the poor law from the parish and made unions compulsory. But the overseers remained, superintended now by the guardians instead of the Justices of the Peace, and the assistant overseer became an official paid to collect the poor-rate. In 1835 the Highway Act abolished compulsory work on the roads; and when in 1867 the North Riding was divided into nineteen Highway Districts, of which Askrigg formed one, the local surveyor disappeared, and in his place a waywarden served on the Highway Board. Finally the Acts of 1839 and 1856 established a paid

L

county police force which in course of time superseded the village constable. As we shall see later these and numerous other moves all led to the establishment of modern local government, with its headquarters in our case at Northallerton and Askrigg.

Though for two or three centuries the ratepayers of Askrigg township had probably held vestry meetings three or four times a year, the first minute book that we have found is dated 1848-83. From it we surmise that the scene would have changed little over the years. There at the Town's House on Thursday in Easter week at ten or eleven in the forenoon the inhabitants assembled, a full attendance 'earnestly requested.' They nominated overseers (in 1850 a woman's name appears) and later guardians, highway surveyors, and eventually waywardens, assessors, and collectors of taxes; and after the Act of 1842 made a list to be laid before the justices of those qualified to serve as constable—the last of such lists being made in 1872.

Sometimes meetings were 'of a stormy nature,' and sometimes others were convened for a specific purpose. At one in 1852 the only business was to draw up a contract with Isaac Bainbridge, who for £7 10s. a year was to catch moles throughout the township. Isaac evidently did not give satisfaction, for after two years his salary was suspended to give him opportunity to 'repair his neglect.' In 1856 it was ordered that a pinfold be built on a plot of ground at Town Head. Regular matters coming up for consideration included decisions upon rating and special cases requiring poor-relief, and the composition of the Select Vestry.

Sworn in on 29th March 1844 four men served Askrigg as constables that year, in 1852 the number was reduced to two, and by 1866 only one was required. Though we know many of their names no record of the activities of any Askrigg constables has been left; but the descendants of the last man to hold that office at Bainbridge, whose constabulary, divided into three divisions, stretched to the head of the dale, have in

		£	s	d
	To the Chief Constable as p̃ 2 prec̃d." ---	39	6	1
May 1	To Expences at private search - - - - -	8	2	8
	To postage of letter - - -	0	0	3
	To the Return of the 14 articles - - - -	0	2	6
	To my journey with freeholders list not acc.d	0	3	6
Sep. 11	To my D.o with D.o — D.o and oath	0	6	6
	To Expences at private search - - - -	0	2	0
	To Return of the freeholders list - - - -	0	2	0
Oct. 9	To my journey with Surveyors list - - -	0	3	6
	To postage of a letter from Clerk of the Peace	0	0	9
Nov. 3	To the Return of the articles - - -	0	2	6
Sep. 28	To journey & Expences with 2 Highway men			
	returning at the Hawes fare as p̃ Rec.t - - - }	2	19	10
	To my journey Horse hire D.o with D.o - - - -	0	10	2
	To assisting poor people with passes - -	0	17	10
	Allow.d Hawes Surveyors for repairing Hayland {	60	13	6
	Rec.d from the Treasurer towards the }	105	10	11
	Repairing Haylands Bridge - }	50	0	0
	£	55	10	11

		£	s	d
	To the Chief Constable as p̃ 2 prec.op.n - -	39	6	1
	To sund.r poor people people with passes - -	0	5	6.
	To journey to Middleham with freeholders art.	0	6	6
	To my D.o to bolton with D.o - - -	0	3	6.
	To my 2 journeys with the 14 articles - - -	0	7	0
	To 1/2 private search - - - - -		4	0
	To Jn.o Cleasor & Wm Johnson journey & Expences }	3	15	6
	to Atterton about Haylands Bridge & p̃ order }			
	To Tho.s moor &c 100 flatstones stones Haylands Bridge	1	9	2.
	To Tho.s Craggs for making two fonderels - - }	1	8	6.
	To Ja.o Warnshill d.o &c. to Mudd Roade &c i 6p.	3	0	0
	To Jn.o Starker 13 1/2 days a 16.d - - - - -	0	15	9
	To Tho.s Morr and &c 12 days a - - - - -	0	16	0
	To Nich. Thweit &c 9 d.o - - -	0	12	0
	To Ben Benton repairing Cawdrud - - - -	0	3	6.
	To Expences at towing Sh.ird s. Roade - -	0	2	8.
	Expences at setting Haylands Bridge -	0	5	10
	£	52	19	6

Page dated 1798 from Bainbridge constable's account-book

their possession an account-book covering the years 1795–1820, and from it we may derive a picture of this ancient official's duties before he passes from the village scene.

By now the constable's oath, sworn before two justices, had lost much of its old phrasing, such as 'blood-sheds assaults and affrays' and 'hues and cries'; only 'watch and ward' remained. The duties had become onerous. The county rate that provided for the repair of bridges and the jail, relief of prisoners, the upkeep of the House of Correction, the treasurer's salary, coroner's fees, and charges concerning vagrants and soldiers' carriage, was by far the largest sum that the constable regularly disbursed. This amount, in the early entries £30 to £40 paid annually by each division, rose during the Napoleonic wars until it reached a climax, over £90 each, in 1816–17, the year following the peace.

Twice a year the constable filled in a return called the Fourteen Articles that contained questions as to the behaviour of the inhabitants. He made numerous journeys to Middleham to deliver to the chief constable both the militia and the Freeholders' Lists. The former gave the names and occupations of all the men in the township between the ages of eighteen and forty-five, and the latter those who were qualified to serve on juries. For the militia the inhabitants provided an allotted number of men either by volunteers or by a ballot conducted at Middleham with the constable present.

Two or three times a year a 'private search,' set down as costing 1s., later 4s., was ordered. The constable and his neighbours met together at night and scoured the district for rogues and vagabonds, who if found were taken before the nearest justice. 'To sundry poor people with passes' is frequently entered as the constable recorded his surveillance of the movements of the destitute, who with a magistrate's removal order were travelling from township to township to their legal places of settlement. In 1806 a new staff, costing 14s., was bought. Perhaps it was the last, for even then the work involved fell too heavily on the shoulders of an unpaid, untrained, local man.

Records of the first union in which the villages joined for the maintenance and employment of the poor have been lost. As we have seen, James Lightfoot the apothecary promoted the 'Union Society,' but he died before plans were complete, and the townships of the district formed a new incorporation under Gilbert's Act in 1812. Between 1809 and 1810 a workhouse was built at Bainbridge and fitted up with utensils for the employment of the poor of Askrigg, Bainbridge, Hawes, Abbotside, Thoralby, Burton, and Aysgarth. The cost, shared by all the townships, was apportioned on a basis of the poor-rates of the previous three years; but for immediate expenses a local loan that was gradually paid off during the next six or seven years was launched. The building was largely erected by local labour at a cost of £1,473 10s. of which Askrigg paid £255 7s. 5¾d., slightly less than the sums paid by Bainbridge and Hawes. 'Rules and Orders for the House' were printed, and a new governor with a salary of £40 a year was appointed.

Constable's staff inscribed Bainbridge Barony 1806 (17½ inches long)

From old ledgers of the Bainbridge Incorporation a picture can be drawn of life in a nineteenth-century workhouse. The place was kept rigorously scrubbed, not only the floors but the doors and woodwork, and 'yallokra' (yellow ochre) adorned the walls. The bedsteads were made by a local joiner, and the bedding consisted of a straw mattress, a bolster in a harden (sackcloth) case, a pair of harden sheets, and a rough blanket. Each inmate was provided with a harden towel and a hair comb. In the 1830's their victuals cost from 2s. 4d. to 3s. 6d. a head per week. On forms drawn up to long tables set with mess tins, knives, forks, spoons, and pewter plates, they sat down to breakfasts of gulls (porridge) and milk, and occasionally treacle, washed down with either coffee or beer, and to meagre dinners that early in the century consisted of broth, pease soup, bread, and cheese. But by the forties and sixties the midday meal had improved, and most days either beast head, mutton hash, beef, potatoes, or fried onions appeared on the menu, and sometimes 'berry pie.' Supper remained a dull meal—'whay sops,' milk, and oatmeal, or tea and bread and butter.

For employment there were two spinning-wheels, stock cards, hand cards, two pairs of looms, and a supply of cotton; and pigs were reared, vegetables sold, and stones broken. The guardians bargained with local doctors to 'attend our paupers . . . so to free the township from any medical expenses.' During the nineties we hear of the first mention of public vaccination, which took place in a room in Bainbridge hired for the purpose. The only books in the workhouse were two Bibles and seven volumes of Burns's *Justice*. A cradle was part of the equipment, and in it often reposed a bastard child. At funerals a cotton shroud wrapped the body laid in a rough deal coffin with rope handles, the only embellishment thin lead initials; and a portion of the churchyard was set aside for paupers—segregated even in their last resting-place. What goes unrecorded is the human misery, the separation of families, and the harshness of some of the governors in this dire time.

On the other hand the minutes of the meetings of the Select Vestries that dealt only with out-door poor-relief give a closer glimpse of reality. A Bainbridge minute book beginning in 1820 shows a state of affairs like the crumbling of a sea wall before the encroaching tide. On the one side an increasing number of miserable, recalcitrant, and desperate poor filtering into or growing up in the township, some returning under removal orders, others finding work with relatives in order to get a settlement; another section losing what work they had, failing in business, or by reason of old age, laziness, or illness being unable to maintain either themselves or their families. On the other side the guardians and overseers, their kindlier instincts stifled by the complaints of their fellow ratepayers and the seemingly endless stream of needy persons, frantically patching up weak places by giving (with strings attached) small pensions, articles of clothing, blankets, coals; offering temporary employment, arranging free medical service, paying house rents; or trying to prevent future erosions by placing boys out as apprentices or sending them to the workhouse to be taught to weave; and as a last resort coercing old people into allowing their children to emigrate.

The wording of the orders sets the tone: this family ordered to give up their house or 'take it on their own bottom,' that family to be 'turned out of the workhouse immediately,' another to employ themselves in knitting 'instead of being a nuisance as at present justly and greatly complained of'; 'John Broderick to give up to the township his horse and cart' and the township to pay him £3 and lend him the same 'on condition that his son leave him as soon as convenient.' So it went on, peremptory dictatorship interposed with kindlier actions such as a young girl set up with 'decent clothes' before going to work on a farm, an old man sent 3s. 'on account of the storm,' and a family relieved with a bottle of wine and a blanket when 'in typhus.'

As the century advanced, and particularly after 1834, a general improvement is reflected locally. By the time we reach 1852, the date of an Askrigg minute book, the waves seem less rough and considerably better under control. In common with others Askrigg Select Vestry made sure that everyone paid his share of the poor-rate or showed 'cause why not.' It held a firm hand on the prospects of work and reduced pensions 'at the commencement of Hay Harvest.' It gave occasional relief such as ordering John Atkinson to 'come with his baskit and have his baskit furnished at the discretion of the guardian at a sum not exceeding 10s.'; but they discontinued his pension of 2s. 6d. a week. Now, on occasion, advice rather than orders was given—that 'William Graham ought to endeavour to place his son William out in service in preference to going to the mines.'

When in 1869 the incorporation under Gilbert's Act was dissolved, the new Aysgarth Union consisted of the same townships as before with the addition of Carperby, Bishopdale, Newbiggin near Thoralby, and Thornton Rust. But unable to see beyond the present, the inhabitants were still too nervous of being overwhelmed with importunate demands to blend an imaginative approach with practical aid. Theirs was a time of temporary expedient.

2. EARLY VICTORIAN ASKRIGG

ON 5TH JANUARY 1841 Fletcher Clarke, bookseller of Hawes, circulated a thousand free copies of '*Clarke's Original Monthly Advertiser* for the market towns of Leyburn, Middleham, Askrigg, Hawes, Sedbergh, and Kirkby Stephen, also for Dent and Swaledale.' This sheet of advertisements eventually developed into the *Wensleydale Advertiser*, sold at 2½*d.* a copy, the first stamped newspaper in the North Riding, published fortnightly from January 1844 until December 1848, when it ceased. Prior to this the newspapers, used by us as channels for advertisements, had been the *York Courant*, the *York Chronicle*, the *Newcastle Journal*, and the *Manchester Mercury*. In this local venture the editor's desire was 'to write about our own loved dales as much as may be possible,' and in consequence Fletcher Clarke left a unique record of events in Wensleydale in the 1840's. From his journal, and a few other sources such as directories, account and commonplace books, inventories, and letters, we may draw a picture of life in Askrigg at the time.

We find some references to poverty in these black years of rising prices. Beggars from other districts were numerous, and vied for charity with the local poor. Oatmeal funds were started, and in winter subscriptions were collected to provide the needy with coal. In January 1847 over £30 was raised in Askrigg township. In the spring of 1845 it was reported that upwards of fifty individuals from Swaledale had passed through Hawes within the week on their way to Liverpool to embark for the United States. In 1841 Alexander Fothergill of Rochdale, the surveyor's grandson, failed in business as a cotton spinner, and severing his family's connection with Raydale sold Carr End. The estate, put up for auction at the White Hart, Hawes, was bought by William Whaley of Gayle for £3,010.

The picture we form is one of a people sometimes deploring lawlessness in the upper dale, but enjoying a rural life coloured by many local events, fairs, feasts, and the new tea-drinking festivals. The editor enlarged on the inhabitants' attachment to the locality, their continuance of ancient usages, and unwillingness to admit innovation. 'Here,' he said, 'may still be found that primitive order of society which is fast giving way before the giant sweep of modern enlightenment.' He viewed with mixed feelings the prospect of a new form of transport that in these years of the railway mania was likely to be brought into the dale, but he fairly took into account the benefits that might accrue.

Each day the Wensleydale royal mail coach set out from Bedale—the post having been brought to it by omnibus from the Leeming Bar station of the new branch line of the York, Newcastle, and Berwick Railway. The coach traversed the valley via Middleham, Leyburn, Bainbridge, and Hawes, to Sedbergh, a route extended in 1844 to Kendal for the conveyance of passengers to the Lake District. Sometimes during winter storms it stuck in snowdrifts above Hawes, and occasionally, as when 'the lead horse slipped and fell with one of the wheel horses upon it,' serious accidents were narrowly averted. If we had travelled outside, we probably dismounted thankfully, for the seats were notoriously hard.

Carriers' carts served the villages well. Two plied from Askrigg to Richmond and one to Kendal, and many passed up and down the dale on the other side of the valley. Trains of pack-horses and donkeys had by no means vanished. The old route from Lancaster to Richmond and Barnard Castle, recorded in a written recollection of these years, followed in part the common way of the monks of Jervaulx Abbey. It passed along Abbotside through Sedbusk, Litherskew, and Skelgill on to Helm, across Slape Wath and, winding up to High Straits Lane, crossed Arngill Beck to Heugh Lane, through Cranehow Knot Nick on Ellerkin, and across Bolton Moor to Richmond.

Accidents with horses, often caused through carelessness, such as driving without reins, letting horses loose in the streets, and allowing them to stand unattended, were prevalent. In May 1844 Thomas Graham, an Askrigg innkeeper, was seriously injured when he was leading turf; and one evening William Preston, unloading iron from a cart at Simpson Little's forge, was hurt when his horse, frightened by the clanging and the glitter of a candle, bolted.

Supposing we had returned to Askrigg in the 1840's after an absence of many years, we should have seen three-storeyed seventeenth-century houses above Pudding Lane, the Pratts' clock-maker's workshop beyond them; Simpson Little's forge near the south-east corner of the churchyard and cottages below it, and across the road from them George Bell's joiner's shop and more cottages where the Temperance Hall and the Wesleyan Chapel now stand. The inns were the Kings Arms, the Red Lion, the George, the New Inn, and the Blacksmiths Arms (the present Crown Inn). Behind the latter, James Sagar, innkeeper and smith, had his forge, and a third smithy was situated at the foot of the moor road. Thomas Little's joiner's workshop and Dorothy Addison's dye-house were on the West End; and most of the cottages in the cobbled yards were occupied.

The four grocers and four other shops still supplied the wants of a country town, such as harness and saddles, to be bought at Richard Butterfield's below Pudding Lane next to Samuel Sykes, grocer and draper, who occupied the present Temperance Hotel. The shop adjoining the Old Hall, lately Joseph Cooper's, displayed in its small-paned bay windows three carboys of coloured liquid, one red and two blue. William Pratt, fresh from Liverpool, a chemist, druggist, and tea dealer, had recently taken over the business. He sold perfumery, genuine patent medicines, teas, coffee, spices, and fruits, and hoped by his unremitting attention and the strictest care in his choice of drugs and in compounding physicians' prescriptions to merit the patronage and support of the public.

The physicians were John Bowman, who occupied a house opposite what is the present Crown Inn, and Thomas Moore Parke, son of Miles Robinson, who lived in the ancient house on the West End. Askrigg had for long supported two members of the profession. In 1717 Thomas Goulding was followed by Thomas Peacock, chirurgeon, and Joseph Smithson, practitioner in physic. There were Francis Wilson, James Lightfoot, and James Brougham, and in 1823 James Metcalfe, surgeon.

Our visitor would see few children in the street. Many would be attending James Burton's private school situated above Winnville; some might be seated before Charles Cay learning to write, others standing up to sing scales for Samuel Halton. After 1842 the majority were taught by Thomas Firby at the new national school, a building adjoining the master's house at the West End. Though children had been taught English and writing at voluntary charity schools, held on Sundays since 1789, many people were still illiterate.

In these years Yorebridge Grammar School, owing to the conduct of an unscrupulous master, Thomas Darnton Milner, almost ceased to function. The Rev. Anthony Wharton, curate of Stalling Busk Church and master of the grammar school for forty-nine years, died in 1843. In his day, according to the report of charity commissioners who visited the premises about 1821, the number of free and English scholars averaged thirty-five and twenty-five respectively. The former paid an old customary sum of 2s. 6d., called a cockpenny, at Shrovetide, and the latter 4s. or 3s. a quarter for reading; all paid 6s. a quarter for being taught to write. The master's salary was then £58.

Due to the exertions of George Winn, a trustee, the rent of the Black Swan, that was enjoying the height of the prosperity of the coaching era, was raised to £200. Mr Milner was appointed master with this salary. Living away and employing another teacher, he neglected his duties so grossly that the number of scholars fell to a mere handful. In 1845 the Lord Chancellor was appealed to, and the heirs-at-law, taking

Old Yorebridge School

charge, dismissed Milner. With the high hopes of the neighbourhood behind him, the Rev. William Balderston, M.A., of St John's College Cambridge, then living at Sedbusk, was given the post, and he took up his duties on 2nd February 1847. A year later a new school, costing £200, was built; this building is still in use for woodwork classes. These years marked a turning point in the fortunes of the school, that with a less fluctuating endowment might have developed into a public school as did Sedbergh and Giggleswick. Instead, Mr Balderston remained as master of a small grammar school until 1891, when his son followed him.

At this time uprisings of religious fervour broke out, to fade away or to leave a permanent mark. The 'deluded followers' of Joseph Barker, and the representatives of Joanna Southcott, appeared in lower Wensleydale. In 1836 the first Primitive Methodist chapel had been built for the community of coal-miners in Cotterdale, that lonely valley north-west of Hawes; and camp meetings, marked by the spirit of revivalism that distinguished the sect, were held in other parts of upper Wensleydale. Later, as we shall see, this movement reached Askrigg.

Meanwhile Wesleyan Methodism established itself as a strong force in the village. An increase of members had coincided with the non-residence of the vicar, Robert Bowman, who in 1811 reported that there were about eighty dissenters, 'denom-inated Arminians,' whose teachers were travelling preachers. A chapel had been established in 1807, and five years later Simeon Holgate made over the building to the first trustees. In 1844 bazaars were being held for the upkeep of chapels in the vicinity.

The spread of education, the formation of Sunday schools, that connected with Askrigg Church established in 1831, and another begun by the Wesleyans two years later, were bringing about a change in manners. Robberies, mostly committed by strangers, occurred now and again, and where poverty pre-vailed in villages, whose inhabitants depended on seasonal work, conduct was rough.

It was evidently a local person who, in January 1848, stole fourteen yards of merino cloth from Rebecca Thwaite's shop in Askrigg. This woman announced her intention of applying to the wise man for its recovery, and early one morning she found the roll on her doorstep. As late as 1860 the Rev. John Winn, vicar of Aysgarth, living at Nappa Mill, was attacked by burglars with a hay-spade.

Although local people found the village constables inade-quate, in 1840 they joined with the rest of the North Riding in appealing against the establishment of a paid police force. Sixty-six Askrigg inhabitants signed a petition suggesting some revision but deploring the inevitable increase in county rates.

However, in 1847 the first member of the force in Wensley-dale, John Pringle, was stationed at Leyburn as 'superintending constable' in charge of a lock-up house. His salary, including a house over the lock-up, was £70 a year, out of which £30 was for providing and keeping a horse. Ten years later a sergeant, William Simpson, at Askrigg, and constables at Hawes and West Burton were appointed.

Undoubtedly drink was still the prevalent vice. A Wensley-dale Temperance Society brought lecturers on teetotalism to the villages; and in 1841 the Leyburn Shawl Tea Festival, that in a few years' time drew as many as three thousand people, was started. Both the Askrigg national school and the Sunday schools began to hold annual tea festivals at which hundreds partook of the 'exhilarating beverage.' There was the occasion such as that on Thursday, 14th September 1848, when a public tea festival was held in a splendid marquee at Town Head. The Askrigg Quadrille Band rendered lively airs, and after dark the players marched round the market cross. Later dancing continued until the early hours of the morning.

There were different progressive movements. Springing from the business of Hutton, Other & Company, bankers of Richmond, Leyburn, and Bedale, the Swaledale and Wensley-dale Banking Company was formed in 1836. Foremost in promoting the company was Christopher Other of Elm House, Redmire. To raise capital twenty thousand shares of £20 each were issued, and eventually bank-notes, with little engravings of Richmond Castle and Bolton Castle printed in the corners, were current in the dale. In 1842 a branch opened at Hawes finally swept away the old system of bonds and borrowings between private individuals, and was of inestimable benefit to the neighbourhood. If any question of it remained, its establishment settled the supremacy of Hawes over Askrigg as a market-town.

Similarly, on 27th September 1843 the first agricultural exhibition in the upper dale was held at Hawes with William John Anderson, of Swinithwaite Hall near West Witton, as president. At first limited to the parish of Aysgarth, the area for competitors was extended the next year to the dale from Wensley Bridge to Hellgill Bridge. We shall speak of the many classes for cattle, sheep, and dairy produce in a later chapter. A light on the times is thrown by the inclusion of a premium of £1 offered to the labourer who had 'brought up the largest family without parochial assistance,' and one of 10s. each to the unmarried male and female servants who had lived longest in the same situation.

Butter and cheese were then stated to be the main products. Market prices, depending on the time of year, gave butter at 9½d. to 11d. a pound, new milk cheese at 63s. a hundredweight, beef and mutton at 5d. a pound, bacon, green and dried, at 5s. 3d., 6s. 6d., or 7s. a stone, eggs at ½d. or sometimes at Christmas time ¾d., ducks at 9d. each, and chickens at 10d. Sharp increases occurred in 1847, when, for example, cheese rose to 67s., dried bacon to 9s., oatmeal to 3s. 2d. a stone, and flour to 4s. 2d.

As the new movements gained support, the old tended to be forsaken. Fletcher Clarke remarked on the lessening of interest in the pleasure fairs. Such a one was Askrigg June Fair, only then beginning to lose its importance as the event of the year in upper Wensleydale. A decade before the street was so thronged that people might have walked from one end of the town to the other on the heads of the crowd. There were boys, truants from school, 'stallions proud with ribbands prancing,' stalls displaying chinaware, many selling cheese-cakes, gingerbread, and tom-trot (a kind of toffee), doubtless tables laden with food in the houses for relatives and friends from a distance; and at night dances, of which the steps have long ago been forgotten, were enjoyed by the young men and girls.

A new date that replaced the June fair in importance was in process of being added to the calendar of the town's and the valley's year. Askrigg Sheep Fair, better known later as Askrigg Hill Fair, grew up, and came to be held annually on

11th and 12th July. A customary fair, having no connection with those granted in the market charter, it originated about 1785 when a few lots of sheep unsold at Stagshaw Bank Fair in Northumberland were shown on Carperby Sleets. Meeting with a ready sale the stock increased year by year, until at the turn of the century the fair was moved to Askrigg Moor where there was better accommodation. In 1819 when the common was enclosed it was held for two or three years above Gayle; then Camshouse, Bellerby, and other sites were proposed; but on a pasture near Askrigg Moor being offered, it returned to Askrigg to the satisfaction of buyers and sellers alike. The fair continued there until, owing to diminishing trade, it was transferred to the market-place, and ended about 1935.

The Fair Allotment, a mile from the village up the moor road, is a long sloping limestone terrace close on 1,300 feet above sea level. Early accounts of the event extol this lofty position, whence those who came for pleasure could see away below them a wide expanse of dale bounded by the fells at the opposite side of the valley. Multitudes assembled from far and wide. The business transacted, with sheep from Scotland as the mainstay, continued to increase. In 1848 Dinmonts sold at 18s. to 24s., Scotch gimmer hogs at 14s. to 22s., tups were in demand, cattle numerous, but horses were 'of a very inferior description.'

Local innkeepers and others, some from distant Stainmore on the fringe of Teesdale, set up drinking booths, the woodwork for which formed part of the stock-in-trade of Askrigg joiners. There were side-shows, displays of crockery, and 'minstrelsy in abundance.' What a sight it must have been! Flinging aside their plaids, the drovers ran to collect stray sheep; their flocks lined the road; the bonnets, ribbons, and print dresses of the women made gay the green pasture. The hillside was 'clad wi' folk'—so many that it was difficult to walk between the couples strolling or sitting in groups.

It was, too, an occasion for the settling up of scores between

Wensleydale and Swaledale men. A written recollection, re-
ferring to these years, states that to those watching the fights
of the six-footers each blow sounded like a horse's kick. In
1848 Superintendent Pringle was dispatched there to keep the
peace. Instead his presence rather acted as an incitement to
worse affrays, and suffering cuts and bruises, he escaped the
mob. Excitement mounted during the night. A party, mostly
composed of miners from Gunnerside, but including James
Pratt Addison, miller and gamekeeper of Askrigg, 'riding the
fair,' that is passing from tent to tent for drink and provisions
as was a custom, in the early hours of the morning ran amok,
threatened a widowed innkeeper, and damaged her tent.

> Have you not heard of Askrigg's famed sheep fair,
> In summer time, when all our folks are there.

Thus wrote Jeremiah Willis of Carperby in his *Beauties of
Wensleydale*, published in 1838. Although Thomas Maude of
Wensley, writing in the eighteenth century, is better known,
in these years local poets had printed slim volumes of verses
either in the hope of monetary reward or to please their
friends. In spite of being derivative, humourless, and riddled
with the sentiment which we associate with minor Victorian
poetry, their verses retain a naïve charm. One of their
number, John Close, a Swaledale man living at Kirkby
Stephen, wrote of a journey into the dales taken about 1841,
and coined these lines on the village:

> And down below old Askrigg queerly stands,
> Built—the Lord knows when, by various hands!

Jeremiah, comparing himself to Tim Bobbin, poor, and conscious of being different from others, was at once the most
pedestrian and the most local. He pictured the villages of
the dale and wrote a description of the 1832 election at
Askrigg that begins:

> What muse shall I call on, if any there be,
> To inspire the pen of a poet like me.

Matthew Willis, living at Yorescot near Bainbridge, whose

M

Mountain Minstrel was published in 1834, aimed higher. He wrote whilst working on his father's farm, was self-taught, and composed a poem 'To the Sun' of almost a hundred verses.

Two others, the Rev. Grover Scarr, who was born at Bainbridge but lived later in Lincolnshire, and Fanny Shaw of Askrigg, a native of Northumberland, sang of the past and relived scenes of their childhood. The latter's *Rhymes and Readings* was published in 1866, and though sentimental and pious, some of her poems have the haunting quality of a Scottish lament. Grover Scarr published two volumes, *Night Musings*, 'received with favour and consideration' in 1847, and *The Eve of St Mark's* in 1871. The life stories of both these two, aliens longing for their homeland, were unhappy.

More mundane than the effusions of the poets are the compilations written down in one or two account and commonplace books that date from these years. Personal jottings throw light on the individuals who kept them. There are lists of family births and deaths, sermons, extracts from newspapers, such as the *Leeds Intelligencer*, on 'for a right temper of mind' or 'the shortness of human life,' and recipes, some again copied, others old and tried, handed down from one generation to another.

From them we learn how to destroy crickets by putting 'Scotch snuff' in the holes where they come out, how to concoct a Prussian dye from, amongst other ingredients, black sealing-wax and soft soap. Here is a recipe containing hog's lard and black lead to make a composition for greasing coach wheels, and a blacking made from coarse sugar, sweet oil, and beer. We read of a paste to stop holes in cooking-pots, of a glass of water being turned to ice overnight, of cures for rheumatism, burns, and toothache. Cellars were evidently lined with English champagne, gooseberry vinegar, punch milk, pop, nectar, treacle beer, raspberry rum, ginger, cowslip, and elderberry wines; and larders stocked with potted char, beef and pork pickled in sugar, saltpetre, and 'bay salt,' napkin cheese made from thick cream covered with nettles until ripe, and queen cakes, gingerbread, raspberry jelly, and rhubarb marmalade. These were the jottings of the well-to-do, the middle class of the village, those who lived in the large houses, employed servants, and kept a carriage and horses.

At the other end of the social scale were the very poor who had few possessions and who owned no clothes but what they wore. From inventories taken at the time we find that their homes contained a minimum of furniture. They had perhaps one or two beds, two blankets, an old rug, a langsettle, a chest, a corner 'cubbert,' tea-things, pots, a coffee-tin or tea-caddy, a candle-box and some snuffers, and, relics of better times, a punch ladle, a looking-glass, or a clock. They possessed the tools of a trade, maybe one or even two looms, a spinning-wheel, a cobbler's stool, and often treasures such as fishing tackle, a large picture, or a bird cage.

But for the majority life was not nearly so harsh. Best clothes of the latest fashion were worn on Sundays and for special occasions. Young ladies of the better-off families sported turbaned caps, and held 'sarsnet parisolls' over leghorn, grass, or ricestraw bonnets. Neck ribbons graced their necks and waist ribbons their pretty dresses that fitted over whalebone stays. In winter they sat down to the piano in confections of 'crape de lion' with ribbon velvet belts. There were plenty of lace trimmings, smart jet beads, 'satton shooes,' and spun silk handkerchiefs. Even little girls clutching six-penny dolls or 'sciping ropes' tripped lightly into the gardens in muslin frocks, or set off sedately down the street in Dunstable or fancy straw bonnets and with tippets round their shoulders; or like Jane, daughter of James Burton Lodge, the brewer, went away to the Misses Bells' school at Richmond on a winter's morning, legs shielded against the cold in 'shiff' boots, or French clogs and worsted stockings, heads cosy in velvet bonnets. Old ladies sat before the fire, the Saturday magazine beside them, perhaps decked in rich black velvet for best or in a 'canton crape shoole' held by a silver pin, mittened fingers busy with knitting that rested now and then on a stiff black silk apron.

In the 1830's Ruth Lodge, Jane's mother, went shopping to Harrogate by staying overnight at Middleham, and at five o'clock next morning boarding the Wensleydale Highflyer that ran through Harrogate to Leeds. In 1845 she would have travelled in the Courier Coach that replaced the Highflyer, and if bound for Leeds, she would have paid 6s. outside and 14s. inside. Perhaps Ruth, who loved pretty clothes, had her daguerreotype taken by Mr McFarlane, photographic artist, who visited Askrigg on Wednesday, 21st June 1848.

Before long, ousted by the railways, the coaches ceased to run, and eventually the turnpike trusts ended. Each year in the 1840's the Richmond to Lancaster Trust advertised the letting of the toll-bars, the one at Askrigg having been replaced by one at Brackenber near Bowbridge. In April 1844 the proposition that a chain or side bar be placed at the end of the Worton Lane where it joined the turnpike, was being considered. It is the last move of which we hear. By instalments the trust was closed: the Eastern District turnpike from Widdale Foot to Richmond Bridge expired under an Act passed in 1868.

By 1845 the railway mania had reached Wensleydale. As rival speculators, George Hudson amongst them, scrambled to claim new ground for main and branch lines, nine schemes were proposed to run through or within the valley. Advertisements of the intentions of the York and Glasgow Union Railway and the Manchester, Liverpool, and Great North of England Union Railway sometimes filled two or three columns of the *Advertiser*. The first was planned to connect east and west by running through the valley, and the second to enter the dale from Settle to Hawes, tunnel under the Buttertubs Pass and proceed down Swaledale to Richmond, so to link up with Durham. A persuasive argument for this was that, due to the difference in the expense of transport, coal cost 8s. a ton at York and 20s. to 22s. a ton at Settle, both equidistant from the pits. A few months later the Lancashire and North Yorkshire Railway advertised its proposed line through Wharfedale and Bishopdale to Middleham, with a branch line from Aysgarth to Hawes.

The notices stated that surveys were being made, and announced public meetings that were supported by leading men in the dale such as the Rev. Richard Wood, the Winns, and Wood Metcalfe of Askrigg. Inspectors were posted to take a check on traffic. Sometimes the facetious remarks beloved of the Victorians were reported, as the answer of one man who, asked where he came from, replied: 'Ah come fra heeam, an' ah'se gaen back t'ut'; or the comment of another that ling would be taken by rail to thatch cottages in London.

As we know, the schemes came to nought. Instead, a private concern, the Bedale and Leyburn Railway Company, launched by residents in lower Wensleydale, brought a line as far as Leyburn in 1856. The directors experienced difficulties from the start, and were soon considering an amalgamation with the North Eastern Company that three years later took over. At the conclusion of the last meeting a resolution was passed that in the interests of Wensleydale the line should be extended farther up the valley. But almost twenty years went by before the railway reached Askrigg.

3. I' THEM DAYS

IN THE SECOND half of the Victorian era, instead of vistas of 'time out of mind,' those within the memory of man approach; and the recollections of living men and women come into play to throw bright but intermittent gleams on to the past. In a sense we have already used this source of evidence in quotations from the depositions of witnesses in lawsuits; for anciently it was usual to call on the knowledge of the very old to assist in the settling of disputes. But whereas such fragments are at second hand, the impressions of the living are told to us by the spoken word. 'I' them days,' 'Sin' I can tell,' 'I've heard mi mother say,' 'When I were a bit of a lad'; these phrases that prelude reminiscences sound as music in the ear of the local historian.

From the mid twentieth century most elderly people return in memory to the 1890's; the really old remember events in their childhoods in the 1870's; and some, repeating recollections of their parents and grandparents, go back a hundred years. These latter memories are rare and remarkable, more than we can normally expect. One tells us that her father, who lived at Nappa Scar as a boy, remembered hearing the horn of the mail coach sounding across the valley; another who died in 1950 aged ninety-one spoke of Low Mill as the 'Tumming Mill,' a name, meaning rough cardings, that was probably used in Agnes Hastwell's day; a third recollects that he attended Yorebridge School under the Rev. William Balderston, and was a fellow pupil with 'Willie Balderston,' who followed his father as master in 1891; and a few remember the opening of the railway in 1877 or remark casually that an event occurred about the time that Jessie Fothergill's novel *Kith and Kin* (1881) was published. Such flashes down the corridors of time startle the mind and breathe life into cold facts.

Askrigg is and has been a place noted for the longevity of its inhabitants. Lord Torrington recorded that here 'people live to a great age.' In 1844 the ages of twenty people averaged more than eighty-three years, and those of twenty-six others averaged seventy-four. In 1859 we had three nonagenarians and others over eighty, and in our own day there were recently two in their nineties, one born at Askrigg living in Swaledale, and several in their eighties. We respect and are fond of these elderly neighbours, most of them well and active to within a short time of their deaths.

The parish can claim four centenarians, two who lived long ago at Bainbridge and one at Worton. Betty Webster, born

Wet roofs

at Thwaite in Swaledale in 1790, occupied one of the Dale
Grange almshouses for some thirty years. She died aged 106
at Aysgarth. Betty's life reflected the times; for she began
work in a Lancashire cotton mill when she was about fourteen.

Marrying and coming to live in Wensleydale, she lost her husband, and brought up eight children by 'charing' and knitting. A small wiry person, her wrinkled face spoke of a hard life. 'I was like a deal mare fond folk; I thought when I'd gitten wed I'd gitten all' was the sad remark that she made to reporters on her hundredth birthday.

But for oral tradition we should know nothing of the Garland Day Sports, that seem to have been a continuation of those organized by the Four Men; for they were held on 16th August and the prizes in part resembled the old ones. The feature of this day was the Garland Race, run over a stiff course from the Fair Hill Allotment in a north-westerly direction to Black Hill Plantation and back; and the first prize was a garland of flowers, the second, a silk hat, and the third, a pair of white gloves. The money for the prizes is said to have been given by a woman who, disappointed in a love affair, encouraged the race as a means of punishing the men; but the tradition does not altogether explain such an ancient reward for prowess as a garland of flowers. After the enclosure of the common the race was run up the village street from Paddock Beck Bridge to Elm Hill Top, and although the event, revived in later years, is remembered, the charity of the prize money, once derived from a field near West Bolton Farm, Carperby, has been lost.

A story, handed down from the eighteenth century, is of the murder of the Scots laird or lord as he is called. Because no one was brought to justice it remains undocumented. The Scotsman is said to have been a cattle dealer, who, after staying the night at Askrigg, set out northwards and was lured up a lane at Newbiggin, and there murdered and robbed. Many incidents are related: of how a couple, by chance witnesses to the murder, were given 'hush money' but did not prosper; of ghosts seen in houses where the Scotsman's body was hidden for a time; and of children calling after the perpetrator 'Scots Lord! Scots Lord!'

Recollections of customs inherited from one generation to

another are not numerous. A belief was held that at midnight on St Mark's Eve the figures of those who would die within the year would be seen going to church. It was a noted date in the calendar: children were sent to bed early on that night. We have been told that whilst some watched from upper windows, two old men regularly sat on the cross. One year one fell asleep, and his companion saw him walk towards the churchyard. He died that year.

In mid-Victorian times, before the coming of the railway, life in Askrigg still moved in its own orbit. Children grew up without stirring farther than within a few miles' radius of their homes, and for many of their elders Carperby eastwards and Hawes westwards were the limits of their world. 'An hardy people,' little touched by sophistication, their roots deep in their native soil, they worked hard and enjoyed simple pleasures.

Although many village trades remained, extensive ones such as hand-knitting gradually ceased to be of importance, especially when Thomas Gill, who had run the worsted mill since 1863, sold it ten years later to Thomas Weatherald for use as a saw mill. The lead mines on the moor and at Woodhall and Worton became less profitable as lead decreased in value. At this time the road to the colliery on Blackstone Edge, heretofore used by donkeys, was made into a cart road that is still to be seen as a green track west of the moor road to Muker. But livelihoods drawn from the land were the real means of sustenance.

At Yorebridge Grammar School new boys faced an ordeal of ragging from the senior boys; and two annual events, the barring-out of the master and a snowball fight between Askrigg and Bainbridge, enlivened the normal routine. The barring-out took place on Ash Wednesday when the boys, locking the master out of the school, claimed a holiday. Both head and under-master enforced discipline by frequent canings, and a page of advanced prose to be repeated correctly before leaving school was considered mild punishment. In 1851 the

Rev. William Balderston built what is still the headmaster's house on school ground to replace an old and poor one.

Most of the children received their education at the national school, where Thomas Firby had been followed by his wife and two daughters, Miss Juliana and Miss Mary, those 'very gentle folk who knew very little.' The schoolhouse, now in part dilapidated, was erected about 1780 by Peter Hutchinson, a carpenter, on the site of an ancient dwelling called Clark Wife House; and the upper room of Peter's 'workshop adjoining' appears to have been used as the main schoolroom. Mrs Firby, who was short and stout, occupied a raised platform with a balustrade that still remains. There were three classes, the A B C segregated in a corner with boards on which the alphabet and words of one syllable were painted in large letters, the Testament class in the middle, and the Bible class on the south side.

A photograph exists of the three teachers and some seventy-five scholars grouped in front of the steps leading to the schoolroom; most of the girls wear pinafores and the upturned feet of the boys sitting at the front are shod in clogs. In the later days of the Misses Firby it is remembered that the children of the better-off families were sent home a little earlier than the rest; and that Miss Juliana, delivering fruit which she sold from her large garden, enjoined a child not to eat any or her father might think she had given short weight. 'And I durstna,' said our informant.

Necessitated by the Elementary Education Act of 1870, a new national school, part of the present building, was planned in 1876. It was built by a firm who did much similar work in the dale, Simon Dougill & Sons of Aysgarth, and when completed with desks and fittings, it cost £504 16s. 10d.

Disaster attended an ambitious church bazaar arranged to raise funds. Three tents, two for the sale of goods, one for luncheon, put up in a field near the school, had been decorated with Japanese awnings, bunting, and fairy-lamps. In the afternoon a strong wind, rising to a gale, blew down one that

School children at Askrigg about 1880. There are seventy-five scholars and at the top are seen the teachers – Mrs Firby, and the Misses Juliana and Mary. The photograph was taken outside the old National School (see page 174).

Teachers and scholars of Yorebridge Grammar School in the school grounds. The headmaster, R C Shorter, has on his right Doris Owens and F E Chevins, and on his left A Meadows and Alice Holden. (1932–3).

Askrigg Post Office about 1908 with Mrs Thistlethwaite in the doorway. Members of the family followed as sub-postmasters until the office was moved higher up the street in April 1963.

A Stationer and newsagent's shop on the West End.

West End, Askrigg, in the late nineteenth century. The Sykes family, grocers and drapers, were in Askrigg in the 1820's. They possibly owned the block, and later moved the shop and Temperance Hotel to the market place. Mrs Sam Sykes may be the lady on the right.

lifted 'like a piece of paper into the air and fell down with a thud on the heads of everyone assembled.' Mrs Winn, an elderly invalid, was marooned in her donkey carriage near one of the central poles. The flower-stall was ruined and crockery smashed. People smile now when they speak of dignified persons crawling from under the wreckage, but at the time consternation must have been intense.

Twenty-one years after the building of the Primitive Methodist chapel at Cotterdale, a second was built at Bowbridge. There followed in 1868 a remarkable revival from which sprang the project for a chapel at Askrigg Town Head; and the next year the revivalist, Miss Hyde, conducted the opening services.

Lacking endowments with which to meet expenses, the chapel trustees were often in need of funds, and they continued the annual tea festivals, sometimes called tea meetings, as a popular means of raising money. Old minute books of Bowbridge and Askrigg chapels record the tasks allotted to the members who acted as 'kettle huggers,' bread fetchers, fire menders, waiters, and of course singers. For a meeting in 1871 the tickets were ordered to be eightpence each, and the provisions 'not to be made so rich as last year.' In spite of this, pastry, spice loaf, teacake, and cakes were baked from some seven stone of flour, twenty-one pounds of currants, and other ingredients. It is remembered that those responsible for much of the food at the Bowbridge meeting held on Ash Wednesday did not go to bed at all on the previous Sunday night. They waited until midnight, then began washing, followed by churning, and after that started to bake; and baked all day Monday and Tuesday.

At the lower end of the village the Wesleyan Methodists were shortly engaged in building a new chapel on the site of the old. In 1878 over three hundred people came to see the foundation-stones laid. A visitor from Leeds was heard to say that 'churches and chapels were an ornament to the town or village, and if in Askrigg he could not speak of beauty, he wished that they would excel in righteousness and let the latter house be more glorious than the first.' On the chapel's completion commemoration mugs were given to the children. The new building was gradually furnished with gifts, such as a

Temperance Hall and Wesleyan chapel

silver communion set, a communion table, and stained-glass windows.

Although now discontinued at Askrigg, the Love Feast, when testimonies of conversion and Christian experiences were given, and, as a token of fellowship, a two-handled mug from which everyone drank water was brought round, was the event of the year. Instead, tea festivals for the Sunday school children, held at the Moor Road Chapel on Christmas Day and at Station Road Chapel on New Year's Day, are important annual meetings.

Gone are the sincere but unlettered local preachers who rode or walked long distances to their Sunday appointments, and about whom many stories are told. There was the one from a lonely farm who, having conducted the service evidently in great anxiety of mind, hurried off, saying: 'Ah mun go; mi yowes is calving and mi cows is lambing.'

These trends, and the opening of a reading-room in the Toll Booth (where the *Yorkshire Post*, *Leeds Mercury*, *Richmond Guardian*, and London journals such as the *Graphic* and *Punch* were read), drew away many of the men from the habits of drinking and fighting then prevalent.

These were as yet the days of individuals whose manners and ways of life fitted an ancient mould. There was Guy Tiplady, the cow doctor and if need be dentist, who, with his long legs almost touching the ground, rode a small pony always at a peculiar canter; Metcalfe Graham, farmer, clerk, and sexton, who rang the church bells, one of which was cracked and was pulled by a looped rope through which he put his foot, so that 'ding, dong, bump' sounded each Sunday; Simpson Little, the blacksmith and the last constable, who, although they struck for him at the forge, carried on a perpetual feud with the older boys; and there were many others oblivious of people's opinions.

The most tragic life stories are those of Thomas Moore Parke and his wife, who now lived in the doctor's house. She became a dipsomaniac, and eventually the doctor, taking to drink, had to give up his practice. Once the sexton, as he was lighting the stoves in church late one night, was alarmed by the approach of a white figure that resolved itself into Mrs Parke, come to ask him to fetch her a bottle of gin.

In these years new forms of communication heralded the approach of the railway. The telegraph system (the single-needle type as used by the railways) was extended to Askrigg in 1871, and later the means of transmittance was improved, until it was replaced by the telephone in 1914.

The postal service, unsatisfactory throughout the eighteenth century, was by now better arranged. Few early records are extant. About 1740 'the Gentlemen Tradesmen and Inhabitants' of the market-towns of Middleham and Askrigg, and of towns and places adjacent, petitioned the postmasters general. They complained that Mr Holmes, postmaster of Bedale, had assumed the right of employing a person to bring them their letters, that he charged them twopence for postage, and that the man employed was often so drunk that he lost several letters out of his bag, and at other times lost the whole bag in the high-road.

An inadequate system, employing letter-carriers between the villages, continued until on 20th February 1812 the residents of Wensleydale petitioned for a better service in a district that had 'served itself three times a week from Bedale.' The post office surveyor recommended the setting up of a daily penny post that, starting from the New Inn, Leeming, 'would reach as far as Askrigg and return in time for the Glasgow mail coach at Leeming Inn.' But in 1823, when William Terry, shopkeeper and auctioneer, was postmaster at Askrigg, there were only four deliveries a week by a riding post that left Bedale at 5.50 a.m. for Middleham, Spennithorne, Leyburn, Askrigg, and Hawes, all penny-post towns. As we have seen, the Wensleydale royal mail coach travelled through the valley in the 1840's, and eventually the mail was brought by train. Throughout the last century, until 1921, 'Askrigg, Bedale' was our address.

In 1877 the salary of the sub-postmaster of Askrigg was £9 4s. a year, plus 4s. 1d. weekly for performing a delivery and station services, and 7s. 6d. for telegraph duties, and a full-time postman received 16s. a week. When in the 1870's Aaron Knaggs, who had had the post office in his shop, became a bankrupt, the postmaster of Bedale came to the village. Choosing a house that was central, he went in and found Thomas Thistlethwaite at work in his cobbler's shop. Offered the job, Thomas accepted it and became sub-postmaster in 1874. His son, his son's widow, and his grand-daughter, Dorothy Outhwaite, followed him at the office that is still conveniently situated in the centre of the main street.

The first route for the railway from Leyburn had been planned high up the hillside north of Askrigg. In 1869 the survey of the present line that runs south of the village was made by the North Eastern Company, and after the buying of land, the invasion of contractors and navvies, and the

The post-mistress

building of embankments and bridges, it was opened for passenger traffic at Askrigg on 1st February 1877 and at Hawes the following year. During this time the inhabitants of Bainbridge failed in their petition for a station at Yore Bridge, and instead the one at Askrigg was built. The line crossed the site of Fors Abbey, where navvies dug up lengths of lead water-pipes and numerous bones that seemed to denote a burial ground. In 1878 the Midland Company completed their branch line from Garsdale on the Settle–Carlisle line to Hawes where the two companies joined in the expense of the

station.   We were now linked with the main lines at Garsdale
on the west and Northallerton on the east.

Greeted with enthusiasm, after 'hopes long deferred,' the
railway was opened amidst scenes of great rejoicing on that
February day.   Several North Eastern Company officials were
present.   The train, whose nine or ten carriages had been
'besieged by delighted crowds at every station,' reached Askrigg at nine-twenty that morning.   It was met by many people,
some attired in fancy dress; and headed by 'a conveyance
containing Gunnerside band drawn by a dozen grey horses'
a procession formed to march up the village.   Here flags,
banners, and flowers adorned the houses, and several triumphal
evergreen arches with models of the engines used by the contractors spanned the street.   The tea provided lasted from one
to four o'clock, and at five the train left packed so full that a
'special' was run about eight.

Anticipating this great day, the inhabitants had attempted
to revive the market on a Thursday of the previous autumn.
An eye-witness recorded a show of pigs, poultry, and seven
hundred sheep, that many tradesmen set up stalls, and that
farmers' wives displayed baskets of butter at the cross.   Sports
held during the afternoon were followed by a tea in the
Assembly Rooms, and a lamp was put in the market-place
inscribed with the words 'Askrigg Market re-opened 1876.'
That year the tolls let before for 1s. 6d. brought in £2.   At
the same time an old house and Simpson Little's forge
were bought for a site on which to build a market hall.
But in spite of the promises of over six hundred people
to become shareholders and a collection of some £700, the
scheme fell through; and two years later the market was
abandoned.

One of the prime movers in these projects was Stockdale
Thompson, who had returned to his native place from Burnley,
and who, living now at Grenada Hall, was a cobbler.   Brimful
of local patriotism, he conducted a lengthy, acrimonious
correspondence with a Hawes man, John Routh, in the

This engine, pulling five small coaches, the front one containing a guard's compartment with a roof-top look-out, opened the last section of the Wensleydale line from Askrigg to Hawes in 1877.

The last trains on the Wensleydale line. On the left Garsdale Thunderbolt with two coaches, and on the right Old Faithful with two coaches, a freight van and a horse box.

Northallerton, and Bedale Times, and published a small paper-backed guide-book to the district. When one of the opposers of the market scheme died, as the funeral passed, he said: 'There he goes a cumberer of the earth.'

To celebrate the reopening of the railway in 1877 Stockdale Thompson arranged a firework display, an event that has been put on record from an outsider's point of view. A boy of fourteen, deputizing for an employee who was drunk, set out from Manchester with the fireworks. Clad in an Inverness cape, he started what was then an adventurous journey by train at five in the morning, and travelled by Leeds and Northallerton to Bedale, where by mistake he alighted. Arriving hours later at Askrigg, he was greeted by the brass band playing furiously, and was marched at once to the cross. Here he lit a few sparklers to everyone's delight, and then let off 'The Devil among the Tailors' that, exploding with loud bangs, alarmed the audience, including the policeman who ordered him and his supporters to stop. Led by the band they adjourned to a field to finish the display; and 'I've never seen people enjoy fireworks so much.'

The boy emigrated to Australia. About fifty years later on a visit to England he motored through Askrigg, and seeing several old men sitting on the cross in the sun, he asked them whether they remembered the fireworks. 'Aye that I do. Was ta theer, mister?' asked one. When he said that he was the boy who had let them off and remembered Stockdale Thompson, the old man, pointing with his pipe to the church-yard, said: 'Yonder's where he lies.'

If all the hopes aroused, such as the market reopening and the increase in the value of land, were not fulfilled, the effects of the railway were far-reaching. Coal that had previously been carted from Leyburn station, or fetched from West Pits or Blackstone Edge, or carried from Durham by donkeys to a depot in the Lodge Yard, now came by train. Falling in price, it was then 16s. a ton. The working of the small collieries eventually ceased except under the duress of wars or

N

strikes. Meal and goods brought to Askrigg station started a regular traffic that daily traversed the moor road to Swaledale. Sometimes as many as twenty carts of badgers and farmers waited in the station yard.

In 1878 a train, arriving in Askrigg at 5.39 a.m., was run for the mail. But the most radical change brought about was the sale of liquid milk that had previously been made into cheese and butter. In the first years of the next century retailers began to contract for milk to be sent by train to Leeds, Manchester, and Liverpool, and in course of time to London; and the great supply of this produce to towns was begun.

The railway developed the then insignificant tourist trade that grew to replace the vanishing industries, and to supplement the farming that by the end of the century was beginning to feel the effects of national trends of cheap food and mass imports. By train came the day trippers who invaded the country from industrial towns and who, no less than the leisurely tourists of a previous age, marvelled at the beauties of the waterfalls. The advertisements of hotel and apartment proprietors emphasized 'well-aired beds,' and extolled the beauties of Mill Gill and Whitfield Falls as the sights to be seen above all others; the Red Lion changed its name to the Railway Hotel; wagonettes plied to and fro; and in the shops souvenirs in glass, wood, and china, with 'A present from Askrigg' or a picture of the Old Hall on them, could be bought. We possess a tiny wooden cradle of antique shape with an oval photograph of Askrigg street printed on the canopy.

Inevitably all this interchange, far more effectively than in the turnpike days, brought in new ideas, swept away local idiosyncrasies, and linked town and country, as motor transport and wars have continued to do.

4. THE END OF AN ERA

IN THE FINAL twenty years of the century and the first decade of the next considerable rebuilding took place, and the appearance of Askrigg's main street, the West End, and Pudding Lane largely assumed the aspect that we see to-day. In the 1880's houses had replaced cottages and the forge

Temperance Hotel and on the right the doctor's house

below the church; two shops on the east side of the market-place, together with several houses on the outskirts of the village, were built in the 1900's, and many others altered and enlarged. With few exceptions they were built by individuals—yeomen, attorneys, apothecaries, hosiers, brewers, grocers, and carpenters—to meet personal need, and so they remain, varied and distinctive in character. Askrigg was now large enough, indeed too large, for its population; some dwellings were unoccupied, and most of the cottages in the yards had fallen into disuse.

In 1873 Dr Baker, who had followed Dr Parke, had left to live in Aysgarth, where our doctors have since remained; and their house in Askrigg became a chemist's and newsagent's shop presided over by 'Stump' Lambert, a little man with a tall wife who wore her hair in ringlets.

Above the chemist's shop the bow windows of the present Temperance Hotel exhibited an infinite variety of drapers', milliners', grocers', and ironmongers' wares; for Samuel Sykes advertised 'the largest general stock of goods kept in Wensleydale,' and indeed here could be purchased dinner services (bought by Samuel in Staffordshire) or wineglasses, boots or hats, Japanese ornaments or wedding-rings. A little below 'Stump' Lambert's, William Handley, in whose family ran a streak of inventive genius, had his coachbuilder's workshops where every part of the carts, gigs, and traps was made. Bright with new paint and varnish the vehicles made a gay show, set out for display on fair days.

Each year up on the pastures the Hill Fair, now held on 1st and 2nd July, drew the crowds. Its character had changed. Due to the cessation of the Scots droving trade, sheep were no longer sold. Instead, horses had taken their place, and those buyers and sellers of horses, gipsies and potters, congregated there. Gradually arriving a week or a fortnight beforehand, they pitched their tents and caravans along the green roads and the lane down to Newbiggin, until every space was filled and the hillside strung with the swarming alien crowds.

Men remember as boys seeing such a gipsy as Cacky Isaac's wife cooking a hedgehog wrapped in clay in the embers of a fire. The prickles peeled off like an egg-shell, and the flesh was white. Women, offering to tell fortunes, and carrying baskets filled with lengths of material and clothes-pegs, pestered every house; and sometimes the men persuaded farmers to buy, for £20 or so, a horse that next morning could scarcely be touched, and that, when eventually let out, careered back to its owners on the hill.

Although at the end of the century not so unruly, in the

1880's the fair was still an occasion for pitched battles. One year a fight between two parties of gipsies necessitated the swearing in of a body of special constables to assist the police in restoring order; and down in the village it is remembered of a famous old gipsy, Peggy Buck, that she knocked a man off his horse, and led it up and down his prostrate body; but the animal avoided treading on its master. At this date a midwife, looking out at dawn, saw the Scots drovers wrapped in their plaids, lying out full length in drunken stupors on the cobbles from Elm Hill down to the bridge. In the inns, open all night, men lay on the floors; and for a week after fair day it was impossible to hire labourers for hay-time. But these scenes, part of an earlier age, were passing.

At the end of the century ancient funeral customs still prevailed. In the hamlets every householder was bidden to attend by a man or boy sent by the undertaker, and at Askrigg, though not all were bidden, a similar procedure was observed. Black crape hatbands and silk scarves for the men, and silk hoods for the women, it is true, had mostly gone; but for some years to come a glass of port, a funeral cake (round like a bath-bun), and a funeral card, deeply edged in black and with an inscription inside it and perhaps a suitable verse, were handed round before the ceremony. Hymns might be sung at the house and at the graveside, especially by the Nonconformists. After the service a substantial meal was provided, ham or mutton, and in older days beer served in tankards, for many would have a long ride home.

What the hearse was like that was bought for £24 from John Drummond of Aysgarth in 1815 we cannot tell. Kept in the Toll Booth it served the parish for forty-three years, and was in the charge of the sexton, who was paid 1s. by the parishioners for its use; 5s. was paid by those living outside the parish to the churchwardens, who also provided a cloak for the driver. In 1858, to house a new hearse, a cottage and some old property at the west side of the churchyard had been bought. At funerals this last horse-drawn vehicle increased the melancholy of the event. On either side raised carvings represented angels blowing trumpets; and with its six bunches of black plumes nodding, it rumbled with a hollow sound over the cobbles. Eventually the green and frayed plumes were removed, and in course of time the hearse itself ceased to be used.

A more cheerful aspect of village life was the enjoyment of music. Whereas neither the arts of writing nor painting have flourished, music was and still is part of the fabric of life in the dale. There was the singing-gallery in Askrigg Church, where, like the characters in *Under The Greenwood Tree* by Thomas Hardy, the musicians performed, and where in 1810 Matthew Thompson first played a bass fiddle that he himself had made.

Melodious voices were a natural gift that, had the population been larger, might have inspired Yorkshire choirs such as those in the West Riding. The Wensleydale Tournament of Song, first held at Leyburn in 1898, encouraged Askrigg to form a choral society in 1899; that year *The Pirates of Penzance* was given, and the male voice choir became noted. Piano lessons and concerts, arranged by the teacher, Miss Maybury, are part of the recollections of the children of these years, and other concerts and soirées in the Assembly Rooms reflected the refinements of the Victorian Age. When the brass band was started, we do not know. Besides those that came from Keld, Gunnerside, and Muker in Swaledale, the Askrigg Band played carols in the village and the hamlets at Christmas time.

The event of the winter, the Conservative Ball, claimed many people's attention beforehand. For each girl there were the new dresses to be bought or made, some fitted by the warm fireside of the sewing-room, an upper room in one of the drapers' shops; and preparations for the supper, always advertised as 'knife and fork,' entailed the boiling of hams and the baking of bread and cakes by those famed for their specialities. After the supper in the Wool Room came a meeting, followed by the ball in the Assembly Rooms. Some of the dances were the eightsome reel, the square eight, and six reel; and whereas they were once accompanied by fiddles, in the early years of the next century two pianos, sometimes assisted by a concertina, provided the music. We picture the colour, the sound, the heat in the room, the farmer's wife who on one occasion led off the ball with eight of her own family behind her, and the girl who each year was accounted the belle of the ball. About four in the morning the dancers left for home, some to mount their horses, the women riding pillion, to return into Swaledale.

In politics most people were Conservatives. Feeling ran high at election times; fights were frequent, and occasionally those who voted Liberal were given notice to quit their cottages. In 1906 Francis Acland, adopted as Liberal candidate for the Richmondshire division, came to live at Colby Hall, and in consequence a strong Women's Liberal Association developed in the village. The candidate worked hard in his constituency and was returned by a small majority. Since when it has remained a Conservative seat.

The turn of the century was a time of remembered poverty, often aggravated by drink and often ameliorated by the kindliness of neighbours. In those days it was said that 'if you had a chair and a bit of a stool, you could marry'; a man who owned a cart and horse was considered well off, and a legacy of £200 was deemed a fortune. House floors were bare except on Sundays when a clip rug made from old clothes that 'had cost nothing' was laid down. People went early to bed to save candles and fuel, and lived on 'gulls,' broth, potatoes, and herrings. A drainer named Nelson with a wife and two children had no work one bad winter, and the destitute family returned in consequence to their home town, Kirkby Stephen. Sent to the workhouse, they were separated; and the man in his despair hanged himself.

Strangers, some of them odd and deformed, who have gone from the modern scene, were the itinerant umbrella-menders, tramping painters, chimney-sweeps, and foreigners, Spaniards or Italians leading performing bears on chains. Catering for these poor travellers, Mark Bett had kept in the main street a common lodging-house that was followed by one run by a Mary Middlemas in a yard at the lower end of the town. Mary hid her money in bags hung from her waist under her ample skirts.

Elderly people speak of the strength and stature of many of their fore-elders. Men fell off horses, breaking their legs, and declared that if they had had more liquor in them they would have avoided accidents; they hugged enormous bundles of hay up steep snow-blocked roads; mowed eleven-foot swathes with great scythes; and walked miles 'over the moor' into Swaledale, where the Askrigg postmaster had for many years to deliver telegrams, and where the grocer, the hosier, the clock-maker, and the butcher sought trade. Though there is no statistical evidence, it seems that in those days men were taller than their present-day descendants. A story of a group of fifteen dalesmen, all over six feet in height, going on a train trip to London, relates that as they mounted a horse-bus, the conductor asked: 'Are they all as big as you where you come from?' 'Nay,' was the answer, 'we're nobbut t'lile ins.'

Characters, some living on into the twentieth century, others remembered from the last, lent a spice to village life. There were the three who stayed in bed for years; one of them, Jane Hunter, lying there supposedly ill for over twenty, who, when mention of the workhouse was breathed, immediately got up and became caretaker at the school. There was Aaron Knaggs, grocer and postmaster, who drank, and being in the way as a funeral approached the churchyard, was pushed into the open grave by the quick-witted sexton; Jimmy Richardson, the rat-catcher, whose traps with their elaborate mechanism were enormous contraptions 'like fortresses,' and who played the fiddle and varnished his hat and his outsize turned-up boots; Mossy Dick, so called because he smoked dried moss, a butt of the boys who once blacked his windows so that, thinking it was still night-time, he stayed in bed; William Thwaite who in his old age traded in keslops, the dried stomachs of calves used instead of rennet for cheese-making; and Dennis Otley the tailor, who came from London and was superior; he locked his wife in when he went out, and wore a frock-coat down to his ankles and a tall narrow top-hat.

Within more recent recollection than these was Jimmy Wood, probably a descendant of James Burton Wood, living in the old brewery house, who hoarded hay, and whose two sisters were seldom seen; and Nancy Willie, the postman, who was terrified of women and whose method of delivering the mail was to kneel on his cap and push the letters under the door. When he died a room in his house was found stacked to the ceiling with undelivered circulars and news-papers.

Lastly there were the practical jokers. One of a sadistic nature blew a powder that induced sneezing into rooms where people were gathered, dropped stones down chimneys at 'toffee joins,' spoiling the pan of toffee on the fire, threw hot pennies to the children, and put housewives' candles in hot ovens; and there is the tale of three men who one Sunday let a donkey into the old chapel, and, it is said, all died violent deaths within the year.

If we had peeped into the workshop of George Thistlethwaite, the Radical shoemaker, who though past work still kept his bench and tools, we might have seen some of the old men as, wrapped in their plaids, they sat talking until the cobbler was summoned to dinner by his wife blowing a whistle. Or in the clock-maker's and antique dealer's house, the present news-agent's shop in the market-place, through a haze of tobacco smoke we should have glimpsed the men gathered there to gossip with old Skiddy, a venerable figure with a white beard, in a medley of sound of the ticking and striking of some fifty or sixty clocks. John Skidmore, though only a repairer, was the last in the line of clock-makers.

Another aspect of the gregarious nature of village life was the children's habit of sitting with old people, usually with the spinsters or the bachelors or the childless. 'Let's go and sit with so-and-so' would be said as they came from church in the afternoons of those dreary, pious, Victorian Sundays. These old people, a few of whom seldom if ever came out of their homes, seem to have accepted their visitors as usual; perhaps they had themselves sat for hours with an older generation; and the children with few amusements found entertainment in the tales of long-past days or in the curiosities to be seen in the kitchens. Peggy Thompson, 'Peggy Mike,' living at Lowlands Farm, regaled the boys with stories, whilst she twiddled and turned the stick in her hand. She went to bed at two or three in the morning, and rose at six or seven.

Up at Town Head in the last house on the moor road lived Faith and Jane Cloughton, Jane who because of a tragedy in her youth never came out, and Jammie, their brother. In the kitchen at the back of the house sat the two old women, clad in bonnets, black dresses, and black laced boots, Jane smoking twist in her clay pipe that was quickly thrust into the oven if the sound of footsteps was heard. From the ceiling hung a string of blown eggs to ward off evil, and Jammie's stove-pipe hat, familiar with its crape hatband at funerals, was suspended in a handkerchief. In the bedrooms witch-stones were hung on the four-posters. If they were dressed in their best clothes, the girls avoided chair and table-legs that were black-leaded.

Many stories are remembered of Faith and Jane. How Faith, when buying paint, was asked what colour she would like; she replied: 'I'll have black, black's as leitsome as owt.' Of how, because their house had been two cottages, they went out of doors and up the stairs in the second cottage. On a wild evening children would say: 'It's a cold night for them to be going to bed.' After their deaths 'all maks and manners' of things, such as lengths of material that the gipsies had persuaded them to buy or barter, and poor Jane's wedding clothes, were found. Faith, Jane, and Jammie, strayed from a past era, died in the 1920's.

In the 1890's the street was seldom empty. There were the occasions when religious and political meetings, entertainments or rejoicings, took place at the cross. At New Year, the bells chimed, Askrigg Brass Band played, the children marched up to Town Head, and afterwards sang songs 'creditably and sweetly.' On Monday, 2nd June 1902, the news of the peace was celebrated, and Corporal Harry Sykes, by chance returning home from South Africa that very day, received an ovation. In August the same year the houses were decorated, and once more the bells pealed, this time to celebrate the Coronation. The national anthem was sung at the cross, and after a free tea, sports, and competitions, a dance in the Wool Room finished the day.

Even on ordinary evenings voices young and old resounded across the street. Women stood knitting and gossiping in doorways; while against the blank wall of a derelict house on the site of a present-day grocer's shop, the young men played a local variety of fives. Below the cross a game of burney ball, a kind of rounders played between two sides, perhaps twenty boys against twenty girls, was in progress. But when dusk fell it was time for the hunt. One boy was given a start and raced off alone; in a few minutes a troupe of perhaps thirty children gave chase. Along the West End he led the way, over the churchyard wall, across the road; with a clatter of clogs and flying sparks the hunters followed. Up Pudding Lane the boy dodged into a dark doorway until the last straggler dashed by. 'Shout!' called the hunters, and waited silent. 'Who hoo!' echoed the answer, and off they clattered once more.

At school childish games included 'Weighing the sheep,' when two of the older girls took hold of a little one and swung her between them. Or the children, collected together in a long line, waited whilst one standing alone recited either of the following verses, and then, shouting and laughing and trying not to be caught, they rushed across to safety.

Widder Widder away
Six and fours ten.
If you're not all off
I'll make you all my men.

Blackthorn butter eggs and barleycorn,
How many geese have you to-day?
As many as you can watch flying away.

At the shops children bought logwood chips with which to dye their hard-boiled eggs for Easter. Perhaps the chips were the last vestiges of the dyers' trade. At winter parties singing games, accompanied by the appropriate actions, were played. Two go thus:

Oats and beans and barley grow
You and I and anyone know
You and I and anyone know
How oats and beans and barley grow.
First the farmer sows his seeds
Folds his arms and takes his ease
Stamps his feet and claps his hands
And turns him round to view the lands.
Waiting for a partner.
Waiting for a partner.
Open the ring
And take one in
And now you've got your partner.
Now you're married you must obey
You must be true to all you say
You must be kind
You must be good
And help your wife to chop the wood.

We'll hire a horse and steal a gig
And all the world shall have a jig
And we'll do all that ever we can
To push the business on.

There were the days in the open spent hunting over the moorland country perhaps up Penhill, Addleborough, Ellerkin, or by the Buttertubs on long runs to the Swaledale border. From 1755, when 'Squire' Pratt brought his harriers to Askrigg, until 1941 hounds were kept in Wensleydale. Amongst several masters of local packs, Christopher Alderson Alderson hunted the Askrigg Harriers from 1810 to 1830. Eventually these, amalgamating with others, formed the nucleus of the Wensleydale Hounds, a 'rummy all-round little pack' that hunted hares, bag foxes, otters, and even water rats. Hounds met about three days a week at several villages, Askrigg included. Foot - followers there were in plenty, not only men and boys, truants from school, but women also who 'rushed about in all directions their knitting in their hands.'

The clerk to the Parish Council

The 1890's saw the end of the old order. In 1889 the North Riding County Council had been created, and under the Local Government Act of 1894 Aysgarth Rural District Council and the Parish Council came into being, the three bodies that still form the basis of our administration. Vestry meetings, except for church government, were swept away, and the Four Men were superseded.

After an election at a public meeting the Askrigg Parish Council met on 3rd January 1895. During their first year of office, the five members were feeling their way. They obtained a book on how to keep the minutes, and a 'standard work for the use of the Council'; they took in the *Parish District and Town Council Gazette,* and drew up elaborate orders regarding procedure to be followed.

As time passed, all kinds of business came under the councillors' direction: the inspection of, repairing, and building of
footbridges, freedom of access to public footpaths, the repair
of stiles, and the prevention of encroachment on public
property.   They appointed the assistant overseer and read
his balance sheet, elected charity trustees and passed their
reports.   Improvements such as the starting of a village library
and the making of a recreation ground were discussed, the
streets were kept clean, and the cross was repaired.

Meanwhile, the Four Men, except James Trotter who refused
to sign the necessary document, renounced their responsibilities,
and with the sanction of the charity commissioners, to whom
had been sent a copy of the market charter, the council took
its place and was allowed the use of the surplus toll money.
In 1898, in spite of 'not liking old landmarks to be removed,'
it was decided to pull down the Toll Booth and auction the
materials.   Then there followed the proposal to spend the
money in hand, £15 17s., on oil lamps to light the village, and
on seats 'for the accommodation of the inhabitants and visitors
of which latter a large number come to the place in summer
time'; and the last of the funds of the market secured for the
town by Peter Thornton four hundred years before was spent
on eight new oil lamps, and four seats for Askrigg and one
for Nappa Scar.

Already, however, in 1891 an old cottage had been bought
to be demolished for a site on which to build a village hall.
Time passed before the necessary funds were collected, and in
1905, due to the efforts of the Band of Hope Society and a
donation of £400 from Henry Tennant of York, a Quaker,
the foundation-stones of the Temperance Hall were laid.   Once
more the celebrations took the form of a procession led by the
Askrigg Brass Band.   A fine roomy building, the hall replaced
the Toll Booth, the Assembly Rooms, and the Wool Room as
the centre for meetings, games, and amusements, and was and
still is of inestimable benefit to the neighbourhood.

In 1908 William Handley Burton, the corn miller, and his

sons harnessed the force of water at Mill Gill Falls and installed the most up-to-date machinery to provide an electricity
supply for the village. Born of the enterprise of one man, it
brought the transition from oil lamps to electricity into the
dale at an early date. As a private company the Burtons
supplied Askrigg, Aysgarth, and Reeth in Swaledale, and
eventually many other places until the national grid system
took over at Askrigg in 1948. Sixpence a unit was charged;
and later a Diesel engine supplemented the water-power. If
we had now looked in on old Skiddy sitting reading at night,
we should have found him with an electric-light bulb, instead
of a candle in his hand moving it backwards and forwards
across the page.

For many years past the corn mills at Bainbridge, Woodhall,
and Nappa had been closed, and Askrigg Mill, grinding oatmeal, supplied the neighbourhood and upper Swaledale, until
it in turn lost trade and ceased to work at a time between the
two world wars. But unlike those at Nappa and Woodhall
that fell into ruin, it continued as the electricity works, and as an
undertaker's and joiner's business where hay-rakes were made.

At Yorebridge Grammar School various Education Acts
culminated in radical changes far removed from Anthony
Besson's wishes for a 'free' school. An Order in Council of
1902 established a governing body of twelve, fixed charges for
the pupils, and one foundation scholarship for every ten
scholars. There were then about twenty pupils, and the
master's salary was £190 a year. Illustrating lessons by relating
them to local people and events, William Balderston had a
peculiar but effectual method of teaching. For example, after
an exposition, he would chant questions in a sing-song, and
pause before each boy in turn, a brush upraised in his hand,
ready to cuff the ignorant. His old pupils, now running
businesses and farms of their own, bear grateful witness to his
sound teaching. Not until 1919, after William Balderston's
retirement, were girls admitted, a very late date when compared with other similar schools.

The girls either went to the national school or to that run by the Misses Thompson.   Here, at the turn of the century, three teachers taught about ten scholars who learnt the three R's, music, and elocution, and who for recreation or perhaps for deportment went through their fan, pole, and hoop drills.

Drill, with wands, featured no less in the national school's curriculum.   The Misses Firby had been followed in 1892 by William Hartshorn and later by Charles Watson, the latter an excellent master but of a similar fiery temper to the two Balderstons.   Due to the many large families, there were over a hundred scholars.   Pupil teachers and sometimes assistant mistresses aided the teaching of the headmaster, whose salary, previously £119 10s. a year, rose in 1914 to £130, whilst the mistresses received £45 to £52 and later £60 a year.

As we have said, the doctor had left Askrigg to live in Aysgarth.   In 1909 the last exciseman, Albert Robson, was transferred elsewhere.   Part of his work, that which had been concerned with licences and agricultural returns, was gradually taken over by the County Council, and the area he covered became amalgamated with other districts.   A year or two later, unfortunately the Winns' solicitor's office closed, but the Aysgarth Rural District Council, to which William Winn had been clerk, kept its headquarters in Askrigg.   Partially the result of chance and partially due to the disruption of village life that had proceeded here as elsewhere throughout the century, members of the yeomen families of the dale who pursued the professions and who had for so long lived and worked in the village fell away.   The Woods, the Metcalfes, and the Lightfoots vanished.   Only the Balderstons at Yorebridge House, and the Lodges, descendants of Joseph Lodge the brewer, remained, and they eventually left the district.

Throughout the century the Old Hall had been occupied by descendants of the Lightfoots, and latterly had been used as a summer residence by Colonel W. Lightfoot Bankes of Liverpool.   His son, R. W. L. Bankes, who died in 1953, was lord of the Manor of Woodhall, and the last collateral descendant

of the Smiths of Camshouse to live in the village.   In 1920 the
Hall was sold, and became a hotel.

About 1903 the doctor, now Dr Hime, drove on his rounds
from Aysgarth in his motor-car, a Daracq.   The beginnings
of this revolution in transport are remembered by the children
of those years who 'earned many a bright shilling,' presumably
accumulated in pennies, by pushing the doctor's car up steep
hills, especially up Howgate.   Others followed.   The Vyners
of Studley Royal, now the owners of Nappa Hall, arrived in
their car for the grouse-shooting season; and in the village
John Gill, son of Thomas Gill the hosier, acquired one of the
first.   They raised clouds of dust in their wake, and sent horses
bolting in the fields; and many many others were to come after
them.

But more than any of these events, either the coming of the
railway or of motor transport, whose effects were slow to be
felt, the 1914–18 war marked the end of an era.   Much that
was good and much that was bad in the ancient ways of life
disappeared.   Drunkenness largely ceased, but the fairs also
faded away. Askrigg men were drafted to far corners of the earth;
fourteen of the hundred and two who joined the forces lost
their lives.   For those who returned, having known little
beyond their own small village world, new vistas opened.

The parish chest

VIII

ST OSWALD'S CHURCH

1. THE HIGH PARISH

IN THE FLAGGED open space at the west end of the north aisle of the church, objects of historic interest have been grouped. It is a modest collection: an early font resting on a millstone hewn from the Greets, a large holy-water stoup once used as a chimney-pot, two pewter flagons, dated 1768, platters, and candle-snuffers in a case, a plan of the eighteenth-century pewing, a model of the building before the 1853 restoration, made by John Rider Wood, and a picture of it once belonging to Stockdale Thompson, and on the flags a small iron box, a so-called Armada chest of German workmanship bought for £1 11s. 6d. in 1828 to hold the parish documents.

One day, as we turned the key in the lock on the lid of the

chest, footsteps sounded overhead; the vicar and a church-warden, successors of the many who have served Askrigg Church, were examining the leads of the roof. They had chosen a still day; on other days the wind swirls round the tower across aisle and clerestory roofs and howls in the bell chamber. The heavy lid fell back to reveal bundles of documents: the deeds of the old parsonage house, of the Firbys' schoolhouse, of the Hearse House, of land bought in Swaledale with money from Queen Anne's Bounty, William Thornton's letter to Trinity College, the faculty for the restoration, particulars of the graveyard extension and of various legacies, and besides other flotsam from the past, the volumes of the parish registers. These are valuable fragments bearing on the church's story but, like a miniature of village history, they have to be added to by evidence to be seen on the walls of the building and in written records that lie afar off in the strong rooms of diocesan registries and Trinity College at Cambridge.

The companionable footsteps faded, leaving a hush in this place where muted sounds, dim figures, and forgotten scenes rise from the past to mingle with the present—the intonings of priests in the chantry, the shuffle of bearers at funerals, the mumble of recited penances, and banns of marriage, citations for the erection of pews, and thanksgivings for victories pronounced from the pulpit. Past the notices on the door in the porch giving news of rebellions, of meetings to oppose new landlords, of enclosures of the commons, a multitude of people have entered these precincts. The story stretches back over eight centuries to a preaching cross in Kirk Close, St Oswald's Cross, to the erection of the Archdeaconry of Richmond in 1090, to the formation of Aysgarth parish, and to the first church built on this site about 1175.

Askrigg is in the parish of Aysgarth in the Deanery of Catterick in the Archdeaconry of Richmond, now in the Diocese of Ripon. It was not always thus. The archdeaconry, once a vast area including the See of Carlisle, was transferred in 1541 to the newly erected Bishopric of Chester, where it

remained until 1836 when it was brought into the new Ripon
Diocese. For three hundred years the bishop in Chester was
our spiritual head; and the Archbishop of York, the bishop,

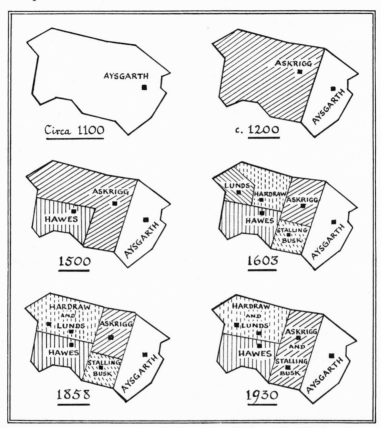

Diagrams showing the development of the parish of Aysgarth

and the archdeacon at Visitations and Church Courts dictated
measures for organization and moral discipline.

Sometime during the twelfth century Aysgarth and Askrigg
churches were built and the parish of Aysgarth was formed;
Askrigg was a chapel-of-ease, and the chapelry extended from
a little west of Aysgarth to the head of the dale—the High

Parish as later we find it called. Gradually with the growth of population in the forest four parishes were carved out of it. Hawes Church was in existence by the mid fifteenth century, and Stalling Busk, Hardraw, and Lunds were built about 1600, all chapels-of-ease in Askrigg parish and Perpetual Curacies under Aysgarth.

As time passed the four chapels threw off the yoke of the payment of dues to Askrigg, and in some cases the right of the appointment of curates by the vicar of Aysgarth. Hawes became separated about 1680 after several suits that cost Askrigg some £200. The case was first tried at the Bishop's Court at Richmond, next at the Archbishop's Court at York, and lastly by Common Law at York Castle, where, so it was said, six false witnesses swore that dues had never been paid, and Hawes won its freedom. In 1722 it is recorded that Askrigg parish consisted of three Quarters, and that Stalling Busk Church, fallen into ruin during the Civil War, was being rebuilt. Some twenty years later it, Hardraw, and Lunds became separated from Askrigg; but a further dispute arising, in 1758 an Askrigg vestry meeting decided that they 'should not be rated to Askrigg Church.'

In more recent years a reverse process began. Hardraw and Lunds were united in 1858, and Askrigg and Stalling Busk in 1930, the latter parish being served by a vicar and a lay reader, and since 1951 by a vicar only. The vicar of Aysgarth, presented by Trinity College, retains the right of appointments at Askrigg and Hawes, and at Hardraw alternate times. To this day the inhabitants of farthest Lunds, remote Raydale, or this village may as residents be married or buried at the mother church.

The story of the church in Askrigg is inevitably linked with that of the parish of Aysgarth, and that of the parish with the payment of tithes. Originally intended for the support of the clergy and the poor of the neighbourhood, they were often granted away—in our case to Jervaulx Abbey and later to Trinity College Cambridge — so that instead of providing livelihoods for local parsons they supported the seats of learning where the clergy received their training. We from the parish of Aysgarth may well feel a personal pride in the beauty of the buildings of the college in distant Cambridge; buildings that to some small extent were raised by money that issued from the crops grown and the stock reared on the meadows and pastures of upper Wensleydale.

Tithes were ever disliked, and many disputes arose from them. The Quakers, basing their refusal on religious grounds, denied altogether their liability to pay them. In 1836 commuted to a rent-charge that by subsequent Acts of Parliament could be paid off, the surrender of a tenth of a man's produce is a burden forgotten by the farmer of to-day, who instead complains of his income tax. For the local historian, however, the story of the tithes is of the greatest interest.

In 1291 the value of the rectory of Aysgarth, the whole of upper Wensleydale, was £100, a very large sum that, owing to the ravages of Scots raids, was reduced in a valuation of 1318 to £66 13s. 4d. Following the de Burghs, the Nevilles of Raby and Middleham castles owned the rectory, and one member of the family held the living of Aysgarth. At that time the priest at Askrigg was in direct receipt of tithes; for in 1301 Robert the Chaplain paid a tax of 13s. 4d. for the tenths of Nappa and Askrigg. In 1397 Ralph Neville exchanged the rectory for the land near Bainbridge called the Barony of Worton, which belonged to the monks of Jervaulx Abbey, and, several difficulties having been overcome in the interval, in 1423 the abbey became possessed of the tithes. An agreement provided that the vicarage of Aysgarth be ordained. It was to be endowed with £30 a year and sixteen acres of glebe land to support two priests, one at Aysgarth and one at Askrigg. The latter eventually received £5 a year paid out of the £30.

In 1434 the rectory was valued at £71. The monks probably farmed out the Great Tithes, that is corn and hay, together with the barns that had belonged to the Nevilles, and took only the Small Tithes, those of sheep, cattle, and so on. There were tithe barns at West Burton, Newbiggin, and Thoralby in Bishopdale, all of which fell into ruin about 1618 when, like the abbeys themselves, they were plundered for stone and timber. Part of the wood of that at Thoralby was given away by Sir Thomas Metcalfe and 'the rest of the tymber was stollen by poore people.'

A custom of tithing had grown up in the parish 'from time whereof the memory of man is not to the contrary' as was said in 1716. The people usually clipped their sheep and gathered their lambs near their homes in the first week after St Peter's Day, 29th June. The representatives of the tithe owners visited each farm and took every tenth fleece from the pile 'so as they take them downwards as they lye.' Every tenth calf was collected during the week after Michaelmas Day. If a man had only nine calves one was taken and a halfpenny returned to him, if eight a penny, until at five, a half-calf being due, money was paid. This complicated system of reckoning applied to foals, lambs, and fleeces; in the case of lambs a penny each was paid for ewe milk, and in 1756 twopence each cow was due for milk. The corn and hay tithes, when taken in kind, were usually collected as the corn stood in sheaves or the hay in cocks. A note on local custom for hay directed that 'when mown you are to knock it out of swathe and then every tenth cock of grass is the tithe men's due.' Later, a shilling for one day's mowing, that is an acre of hay, was paid, and in 1787 two shillings. Lastly twopence was paid by every inhabitant over sixteen at Easter.

After the Dissolution the tithes, valued at £160 a year, were impropriated to Michael Wentworth for a term of years, and in 1554 Queen Mary granted them to Trinity College. For a time small areas were farmed out by the college to individuals. In 1563 Christopher Tatam and others held the tenths of sheaves and grain worth £6 a year in the fields of Askrigg, called Mydcuple (Middle Chapel) Tithe.

In 1571 the whole rectory was leased out to Sir Christopher

Metcalfe, and it remained in the family's hands until Sir Thomas and the yeomen of the forest became involved in the hay tithe suit at the beginning of the next century. At this time, due to an Elizabethan Corn Act that ordered a third part of tithes to be paid in wheat and malt, the rent was £106 13s. 4d., and a quarter of wheat and 212 quarters of malt to be delivered at the college bakehouse or paid for at prices current in Cambridge market.

When prosecuting Sir Thomas for not paying the rent, the college pleaded, in the form common in such cases, that Aysgarth Rectory was a great part of their revenue, and that they needed the sums due 'by reason of ye greate necessary costs and expenses of buildings and reperations.' But from thenceforward with the additional payment of hay tithe in the forest the value of the tithes rose to £320 a year, and as farming improved they continued to increase. In 1655 they were worth £450 a year, and they were leased out to local men, sometimes groups of yeomen, such as Alexander Smith, Augustine Metcalfe, and Josias Lambert.

During this century and the early years of the next, when new churches had been built in the parish and the provision of adequate stipends for curates was difficult, the Master and Fellows of Trinity were besieged by letters from the inhabitants. In 1711 Hardraw pleaded for an increase in the £2 a year previously allowed them, and Hawes came to an agreement for £10 three years later; then there were appeals for the up-keep of the chancel in Aysgarth Church and other fabrics. We have already referred to a letter that described Askrigg as a great market town written by the yeomen about 1655. It reveals the general plight in the years of the Commonwealth:

At Askrigg . . . they have noe other maintenance for a minister than the £5 per annum and other £5 allowed by your Worships the twoe last yeares soe that sometyme they have none and when any they have heretofore commonly sold ale and used other means to gaine a livelihood unbeseeming the Ministers of the Gospell of Jesus Christ.

That at the other 4 Chapells they have not for many yeares

last past had any to preach or read divine service to them wherby many of the inhabitants scarce ever in severall yeares repaire to any publique place of Gods Worship soe as ye Sabbath is comonly prophaned and the people live and die in such grosse ignorance as we forbeare to mention.

Do humbly pray that in tender compassion to your petitioners who notwithstanding your great neglect of us hitherto have constantly and freely paid our tithes to you not doubting but that you (who are Men and Ministers of God) will inlarge your bowells towards us and minister to our necessity.

After this the college remitted the payment of fees for marriages and funerals, previously claimed by them, and subscribed a further £5, so that the stipend of the curate of Askrigg rose to £15 10s. a year. Short of the college giving up all its income, it was difficult to do more. It remained for Queen Anne's Bounty in the next century to improve conditions at all the chapels.

Besides Sir Thomas's lawsuit, one against Bernard Smith and other yeomen came before the Court of Exchequer in 1661. It hinged on the fact that Camshouse, as a former grange of Jervaulx Abbey, was tithe free; for the Cistercians and Praemonstratensians had obtained this privilege for their lands. In consequence, when occupied by their owners, several estates on Abbotside, including Camshouse and Cross Close at Askrigg, Woodhall Park and, for some different reason, Nappa did not pay tithes; but this exemption had at times to be established as in Bernard Smith's case.

In the Restoration years, as we have seen, many Quakers were thrown into jail, some for the non-payment of tithes. For this reason Alexander Fothergill, the surveyor's grandfather, was imprisoned in York Castle, and he died shortly after his release. In 1757 the Quaker tithe in the rectory was valued at £50; and according to the minute books of the Society of Friends, two justices assessed the annual amount due from individual Quakers, who had their goods distrained. In 1766 forty-seven people had taken stirks, stockings, cheese, hams, shoes, and other personal property; and there seems to have been a sale of such goods at Askrigg in the spring of each year.

After 1760 confusion resulted from the tithes being in the hands of the college receiver instead of being leased out. For the most part moduses, that is money payments, first mentioned in 1717, were being made, though Askrigg High Field and the Holmes were remarkable in that hay from them was still paid in kind. Cases came before the Consistory Court at Richmond for non-payment, and in 1784, when John Rider Wood obtained the lease, long and complicated lawsuits followed. Many people who, as it was said, 'battled with the obstinacy peculiar to them,' were prosecuted until agreement was reached. In 1816 the tithes were valued at £747 11s. 11d. a year, and in 1839 when the whole system was altered to a rent-charge and the tithe award was made, the value was £1,196 7s. 6d., of which the apportionment of Askrigg township was £84.

These facts, inseparable from our story, have taken us far from the chest in the north aisle of this the oldest building in the village. We look round the familiar interior at the spacious aisles, the lofty nave, and the open chancel, not separated from the rest by an arch. There is nothing to be seen of the first church. Rebuilt in the fifteenth and early sixteenth centuries to accommodate the increasing population in the forest, it was ever a plain structure; and as we have seen, the adornments of medieval days, the images, and the rood-loft that divided the nave from the chancel, were destroyed after the Reformation. The round pillars of the north arcade pose a lasting problem, for they are too tall, so that the arches they support have had to be depressed, and too narrow to fit naturally the wall above them; yet that they came from the monks' chapel at Dale Grange is an unlikely supposition.

In the disastrous restoration of 1853 the character of the church was spoilt by replacing the simple Perpendicular windows with a mock Gothic style, by fixing a reredos of tiles in the chancel, and by clearing away the singing-gallery and the crowded horse-box pews of the eighteenth century and drowning the pillars in a sea of pitch-pine. The church's merit lies in the fair proportions of the building, the dissimilar pillars with their warm-coloured stone-work, the clerestory windows that the restorers left untouched, and the carved beams of the Perpendicular roof.

The ancient structure has needed constant repair. In 1665 the vicar and churchwardens were admonished that 'the leads of theire Chappell wante repareing and theire Chappell not beutified,' an order repeated three years later. In 1673 the windows were in great decay, but by 1707 all was 'well done and repaired only the church is not yet whitned but wee hope it will be shortly done likewise the sounding board is undone.' In 1657 a peal of three bells had been hung, a paten (now lost), and a silver chalice with the misspelt inscription 'Askrigg Chuch 1666' engraved on it, were presented, and many oak pews put in by the yeomen. These were six-panelled, with the initials and dates of the owners and their wives carved on the top panel.

Silver chalice

Throughout the next century the building was gradually filled with pews, some of them common stalls, but most erected by private individuals. Many encroached on the chancel, the pulpit and the clerk's pew were put in the nave, and the Nappa Hall pew, the Hall servants' and the tenants' in the Metcalfe Chapel. Permission had to be obtained to erect a pew. On a parishioner's behalf the vicar and churchwardens, stating the size and position, applied for a faculty or licence to the Archdeacon's Court at Richmond. Then a citation, enjoining any who might have rival claims to the space to appear at the court, was read during the service; and if no objections were lodged, the licence was granted.

In 1790 long and expensive litigation resulted from the

application of Henry Metcalfe, a collateral descendant of the Metcalfes of Nappa, and George Dinsdale, servant to Dr Lightfoot, both owners of property. They averred in the usual phraseology that there was a 'publick voice and fame' for the truth of their statements, but the rival claimants said that their ancestors were buried under the old pews already there. 'They had paid at these funerals 5s. to the curate and 2s. 6d. to the

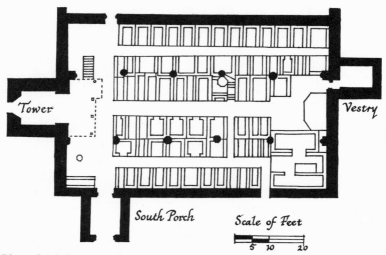

Plan of Askrigg Church, showing the eighteenth-century pews, the vestry, and the singing-gallery with steps leading up to it, prior to the 1853 restoration

clerk for their fees and 6d. to the sexton for making the grave and taking away the stalls and the flags underneath and paid for replacing the same.' The verdict, given in favour of the applicants, enjoined the opponents to 'perpetual silence' and ordered them to pay costs.

In 1750 ninety-one people gave varying amounts, in all £9 17s., to erect the singing-gallery in front of the tower; and in 1749 eighty-seven people subscribed £15 16s. towards 'a new good and substantial clock' to replace one so old that it was deemed beyond repair. For this a church rate had been proposed, but Thomas Metcalfe advised that it might be illegal, and voluntary gifts were made. To avoid trouble in this town of several clock-makers Mary Pratt of Cams-house, who had subscribed £8, was nominated to choose 'the clock-maker as she shall think most proper to be employed.' Unfortunately we are not told the makers of either the new or the old clocks; but one of the dials with the inscription 'Deface me not; I mean no, ill I stand, to serve; you for good will' remains on the wall over the south door.

The time of the town's heyday marked a period of progress for the church in Askrigg. The curate was resident, the Quakers were not increasing, and the Methodists not yet established. In June 1755 four hundred and twelve people were confirmed in Askrigg Church, though probably this meant that the bishop had not visited the parish for many years. There were a hundred regular communicants compared with thirty-five in 1811. Besides the new pews, the curate's stipend, as we shall see, was put on a reasonable footing, and a restoration that included the rebuilding of the south aisle and the erection of a vestry was undertaken in 1773.

James Lamb, the minister, proudly described the improvements: 'The Chapel is a large building in very good repair, containing within one Communion Table with a covering of blue cloth, also one linen cloth with two napkins, two pewther flagons, one silver chalice, one silver patin, two pewther plates for the offertory. A pulpit, reading desk, and clerk's pew all new, a pulpit cushion covered with blue cloth, the King's Arms newly drawn, the Creed, the Lord's Prayer, and Ten Commandments lately set up in frames, a large gallery for the singers, one clock two dials the one within the other without, three large bells with their frames, a new and beautiful font made of hewn stone, one bier, one horse cloth, two surplices.' The church had also a library of thirty-five theological works, some in several volumes, such as *Erasmi Ecclesiastes*, Bray's *Martyrology*, and Nelson's *Festivals*, all of which have now disappeared.

But the ravages of time continued and year by year the

churchwardens carried out repairs and improvements. In 1813 it was decided to plant the churchyard with 'popular trees,' a project that either was never carried out or the 'popular trees' died, for old pictures show a bare churchyard and the present trees are sycamores. In 1824 the lead roof of the north aisle was recast, the position of the stiles into the churchyard was altered, and iron gates were made. In 1831 at a poll taken at the Town's House 125 voters against 124 defeated the proposal to install a peal of six bells, and instead the old ones were repaired. It was not until 1897 that these were recast and three new ones hung. In 1850 the singing-gallery, then in a ruinous condition, was repaired and underdrawn; and when Hawes Church was rebuilt the following year, the pulpit was brought from it and temporarily fixed in Askrigg Church.

A year later public notice was given of a meeting to consider repairs to the whole building, once more in a dilapidated state, and by means of levying a rate throughout the parish, funds were raised to complete the restoration. At this time a small piece of fifteenth-century German glass was presented to the church, and set in the west window of the north aisle. One curiosity that could scarcely have remained for ever was the ash tree that had grown on the vestry roof; both it and the vestry were pulled down. As for Mary Pratt's clock that in 1840 had been given a new mahogany face, painted and gilded, it was replaced. In 1902, when all the local makers had gone, Messrs Potts of Leeds fixed a new clock.

2. PARSONS AND PARISHIONERS

FOR SEVEN centuries the parsons of Askrigg have ministered to their parishioners. Uctred, priest about 1200, and Robert the Chaplain in 1301, are the earliest names we know. In the fifteenth and sixteenth centuries many of them were local men who lived humbly amongst their neighbours. One of their number, Percival Atkinson, curate for many years, dying in 1587, left all his goods 'unto my host Nynyan Metcalfe and Agnes his wife in consideration they have been good unto me, and keepte me and releved me in this my great need and miserie with meat drinke and apparell and other necessaries when all other did refuse to do yt.' Tristram Janson, probably a son of the vicar of Aysgarth, followed him, and in 1633 the

The church from the west

parson, Henry Hodges, was brought before the Quarter Sessions for brewing ale without a licence. In the late seventeenth century the sons of the yeomen, educated at Yorebridge School and at Caius, St John's, and Christ's College Cambridge, held the living, and two of them, William Thompson and James Metcalfe, were also masters of the grammar school.

Up to a very late date many parishes had no house for the incumbent. But in 1686 Dorothy Fothergill of Burghill near Bainbridge gave £20, and the yeomen, including her nephew Anthony, subscribed the same amount to buy a house for the curate at the west end of the town. It was a small place thatched with ling with 'two rooms up and two down and not ceiled.' In 1811 it was described as a 'mere cottage let to a pauper,' and twenty-three years later, though still not lived in by the vicar, it was rebuilt by the Rev. Richard Wood.

Until 1739 the curate's stipend was £15 10s. a year, supplemented by 'four pence for every house yearly.' In that year it was augmented by £200 from Queen Anne's Bounty. Then in 1755 Dr Stratford, Commissary at the Archdeacon's Court at Richmond, left £100 to Askrigg Church, and at the same time one of the many local subscriptions raised a similar amount. The list of names is headed: 'Mr Samuel Lindsay of Camshouse and James Lightfoot of Askrigg were solely concern'd in applying for and collecting the money . . . and succeeded.' In consequence a further bounty was granted, and an estate was bought in Swaledale as an investment. In 1808 the stipend was £67 13s. a year. Three years later the curate, Robert Bowman, stated that because there was no suitable house, he lived at West Witton, and employed a stipendiary curate at Askrigg at a salary of £40 a year.

In the 1830's a remarkable number of clergy lived in the township: the Rev. John Lodge, a former librarian of Cambridge, Rev. Henry Overend, incumbent of Stalling Busk, living at the Flax Mill, Rev. John Winn, vicar of Aysgarth, at Nappa Mill, and Rev. James Suttel Wood, and Rev. Richard Wood, at Woodhall. The latter and Canon Christopher Whaley, a much-loved parson who wrote the *History of Askrigg*, between them, as vicars of Askrigg, almost spanned a century. Canon Whaley lived at the Manor House, for it was not until 1912 that the present vicarage was built. Meanwhile grants from church funds had brought the stipend up to the moderate standards of the present day; and even now the vicar of Aysgarth, by virtue of the agreement made in 1423, hands over to the vicar of Askrigg £5 a year.

Here at our feet in the Armada chest lie the parish registers that contain the long lists of baptisms, deaths, and marriages of the parishioners. Though registers should have been kept

Askrigg market-place with trees half grown, and on the left the toll booth pulled down in 1898.

Laying the foundation stone to the vicarage in 1912.

after an order issued in 1538, there are no early ones. The first Askrigg registers are preserved in the transcripts that had to be sent to the bishop after a further regulation of 1597; and in the Ripon Diocesan Registry we find the records of civil marriages performed by magistrates during the Commonwealth between 1655 and 1660. The banns, certified by Benjamin Janson, the 'parish register' or keeper of the registers, were read not only at Askrigg Church but at the market cross at Richmond on three market-days, and the comment 'no objection at all by anyone' is usually appended.

In the chest are ten volumes of registers, five bound in smooth brown suède calf. The earliest, written on vellum, the pages loosely sewn together, is for the years 1701 to 1728. Besides these, nine volumes contain lists of the baptisms and burials that took place between 1729 and 1876, and the marriages to 1837. One book beginning 25th April 1754 has, under the Hardwicke Marriage Act, the first printed forms signed by the contracting parties. Occasionally explanatory remarks were written against the names—Quaker, Papist, stranger, pauper, of the workhouse, bygitt, an apprentice, or 'buried in woollen' and 'lead coffin.' Ages were noted spasmodically, and occupations were added every now and again in the eighteenth century and fairly regularly later.

Throughout the centuries baptismal records show the popularity of biblical names in the parish. There are over forty, including Aaron, Azariah, Emmanuel, Ezra, Levi, Obadiah, Solomon, and Susannah. The Nonconformist influence is shown in the names Barzillai, Bezaliel, Eleazer, Tirzah, and Zipporah; and John Shaw, a clogger, and his wife Mary christened their six children, Peninnah Victoria, Zillah, Azubah, Elizabeth, Shelometh, and Jabin. Fortune Wellbank, Ferdinando Murrel, Lanty Fulart, Mullin Taster, and Bartholomew Verity seem to step straight from the novels of Charles Dickens or Wilkie Collins.

We learn isolated, often tragic, facts about the strangers who wandered into the parish. On 19th August 1719 the

P

christening took place of Elizabeth, 'daughter of Mary Dakar
a traveller intending to follow her husband John Dakar who
has left her into Scotland,' on 29th November 1739 the burial
of 'a person whose name was not known dying at Leo. Terrys
in Askrigge,' on the 3rd December 1780 the christening of
'Luke Stones a foundling left at Askrigg upon the Hard Stones
by a woman unknown on St Luke's Day'—he died seven years
later—and one winter a traveller was 'found dead upon Cam.'
We read of William Coultherd of Worton, 'killed by lightning
aged 20,' and of a child of two who was 'burnt to death.'
Here a man was 'lost in the snow,' there another was 'killed
by a wagon.'   In the autumn of 1841 eight people died from
smallpox 'all being unvaccinated.'   A note recounts that at
the time there were eighty cases in Askrigg but that only one
person died after vaccination.   Sharp rises in the graph of the
deaths made from the registers point to other epidemics in
1727–9, 1740–1, 1745, and 1765; but we do not know what
diseases caused them.

Of the several Askrigg charities two of the oldest, given by
William Thornton and Margaret Holmes, have been lost.
William Thornton, who died in 1740, left the yearly profits from
a close at Dale Grange, called Burtrees Steel, to be distributed
each Christmas Eve to the most needful inhabitants within the
chapelry of Askrigg.   Margaret Holmes, a Wetherilt before
her marriage to Anthony Holmes, victualler of Wapping, in
1725, then a widow, acquired an estate at Nappa Scar for £800.
In her will Margaret charged her Nappa Scar property with
the weekly payment of two shillings with which to buy bread
to distribute 'amongst the poor of Askitt' every Sunday for
ever: and in a codicil she left half a guinea to the minister to
preach a yearly sermon on her account in Askrigg Church.

On 28th May 1748 John Wetherill of Birtley left £50 to be
invested by 'the Gentlemen of the twelve for the Chapelry of
Askrigg,' half the yearly interest to be given to the parson and
half to needy families.   Of this £25 has been lost.   The
charity known as Alderson's Dole, given by James Alderson of

The church before the restoration of 1853, drawn from a water-colour. The picture shows the vestry with the ash-tree growing on the roof, and also the Toll Booth on the left

Bull Close, Halifax, in the eighteenth century, is 12s. a year paid out of the close, Seata End.   In 1791, in a letter reminding the owner, John Rider Wood, that the sum had not been paid, James Lightfoot wrote: 'I am very certain your mind will be much hurt that ye poor people should be in want of its distribution.'   The interest on £200 left by Juliana Firby in 1915 was to be spent on coals to be given to the poor of Askrigg each Christmas; and Margaret Winn left £300 in 1932, the interest to be divided amongst the needy.

Some of the most valuable evidence for the story of the church's building, the parsons, and the parishioners is to be found in the replies to questions put at the Visitations of the higher dignitaries of the Church to their deaneries, and connected with these, the books and papers from the ecclesiastical courts, accumulated over the centuries in the registries.   The latter were important offices where, besides housing these documents, the registrar issued marriage licences, and licences for parsons, schoolmasters, parish clerks, and midwives to practise their professions; and granted faculties for the alteration to church fabrics and the erection of pews.

The Archbishop of York's Visitation for the Deanery of Catterick was usually held every three years at Bedale, the Bishop of Chester's at Richmond, and the Archdeacon of Richmond sent his officials each year to every parish.   At these Visitations the clergy answered questions about themselves, attendance at church, schools, Papists, Quakers, and in course of time Methodists, and the churchwardens replied to articles of inquiry concerning the state of the building, the 'life and conversation' of the minister, and the behaviour of the inhabitants.   We have already drawn on many of these particulars that sometimes included terriers, such as James Lamb's inventory.   Following the Visitations, orders summoned transgressors to appear at the courts.   Men and women from the farthest corners of the High Parish had occasionally to journey to York, and frequently to the Bishop's and Archdeacon's Courts at Richmond.   This latter, presided over by the commissary, was held in the north aisle of Holy Trinity Church in the market-place there.

The power of the ecclesiastical courts, like the burden of tithes, is now forgotten. Their system unimpaired by the Reformation, their measures strictly enforced in the reign of Elizabeth I, they suffered a gradual decline after the Restoration, until in 1860 they ceased to have legal hold over the laity. In them wills were proved and letters of administration given. People were fined for non-payment of church rates and tithes, non-attendance at church or communion, and were ordered to perform penances for moral offences such as usury, slander, and fornication. As a last resort if they persisted in not appearing to answer the charges, or refused to take communion, they were excommunicated. In the pages of the court books occur ancient phrases, their wording and the penances unchanged since medieval days.

The system of strict surveillance that scrutinized the public and private actions of each individual is out of sympathy with the modern mind. But in those days the people, even the outspoken Elizabethans, accepted it as customary; the punishments were intended for their 'Soul's Health and the reformation of their manners,' and on the whole were meted out with justice and consideration.

It was in 1571 at the Archbishop's Court at York that the order was given for the destruction of the rood-loft in Askrigg Church. From later records of the court we learn that in 1578 Austyn Metcalfe of Askrigg 'beinge furthe of charytye cometh very seldome to churche and did not communycate at Easter last past,' and again in 1590 'he cometh not to church but kneleth in a corner.' In 1578 two adulterers were ordered 'to perform penances in the public market-place of Ayskerigge on Thursday next, in the chapel of Ayskerigge on Sunday next following and in the church of Ayskarth on the Sunday after that.' They probably stood in church, as was usual in similar cases, with sheets wrapped about them 'from the shoulder to the foot.' The same year two more, presented by William Thornton, one of the sworn men (sidesmen), were ordered to go before the commissary with 'for him seven handed of honest persons his neighbours, for her three handed of honest women.' This meant six others and himself, and for the woman two and herself—witnesses willing to assert that the offenders were innocent. At the same time Lionel Thistlewood, who had lent Thomas Metcalfe, a churchwarden, 'fyve marks for a year for the occupacion of a close worth fyve nobles durynge the same tyme,' was charged with usury, but was dismissed with a caution.

In 1633 several people from Gayle and Appersett near Hawes were presented for not attending Askrigg Church, others for not receiving holy communion, one of whom, Matthew Thwaite of Litherskew, pleaded that he was over eighty and unable to travel and that the minister had neglected to come to his house. Old Matthew was instructed to receive at Christmas next. There were cases of 'vehement suspicion of adultery'; people living away but having land in the parish, were accused of not paying church rates, and Adam Foster of teaching at Yorebridge School without a licence. Lastly under Aysgarth, James Nicholson of Carperby was presented for 'abuseing the Ministrie in these and the like termes viz. The preaching of the Gospell is but bibble babble and I care not for anie blacke Coate in Wensleydaile. I had rather hear a Cuckowe sing.'

Similar charges came up before the Archdeacon's Court. In 1668 seventeen men of Askrigg owed small sums from 1d. to 4s. for their church assessments; Christopher Alderson, the dyer, was fined £4 for 'hanging out his stockings to dry upon Sondayes,' and the churchwardens fined 2s. 4d. for not exhibiting 'a transcript of their Register booke.' Jane Hird was charged with bearing a bastard child whose father had 'since fled into Ireland,' and Anthony Swithenbanke 'clandestinely married' and his child 'yet alive and the woman dead' was absolved. Five years later eleven 'negligent comers to church,' two Recusants, John Lambert and

William Terry, and six Quakers, three of them Rouths, were named.

There were cases of 'injurious scandal,' sometimes described as the hurt of another person 'contrary to good manners and the rule of charity.' Women and sometimes men accused women 'in an angry reproachful and invidious manner' for moral offences. In 1719 when the townspeople were quarrelling over the market tolls, Guy Warwick, Jeffrey Clarkson, James Wadeson, and William Terry defamed William Thornton. Found guilty, William Terry was ordered to go to the Toll Booth and in the presence of the curate and the constable to say that he was heartily sorry and ask forgiveness for saying that 'Mr Thornton did rogue and thieve, and denied his hand to a paper relating to the tolls of Askrigg.'

After a death the will of the deceased had to be proved and letters of administration obtained. On 13th December 1750, following the death of William Alderson, a dyer, an announcement 'peremptorily' ordering his next of kin to exhibit his will was read in Askrigg Church. On another occasion John Caygill brought a suit against Ann, widow of William Leeming, yeoman of Askrigg, whose debts amounted to £40 of which £22 16s. was owed to Caygill. An inventory of William's property, including shop goods, chests, boxes, scales, and weights £80, a black galloway £1 10s., and a silver cup £1 5s., totalled £160 5s. The wills and often inventories, dating from Tudor times, are preserved in the Borthwick Institute at York.

In them and in the court cases are many names familiar to us. Bernard Smith was sued for alimony before his case went before Quarter Sessions; Margaret, widow of Alexander Colby, applied for new trustees for her husband's estate; Christopher Caygill, the clock-maker, wished to erect a pew. In a case connected with John Rider Wood's tithe dispute John Metcalfe of Marsett, near Semerwater, was excommunicated 'in churches and chapels on Sundays and Holidays in time of divine service for his manifest contempt in not appearing.'

Three years later he was absolved. Tried first in the Archdeacon's Court, cases often went on to the others, and sometimes ended, like the early Yorebridge case, with an appeal
to the Council of the North, or, like Agnes Hastwell's quarrel
with her stepdaughter, in Chancery.

Lastly we come to those parishioners who filled the offices
of churchwarden, parish clerk, and sexton. Only one old book,
containing the warden's accounts from 1811 to 1921, remains.
Its leather back as soft as velvet, it measures 15 inches by 9½
inches and is too large to be kept in the small chest in the north
aisle.

On the first page is a note written by George Winn, who
was churchwarden from 1840 to 1873, on the custom of
appointing these officials in the ancient chapelry of Askrigg.
'The inhabitants of each township nominate or propose three
persons, and the Perpetual Curate or Incumbent elects any of
the three for Warden during the ensueing year.' No doubt
this was the method adopted in those days when the parish
reached to the limits of the dale. As we know, this area
had dwindled, and at the date when the book begins Askrigg parish consisted only of Askrigg, Bainbridge, and Low
Abbotside.

The expenses of repairs to the structure, salaries to the parish
clerk, sexton, and so on were shared; Askrigg paid about half,
Bainbridge less, and Abbotside the least. The outstanding
feature of the account-book is the lavishness of expenditure
before 1868, the year church rates were abolished by Act of
Parliament, and the economies that had to be practised after
that date. Before, we read entries such as: 'To John Thwaite
for ale etc. for workmen when repairing the church 19s. 6d.';
'The female singers to have a present of 10s. 6d. divided
amongst them every Christmas Day'; 'To Benjamin Crowther
a present made him with the consent of the Vestry on account
of his having done his work to the satisfaction of the chapelry
£1 10s.' In spite of a meeting having to be called in 1834 to
consider the steps to be taken 'to compel payment of Chapel

Rates' open-handed dealings continued, until immediate economies became necessary, and in 1870 the offices of parish
clerk and sexton were amalgamated.

Long and faithful service was traditional. In 1767, following
John Sagar as parish clerk, Warwick Sagar remained in office
forty-seven years. Charles Wright was sexton for forty years,
John Graham, junior, for fifty years; and Metcalfe Graham
combined the two duties for thirty years. When the grammar
school was founded, the parish clerk, taking on the duties of
usher there, was paid a salary of £6 13s. 4d., but for how long
this arrangement held we do not know. From 1811, the clerk
received £1 5s. annually, until on his 'ceasing to collect the
Easter dues,' it was raised to £5. The sexton was paid 10s.,
later £1, and when the offices were combined, Metcalfe
Graham received £1 as sexton and £2 10s. as parish clerk.
Money was continually earned by them for extra work 'for
washing surplices 10s.,' 'to cleaning flaggen and cupp 3s. 9d.,'
'whitewashing, cleaning, colouring, and cleaning windows
7s. 9d.,' 'assisting in repairing gallery 1s.' 'shovelling snow
sundry times 2s. 6d.,' and 'cleaning yard 3s.'

As well as the large sums spent on the church fabric and
alterations to the churchyard, there were smaller expenses, of
which the oddest was the reward offered by the churchwardens
to keep down vermin. 5s. for '2 fox heads' is an item that
occurs for the last time in 1823. A register book for burials cost
19s., and new bell-ropes bought in 1828 for £1 5s. lasted for
twenty-three years. Other regular expenses included sand for
the church floor and 'Bishopbrig coals.' Yearly the minister
received 6s. for copying the register, the ringers 10s., and
William Pratt £2 2s. for winding and repairing the church clock.

Many of the craftsmen, masons, joiners, blacksmiths,
plumbers, and glaziers were paid for one job or another;
and the shopkeepers, Samuel Sykes, Rebecca Thwaite, Aaron
Knaggs, and later Sarah Banks, supplied candles, oil, besoms,
and lengths of material to make surplices. Thomas Thompson, the tailor, repaired the mats, James Robinson painted the

doors, gates, and the weathercock, and the village innkeepers provided vast quantities of sacramental wine and ale. In one year John Thwaite was paid for '5 bottles of wine 21s. 6d., ale for the singers 10s., and ale for the workmen 7s.'

Then there were the singers who since 1750 had sung in the gallery. They received their accustomed fee of £1 1s. at Christmas, and £5 that, divided among them, came from an annuity left in 1827 by Christopher Place of Askrigg. For five weeks, in 1813, Samuel Halton, the singing master, was engaged at £1 4s. a week to instruct them. In the early half of the century they were accompanied by five 'Musick Men,' two bassoon players, paid £1 1s. a year, and three other 'music men,' namely Francis Thompson the joiner, Christopher Lee the blacksmith, and John Tiplady, a miner, who had each 16s. Sometimes the instruments themselves needed replacements, such as a reed for the bassoon that cost 2s. and a string for the bass violin 6s.; and the players had their own music, for 9s. 2d. was paid 'John Metcalfe for pricking tunes in the church book.'

Gradually the 'music men' fell away. In 1847 they were reduced to 'one bassoon or bass violin' and three other players; four years later there were three. In 1858 a harmonium 'having been subscribed for,' it 'entirely superseded the other instruments.' Only one performer remained, the 'harmoniumist.' An organ bought eleven years later was in its turn replaced by a large organ made by Hopkins of York, erected in memory of Canon Whaley in 1906. It fills the Metcalfe Chapel, and the electric blower, installed in 1946, rests on the stone under which James Metcalfe and his wife were buried about 1472.

In this north-west corner, on the wall above the parish chest, a familiar name, Christopher Alderson Alderson, stands out in black lettering on a decayed marble wall-tablet. Near by part of another, that of Christopher Alderson who endowed the almshouses, has fallen down and lies on a window-sill. Other memorials remind us of those who, leaders of the village in their day, have stepped into the pages of this book. We learn from a brass plate on a pillar that William Thornton the younger was 'a loving husband, an indulgent parent, and a kind master.' Here is the wall-tablet of Sarah, his daughter, there that of Samuel Lindsey of Camshouse, near whose memorial is Margaret Lightfoot's, sixth daughter of Alexander Smith, and beyond, that of her son, James the apothecary in whom 'the Parish lost a benefactor and the poor a Friend.' On the wall of the south aisle John Pratt and his wife have each a fine green marble memorial adorned with their coat of arms. Wood Metcalfe's tablet admonishes the reader: 'Boast not thyself of to-morrow, for thou knowest not what a day may bring forth.' Besides these, four stained-glass windows, including the East Window in memory of George Winn who in 1876 was drowned when fording the river near Aysgarth, commemorate members of the Winn family. It is sobering to read these affectionate tributes to men and women who are 'now all gone, one generation vanishing after another, gone as utterly as we ourselves shall shortly be gone like ghosts at cock-crow.'

Beezy lead mine

IX

HOUSES, CRAFTS, AND TRADES

JOHN THE SMITH, John and Alan the carpenters, Ralph the weaver in 1301, and William the cobbler in 1332, are the first names vouchsafed us of a long line of individuals who practised the crafts and trades in Askrigg. Skill was handed down often in families, or after the Statute of Artificers in 1563 by means of apprenticeship. In their time the dyers and hosiers, engaged in trade, were conspicuously the most prosperous, followed by the millers and the carpenters. The smiths, masons, shoemakers, and even that renowned group, the clock-makers, emerge as people whose work brought in only moderate monetary reward.

The building of stone houses instead of wood in the sixteenth century, and the gradual replacement of ling thatches by stone slates, were revolutionary changes. Sandstone was quarried in the gills; and material for most of the old houses in Askrigg came from Arngill that, set aside as a township quarry where stone could be obtained free for the hewing and carting, lies half a mile north-east of the village. It was last quarried for stone for the vicarage, built in 1912, and a grass-grown track still runs by the side of the stream to the exposed rock.

During the building era in the last century other sources, chiefly Burtersett, Sedbusk, and Simonstone quarries, all near Hawes, were drawn on. The first supplied flags, slates of a poor quality, and soft stones suitable for fire-place surrounds. Stone for the front of the Temperance Hall and the new Yorebridge Grammar School came from Sedbusk, and that for Winnville from Simonstone. On the other hand material for the station buildings and the Wesleyan chapel was carted from Mill Gill, and Haworth stone from the West Riding built Thornsgill House at the foot of the moor road.

Freestone, the millstone grit exposed on the summit of the moor, was used for the carved door-heads, mullions, rigging, corbels, and through-stones of the yeomen's houses. At the Greets above Ellerkin millstones were hewn and dressed, and three that for some reason were abandoned still lie below the rampart of dark rocks. In 1677 it was stated that 'there is a place called the Greets in which mill stones have been got at several tymes by leave from the King's Steward of the Mannor of Bainbridge and Lordship of Middleham.' It will be remembered that this area is in the Manor of Woodhall that was once the property of the Crown.

Beds of rock that split into thin flags provided roofing material. These quarries were situated alongside High Straits Lane, and one above Arngill was called Patty. From the former stone slates were supplied over a wide area.

A yeoman building a porch in a neighbouring village in 1702 bought the materials, and employed workmen at eightpence a day 'with meat.' For house building, wood for oak door-mans (large beams), spars, bedroom floors, doors, and later windows had to be fetched from farther down the dale, and sometimes from as far afield as York. Tradition relates that the massive beams in the house that we have called for convenience the Scropes' were brought from Pendragon Castle fifteen miles away in Westmorland. (When the house was

Fire-place at Newbiggin removed in 1952

repaired recently, plastering over rushes was disclosed.) In 1760 a yeoman rebuilt his house for £85 and employed a mason, slater, plasterer, joiner, glazier, and a smith. The kitchen range cost 18s., the parlour range (encased in a wooden surround called the firestead that was a separate item) 8s. 9d., and a chamber range 3s. 8d.

Though now we deplore the scarcity of skilled masons, they have long been depleted in numbers, a dwindling band of men since medieval days. Nappa Hall, erected when masons were still engaged in church building, is the finest example of their work in the neighbourhood and a national heritage. In later domestic architecture their art flowered in the embellishments

Doorway, John Pratt's house

carved for the yeomen's houses, none of which remains intact in Askrigg itself. Three of the arched fire-places at Colby Hall exhibit masons' marks; Anthony Besson's house at Worton had originally a central fire-place arch, flanked by two small arches, adorned with fluted carving; and the Scropes' house and the Temperance Hotel, old houses with new fronts, retain their spiral staircases. Good work of the eighteenth century may be seen in Robinson's Gateways and in the vaulted cellar, the window surrounds, the main doorway, and a staircase built on the cantilever system in John Pratt's house (the Kings Arms Hotel and the Manor House); in two other houses are similar staircases, and the thick blocks of polished stone that make doorsteps give pleasure by their very size.

It is said that the mason, Philip Dinsdale, alone undertook the stone-work of Winnville, and if this is so, it remains a monument to his skill. The walls are water-shot, that is the outer stones tilt downwards and project slightly the one above the other. These dressed stones were laid so close that they have never needed pointing. Several other houses in the village and one at Bainbridge near the Manor House were built in a similar manner by the same man.

From about 1730 the Askrigg joiners were for over a hundred years the Thompsons—Johns, Matthews, Edwards, and a Francis. They repaired and provided market gear for the Four Men; in 1788 'Nedey' is noted as a wheelwright, and an Edward took a large share in the building of the new workhouse at Bainbridge. They were employed by the churchwardens, and it seems likely that they were responsible for the excellent doors and panelling that remain in some of the Georgian houses.

At the time of the church's restoration the Thompsons had gone, but they had intermarried with the Littles. When the first Aysgarth School near that village was built Thomas Little undertook the woodwork. He breakfasted on porridge, walked the four and a half miles there, and lunched on cold porridge carried in a bowl. Thomas Weatherald, who bought Low Mill for a joiner's shop, 'served his time' in London in the 1860's; and coming home for holidays, he trudged the twelve miles from Leyburn station with a carpet-bag slung over his shoulder. Thomas did work in Swaledale, and once, with a laden cart and horses, took seven hours to reach his destination at the head of the dale. His biggest job was designing and building the Wesleyan chapel, that complete with the pewing cost £800. Others followed: the Handleys, skilful craftsmen making traps, gigs, and carts; the Burtons

at West Mill, combining milling, joinery, and electricity work;
John Henry Lomax at the Temperance Hotel; and at Low
Mill Thomas Weatherald's son and grandson, now building
contractors and the only joiners in the village.

At least as early as 1730 and no doubt long before, Askrigg
supported two smiths, who in later years often combined the
occupation with that of innkeeper. Lees, Dinsdales, Sagars,
Littles, Metcalfes, and Calverts plied their craft during the last
hundred and fifty years. In 1788 a memorandum of a year's
agreement in the Bainbridge miller's ledger reads: 'Be it greed
betwixte James Dinsdale blacksmith [of Askrigg] and George
Terry that James Dinsdale is to shou 4 horses at 10 shillings
per horse and one horse 12 shillings and if aney should be loste
the sade James Dinsdale is to pay for them.' A later bargain
included the sharpening of picks, chisels, and gavelocks
(crowbars).

The smith's work followed the round of the seasons. In
winter during frosty weather he 'sharped and spurned' horses'
shoes, that is each shoe was removed, sharpened all over, and
the spurn, a bar, was fixed across the toe to prevent slipping.
In late spring he made horn burners and tar markers for sheep;
in June he supplied new shears for clipping and ground old
ones; and in July sold scythes and hay-forks, and repaired
mowing-machines when they came into use. He 'carkered'
clogs, that is fixed irons on the soles. He made iron-work for
carts, snecks and hinges for houses, loops for coffin handles,
parts for mill-wheels; he fitted new ranges in houses, and
'landered' the fronts, that is fixed spouting, whilst for the
women he soldered teapots, mended candlesticks and kettles,
and fitted keys to locks. The smith was indispensable in the
village, not only for basic needs but for the smooth running
of households.

Apart from Skipton, Askrigg was the most flourishing
centre for the making of grandfather's clocks in the north-west
dales of Yorkshire, and at times during its heyday it supported
as many as five makers. The first, John Ogden, a Quaker,

Q

came, it is thought, from Halifax about 1681. He settled at Bowbridge, perhaps eventually living at or in part of Colby Hall, for some of his clocks bear the inscription 'Bowbridge Hall.' Mark Metcalfe (1693–1776), his apprentice, lived at Askrigg, and is strictly the first Askrigg maker. Others, well known in their day, followed: Christopher Caygill and James Wilson, Metcalfe's apprentices, John Stancliffe and James Pratt, Caygill's apprentices, a few who settled in the town for a time, and some Askrigg men who pursued their craft elsewhere, chiefly Skipton. The Pratts, James and his two sons of whom William was a wastrel, so jealous that he once smashed a clock better than his own, were the last upholders in the village of a craft that faded away in the middle of the nineteenth century, ousted by cheap American and other foreign clocks.

Clock-maker's advertisement

What is known of these men of inventive skill has already been set down, so that little more need be said.[1] Most information derived originally from John Skidmore, a nephew of William Pratt, who followed his uncle as a dealer and repairer rather than as a maker. Until 1935 the clock-maker's workbench stood under a window in the antique shop in the market-place. To see it set out with an orderly array of tools invoked thoughts of a quieter age than this, when hand-made work well done gave pleasure to both craftsman and buyer.

As we have seen, lead- and iron-mining were part of the activities of the Abbot of Jervaulx's men in the forest; the grassed-over cinder heaps near the river-bank alongside the site of Fors Abbey bear witness to the extent of the smelting

[1] *The Old Clock-makers of Yorkshire*, N. V. Dinsdale.

of iron. The lead mines, with rich veins of ore at Woodhall and on Askrigg Moor, were worked for many centuries. A hundred and fifty years ago Woodhall was composed largely of miners' cottages, and there were once two inns, the Fox and Hounds in the hamlet, and the other on the old road on the hillside. The ruins of the buildings of Beezy Mine, already so called in 1765, named after the Beezon family who evidently worked it, are to be seen on the moor east of the Muker road. At Worton a small mine was opened in the last century and ceased working in the 1880's.

We have found few records of the dyers and hosiers. In Elizabethan times the trade was linked with that in York, and it was the mainstay of prosperity in Askrigg for some two hundred and fifty years, from the latter half of the sixteenth century to the first half of the nineteenth. Woods, Burtons, Smiths, Aldersons, Caygills, Tipladys, Metcalfes, Addisons— all were dyers. They knew the secret of processes that about 1700 employed alum, tartar, argol, cochineal, madder, 'fasdick,' redwood, galls, and in later days logwood. Christopher Alderson, who failed in business, 'exercised the trade of dyer in the buying and selling of diverse goods wares and merchandise as other dyers used to do in his late dwelling-house and shop at Askrigg.' An inventory of the goods of Thomas Burton, taken in 1635, included '8 dying fatts for dying' worth 16s.; and in 1743 William Alderson's dye-house contained four cisterns, one with a copper bottom, and was adjoined by drying yards. In the eighteenth century the Caygills' dye-houses were situated on Mill Green, the Burtons' was near the High Bridge, and a third once stood on the site of Grenada Hall.

Meanwhile the knitters, employed by the hosiers who often combined their trade with dyeing, pursued their automatic monotonous task. 'An idle work, for the workers go where they like, talk, saunter, and sit down . . . I bought a pr. of coarse stockings for my wet expeditions; or to put on when wetted; they cost me 8½d.', said Lord Torrington. The full story has been told in our book *The Old Hand-knitters of the Dales*, so that a brief mention will suffice.

The magnitude of the industry in the dales' economy is seldom given its full prominence. Centred first at Richmond and later at Kendal in Westmorland, hand-knitting flourished as a trade in the north-west dales from the reign of Elizabeth I until it declined in the nineteenth century.

A skilled traditional craft, the method of knitting was essentially the same as that generally followed in England to-day. The difference lies in the fact that with the help of a knitting sheath and curved needles great speed is attained. The knitter fastened a belt tightly round the waist, tucked in the sheath (in the dales the goose-wing-shaped variety) slant-wise at the right-hand side, and fixed one needle into the hole at the top of the sheath. The forefinger of the right hand, held on top of the needle and as near to the end as possible, plied the wool, while a finger of the left hand pushed off the loops (stitches). The secret of the method was the rhythmic motion of arms and body, and the art of 'striking the loop' without any hesitation.

While caps, gloves, mittens, and jerseys were made, stockings were the mainstay of the industry, and up to about 1800 thousands of pairs of different qualities and sizes were sent year by year out of Wensleydale alone to supply the army and private individuals. Thomas and John Gill, working in Agnes Hastwell's worsted mill until 1873, represented the last of the hosiers in Askrigg, though at the end of the century William Metcalfe, Pack Willie, kept a shop on the West End, and regularly tramped into Swaledale to sell yarn and buy stockings.

Spanning the years 1771 to 1828 the account-books of the millers of Nappa and Bainbridge, John Broderick and George Terry, give an insight into one of the oldest trades. The millers were important enough to be in a position to lend money and take up mortgages. As owners of horses and carts they went farther afield than most folk, and going to markets

up and down the dale, often to Richmond, executed commissions for their customers. Accounts ran on for a year or
more, and were balanced at the year's end against the millers'
purchases; thus sometimes very little if any money changed
hands.

Their greatest trade was undoubtedly in oatmeal, but the
baker, James Metcalfe of Askrigg, bought 'flower' and wheat-
meal. In six months he spent about £13 on these com-
modities. The Rev. Anthony Wharton, who as master of
Yorebridge School took in boarders, evidently fed the boys on
quantities of porridge, for he regularly bought oatmeal by the
load or half-load. (A load was a variable amount, and here
seems to have been about five bushels.) Prices varied considerably from month to month and year to year. A sharp
increase occurred in 1800 when, owing to bad harvests, oatmeal, previously ranging from 1s. to 1s. 10d. a peck, rose to
3s. 2d., 4s. 3d., and finally 5s. for the same amount. Other
goods obtainable from the miller included malt, barley meal,
maslin (a mixture of different grains), ryemeal, salt, tar, peas,
apples, potatoes, and sometimes bacon.

Life at Nappa Mill was quiet, concerned with the slow
grinding of corn and the daily round on the farm. At Bainbridge George Terry, not content with normal trade, took on
any job that offered. He carted coals from Tan Hill and
West Pits, carried loads of wood to Leyburn, or undertook to
provide almost anything from yards of linen to a shoulder
of mutton. He supplied milk to his neighbours and
'miln butter,' and sold cheese by the hundredweight,
paid for sometimes part in cash, part in kind, once by
'shuger,' 'candels,' and tea. He bought and sold cows and
sheep, kept a bull, pigs, and geese, and let his fields for
grazing.

In 1797 a new mill was built at Bainbridge and the miller,
conscious of the importance of the event, recorded the progress
of the work. A few prices are given; but unfortunately not the
total cost.

June th   20   I George Terry lefte over grinden at the owld mill
                at Bainbridge
June   21   The owld mill was taken downe by Thomas Met-
                calfe of Gunrsgatte
June   26   the ground works was layd of the mill by Do.
Sept th   9   the new mill was reared & spente at Do.   £1.
Octr th   25   John Sayre putt in the cogg wheele & axle tree
Novbr th   3   John Sayre putt in a parte of the water trouf
           28   John Terry glazed mill windowes   £3
Decbr th   9   Peter Huthison putt joists & dormon runde the mill
                & bargend for Do   £9 9s.
           18   the Blue stones was sett to grinden
Janry th   12   a new stone came from Addingham
           23   the other new gray stone came from Addingham
            —   Do the new mechine came the same time
Febry th   5   the gray stones was sett to grinden and the silender
                at the same time
July th   16   Payd for paynting 2 sash windowes   2s.
                for Peter Huthison
                Do for douers & window slides   £1

In the eighteenth century, one generation succeeding another, the Weatheralds were with others the shoemakers in
Askrigg; and during the next century these most numerous
of craftsmen included Caygills, Storeys, Grahams, and Thistle-
thwaites.   Amongst them Stockdale Thompson won a prize at
Manchester for a pair of clogs that had french-polished soles
and silver buckles and calkers, and Robert Hunter, known as
Black Bob, supplied customers at towns as far away as Richmond and Northallerton.   In an undated letter John Daykin
of Bedale wrote to the latter thus:

Sir, I have enclosed the measurements of my foot the right foot
I want them strong ones same as the last I am wanting them has
I am wet every day can you send them by Wednesday has I shall
be getting cold make them good ones and tidy send them to
Leeming station.

The ledger that Robert Hunter used from 1845 to 1859 has

been preserved. In 1851 the Rev. John Winn paid 1s. 6d. to have his 'shous heeld and spect' (patched), and James Sagar, the blacksmith, brought his bellows to be mended and his boots to be 'sould and vampt' (new fronts put on). Juliana Firby bought a pair of new shoes for 6s.; John Banks of Cams-house had his leggings mended; and Richard Mason, landlord of the Kings Arms, bought a new whip. Sometimes for clarity individual names were set against the items as in the case of the children of William Bell, the joiner. '1844, New boots John 12s. 6d., Shous soald James 3s. 10d., New shoes Simon 8s., New boots James 8s. 10d.' Clogs at 3s. 3d. to 7s., boots from 6s. to 19s., leggings at 8s. 6d., blacking at 3d., and 'elastict' boots formed part of his stock-in-trade.

The account of James Trotter, farmer and bacon factor, illustrates the method of barter. In 1890 James, besides pur-chasing new footwear, had his 'wife shoe stitched up heel 2d.,' 'trappins and reins mended 5s.,' 'boy Sunday boots soald,' 'back can strap stitched,' 'cart saddle girth buckle stitched on,' that in all amounted to £5 9s. 10d. Robert bought from James a pound of butter for 1s. 1d., one backbone 1s. 3d., two pounds of pork 1s., a bottle of brandy 4s. 6d., one sweet loaf at Christmas 1s., and many cash items that totalled £5 8s. 2d. This left a balance of 1s. 8d. to be carried forward.

These notes picture only a few of the occupations that the inhabitants of Askrigg once pursued. Most of the trades and crafts are lost to the village. The lead mines and quarries lie disused and overgrown; those who take up mason-work are seldom called on to build a house, and one of the most skilled of their number is employed as a roadman. One blacksmith suffices for both Askrigg and Bainbridge. The mills in the township no longer grind corn. Dyers, hosiers, knitters, and clock-makers are all forgotten. The shoe repairer's wife (due to the death of her husband) retails footwear for a Catterick firm.

To take their place there are the dairymen who make cheese, the coal merchant and the carrier with their lorries, the

electrician with his stores in the corn mill, the garage proprietor, part of whose premises is the Wool Room, the provision
merchant who, employing several men, grinds cattle food by
a mill driven by electricity; and two haulage contractors, the
one with two lorries for the transport of farm stock, the other,
whose garage occupies the brewery buildings near the High
Bridge, employing some eight men to drive milk lorries, cattle
trucks, and other vehicles.

Hay-making on Croft Hill

X

FARMING

THE FARMING pattern that is visible around us seems age-old, yet not until after 1819 when the hillside pastures were enclosed with walls was it shaped as we see it to-day. The first farmers and the first villagers were the Iron Age folk who lived on the hills. These people, as we have seen, settled here in the third century before Christ, and later belonged to the tribe known as the Brigantes, the people whom the Romans found in the north of England. On the sides of Addlebrough at heights such as 1,400 feet above sea level may be seen the ruinous walls of their little fields, where during wild wet months and a brief summer they tended goats, sheep, and cattle. At farms and villages on lower ground, indicated on the map on page 11, corn also was grown. They made little mark on the landscape, and they appear to have moved to lower country after the Roman occupation ended.

Next, in the seventh or eighth centuries the Angles, settling in the valley on terraces above the river, divided the land into areas of high and low ground (roughly the present townships). They introduced a communal system of farming. Askrigg and

R   237

every place east of us had its large ploughed fields cultivated in narrow strips. In this hilly country the strips usually formed ridges called ranes, and grassed over now, they can be traced around Aysgarth, Carperby, Thornton Rust, Redmire, Castle Bolton, and other Wensleydale villages. The hamlets of Newbiggin and Nappa in the township each had their own systems.

At Askrigg there developed the East Field and the High Field, named in documents, what was probably called either the West or the Mill Field, and a smaller area to the south. Referred to as the fields of Askrigg or the townfields, they eventually covered at a rough estimate 250 acres. Not all of this acreage can be counted as arable land; for part was taken up by ground difficult to plough and by the sides of the terraces banked up with boulders cleared off the ground.

Descriptions of the method of cultivation can be found in numerous books, in particular *The Open Fields* by C. S. Orwin. Suffice to say that here probably oats, barley, rye, beans, and peas were grown; the fields were alternately autumn and spring sown and laid fallow, and after harvest right of shack allowed the cattle to be turned on to the stubble. Each man had his allotted amount of land called a virgate, consisting of strips scattered about the fields so that good and poor land was shared. He was responsible for a length of the outer ring fence (a mound topped with stakes or brushwood) where his land adjoined it, and he ploughed with one to two yoke of oxen. As will be seen from the map of the fields, groups of strips, due to the configuration of the ground and for drainage purposes, were arranged at all angles, and some in the High Field ran up and down a steep hillside.

As land was cleared there were established, besides the townfields, the hay meadows in the low-lying land by the river, the Cow Close on the hillside north of the village, and the common beyond for sheep. The meadows also were divided into strips that can still be traced in Askrigg Holmes. The Cow Close was no doubt enlarged at various times, and in

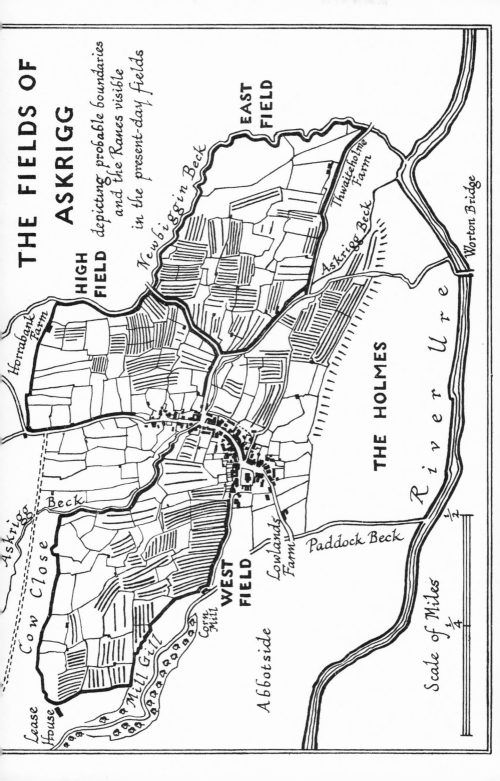

THE FIELDS OF ASKRIGG

depicting probable boundaries
and the Ranes visible
in the present-day fields

HIGH FIELD

EAST FIELD

WEST FIELD

THE HOLMES

Newbiggin Beck

Thwaiteholme Farm

Askrigg Beck

Worton Bridge

River Ure

Horrabank Farm

Askrigg Beck

Cow Close

Mill Gill

Corn Mill

Lease House

Lowlands Farm

Paddock Beck

Abbotside

Scale of Miles
¼ ½

1819 when it was split up it contained 479 acres and 2 roods. Similar areas of rough grazing may still be seen at Redmire and Castle Bolton where the Cow Pastures are farmed communally. A holding consisted of a house, strips in the open fields, rights in the Cow Close and roods of land in the hay meadows in proportion, and pasturage on the common; and on his produce a man subsisted.

Stock had to be well guarded. About 1156 Earl Conan was angered because his men had allowed a multitude of wolves that attacked both men and their beasts to gather in the district. It is usually assumed that few wolves survived after the fourteenth century.

In the tenth century the Norsemen established their sheep farms in the primitive country west of Askrigg. They had winter homesteads on valley terraces and summer seters on the hill pastures in the side valleys at places such as Thwaite Bridge, Forsdale, Sedbusk, Marsett, Countersett, Burtersett, and Appersett. The termination 'sett' from the Norse *saetr* (sheiling) was still used at a much later date in the name Seate House, meaning a farm.

The cattle ranching of the lords of Middleham and the sheep farming of the abbot and monks of Jervaulx in the Forest of Wensleydale followed in the late twelfth century. Briefly we may fill in a few details of the farming that was pursued around Askrigg at that time. In 1218 it was agreed that the monks might make folds for their horses throughout the forest, and establish cattle farms and places for their swine on the south side of the Ure wherever convenient to them; and on the other hand the men of the lord's demesnes at Bainbridge might graze their cattle south of the Ure, herding their young and sick cattle in suitable places, but driving back the strong cattle each night to lie within the bounds of Bainbridge.

In 1307, when the ownership of the forest had reverted to the Duke of Brittany, John, Earl of Richmond, amongst other grants gave the monks common for 1,100 oxen, cows, and horses, pasturage in Cragdale beyond Semerwater for 1,200 sheep, and pasturage on Cam for 600. The deer were not to be excluded from the meadow land. This condition, the custom of the forest, hindered the farming of the yeomen in Raydale in early Stuart times.

Before the Dissolution the abbot still pastured on Cam a 'greatt floke of weathers which were used to be wyntered at Symon Stone'; the cattle of the abbey grazed at Sargill Park and at Spen on Low Abbotside, and stallions and mares were kept at Cotterdale Bank and at Rigg under Cotter End. There were also farmers with their own stock paying rents to the abbot.

At Askrigg the tenants of the FitzHughs and the Scropes held land under their lords. The terms of tenure, based on the custom of tenant right, consisted of a small yearly rent, and fines when a lord died, when a farmer died, and when his son or a new tenant succeeded to the holding. It may be, though we have no direct evidence, that every tenant was bound to furnish an able man in war-time for service in the north, as was customary in Swaledale and in the lordship of Middleham. About 1614–20 Sir Thomas Metcalfe reorganized the rents of his farms at Askrigg. The ancient rents were abolished, boon-works (probably work on the manor farm at hay-time and harvest) and services were commuted by a money payment; and instead the tenants, given leases of two thousand years, paid a yearly rent and a penny in lieu of boons at the feast of 'St Michael Tharchangel.' Some rents at Askrigg were anciently paid at the feast of St John the Baptist 'commonly called Mydsomer day' and at the feast of St Martin the Bishop in winter.

At the end of the sixteenth century we suffered our own small agrarian revolution, part of a widespread movement. The large open areas of the townfields were divided by walls into many closes. We have found mention in 1608 of '2 parcels of land in the Eastefield of Askrigge containing $3\frac{1}{2}$ roods' and in 1637 a reference to 'the Common Ranes neare unto Nappey Park.' But thenceforward land is invariably described as in closes. Gradually the growing of corn ceased. In 1637 a field of three and a half roods, Skewbank Close, was ploughed, and as late as 1785 oats and 'other corn' were grown extensively at Nappa.

At the time of the enclosures, adjoining strips had doubtless become the property of one man, and these groups, often called flatts, were walled round, making the fields that we see on all sides of the village at the present day. Strangely shaped, the meadows still define the ancient arrangement of the strips. Old field names, some forgotten, some in use, originate from that time: Great Stripe, Little Stripe, Pease Flatt, Peslands, Long Roods, Three Roods, Scabbed Roods, Langacres, Flatts.

This change and the other important developments that took place at a similar date—the establishment of the market and fairs, the splitting up of estates, and the rise of the yeomen—laid down the pattern of life and farming at Askrigg for two hundred years. The ancient system of rents virtually disappeared except where it survived in fee farm rents. Land continually changed hands. As an illustration, Gill Close in what had been the East Field was transferred from one owner to another six times, once because of a death, between 1614 and 1661. Consisting of 3·773 acres it was worth £32 at the latter date. Probably the hay meadows in Askrigg Holmes were enclosed gradually at the same time as the townfields. In 1673 Thomas Pearson sold Edmond Tiplady 2½ roods of ground in Askrigg Holmes, 1 rood adjoining the Strans, and ½ rood taken out of Kittle-a-bank bottom.

Horses, notably greys and perhaps of the famous breed of the monks of Jervaulx, were bred by the yeomen-gentry such as Bernard Smith; and large farms usually had a stoned horse paddock (stallion paddock). Adam Middleham of Gill, near Aysgarth, owned at the time of his death in 1622 two bay mares, eleven grey mares, and one bay nag valued at £10, and one grey mare, one sanded mare, one grey nag, one young grey mare, and one grey colt stag valued at £8 6s. 8d. He also had hens (pullen) worth 11s. 6d.

In 1624 George Bell of Askrigg farmed a small place known as 'Six Shillings Rent' that was stocked with one grey nag valued at £1, three cows at £6, and forty sheep at £11. He may have had another occupation. In a list dated 1675 containing the names of forty people who paid the small sums due besides stock for tithes, we recognize the names of many tradesmen; only two men, William Thornton and Giles Metcalfe, paid tithes on foals, and for most cattle were plainly of more importance than sheep.

The Askrigg yeomen, whose ancestors as they said had been breeders of cattle from 'tyme whereof the memory of man is not knowne to the contrary,' were involved in a lawsuit about bulls in 1682. The case, that came before the Court of Chancery, records a project instituted eighty years or more before.

At that time the yeomen banded together in an agreement that was designed to improve the quality of their stock. Instead of individuals keeping inferior beasts it was arranged that two bulls 'of great value and of good breed' and land on which to maintain them should be purchased and held in common. Almost £100 was raised; fields that became known as Bull Farmer and Bull Ing and two bulls 'to the vallue of fifteene pounds' were bought. Two bulls were to be kept in summertime and one in winter. Each man concerned took turn according to houserow to look after them for a year, and during that time he had the use of the land. A running stock composed of money from the sale of old bulls and any profits that might arise from the fields was to provide for the purchase of young ones, and if any surplus accumulated, it was to be distributed amongst the poor. Lastly four men, 'fowre of the best in the towne,' had charge of the money and the election, if necessary, of the keeper of the bulls.

The suit was brought by thirty-six yeomen, including William Thornton, and two women, against Christopher Alderson and Thomas Pearson. It arose because the latter, holding the fields, claimed them as being rented from Thomas Metcalfe

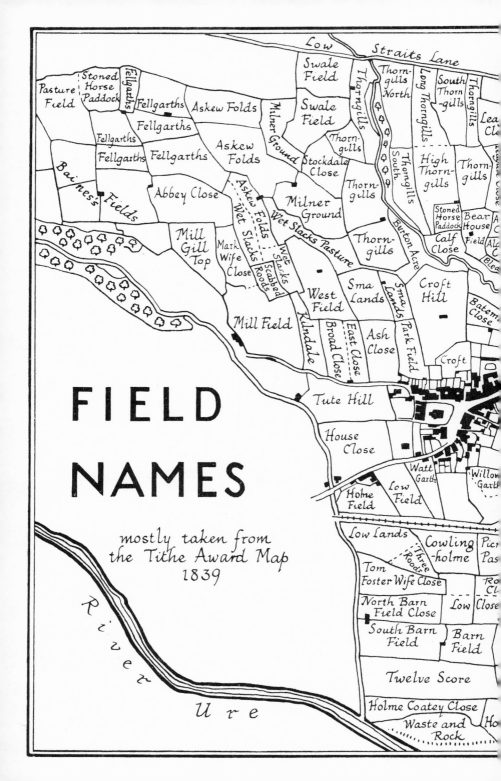

FIELD NAMES

mostly taken from
the Tithe Award Map
1839

Low Straits Lane

Swale Field

Swale Field

Thorngills

Thorngills North

Long Thorngills

South Thorn -gills

Thorngills

Lea Cl

Pasture Field

Stoned Horse Paddock

Fellgarths

Fellgarths

Askew Folds

Milner Ground

Thorn- gills

Thorngills South

High Thorn- gills

Thorn gills

Fellgarths

Fellgarths

Fellgarths

Fellgarths

Askew Folds

Stockdale Close

Thorngills

Baines's Fields

Abbey Close

Askew Folds Wet Slacks Roods

Milner Ground

Wet Slacks Pasture

Thorngills

Burton Acre

Stoned Horse Paddock

Bear House

Calf Close

Mill Gill Top

Math Wife Close

Wet Slacks

Scabbed Roods

West Field

Sma Lands

Sma Lands

Croft Hill

Batem Close

Mill Field

Kiln dale

Broad Close

East Close

Ash Close

Park Field

Croft

FIELD

NAMES

Tute Hill

House Close

Watt Garth

Willo Garth

Holme Field

Low Field

Low lands

Cowling -holme

Pic Pas

Tom Foster Wife Close

Three Roods

North Barn Field Close

Low Close

Ro Cl

South Barn Field

Barn Field

Twelve Score

River Ure

Holme Coatey Close

Waste and Rock

Ho

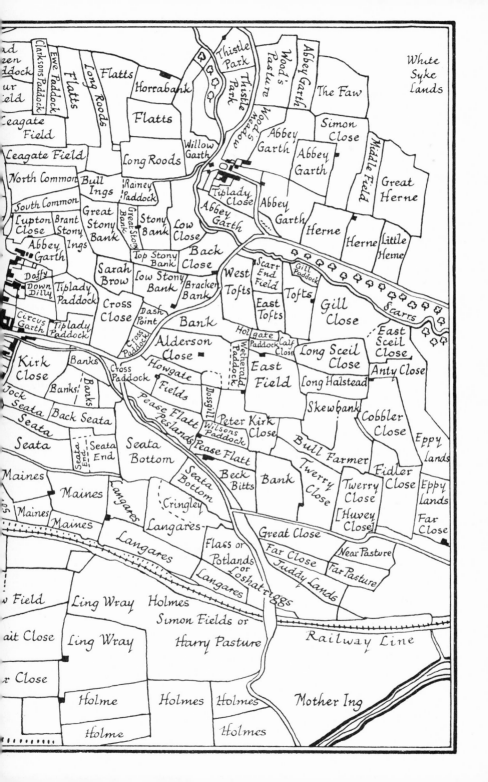

of Nappa Hall, the same Thomas who quarrelled with
William Thornton over the Woodhall Mines. The yeomen
won their case, for in 1819 the land was still the property of
the town.

In the seventeenth century many fields contained outhouses
where stock, to be fed on hay, was kept in winter. As small-
holders with other occupations, the majority of the men had
near their homes a stable for a horse and, save for a garth,
little land. Up to a late date some of these outhouses,
unlike the present-day two-storeyed barns that hold cattle
and hay, were low buildings for cattle only. Stacks and
'lumps' of hay are listed frequently in the inventories of the
yeomen.

In 1793 James Lightfoot built a little cowhouse that cost him
without timber £10 0s. 7d. In 1774 Alexander Fothergill
gave particulars of the building of another that held four cows:
'Dimensions 4½ yards long by 3½ wide and 2½ high to the
square to be built with a ridging to stand part in and part out
of the Stackgarth, beast heads to the Stackgarth, two holes
2 feet square each to fodder thro' splayed like windows on the
inside, one door to the north with stone made cheeks. The
undertaker to provide the stones, lime, and sand, digg the
foundations and build the house very well, and provide good
sound slates led to the place. For which I agree to give
Baynes 5 guineas to give him 10 load of lime now on the place,
and 2s. for Worton Quarry flaggs for the tops and bothams
and sides of the foddering holes.'

At the beginning of the nineteenth century a rough estimate
of the number of cattle gates in the Cow Close may be deduced
from a tithe survey that lists 187 cows and 20 heifers at
Askrigg. The gates [1] had long been separated from the land
to which they had belonged. Over the years the prices at
which they were sold, increasing as the value of money fell,
reflected current demand. This was noticeable in 1815 when
the allotment of land by enclosure to the owners of gates was

---

[1] Right of grazing for one cow.

imminent. The following list of the prices of cattle gates is taken from deeds:

1675	£2	1770	£12 16s.	1785	£9 5s.
1724	£5	1775	£12 12s.	1790	£10 13s. 4d.
1767	£8 10s.	1776	£10 10s.	1804	£14 7s. 6d.
1770	£9 10s.	1783	£ 9 9s.	1815	£37 5s. 6d.

The plans to divide Askrigg Cow Close into separate fields took long to crystallize. Although the proprietors met for discussion on 26th September 1805, difficulties respecting the claims of Lord Grantham, the owner of the Nappa Hall estate, caused postponement. Again on 2nd July 1811 a meeting with Parson Wood in the chair was held at the New Inn. Not until 1816 was the Act passed for enclosure. It covered the cow closes at Askrigg and Newbiggin, Askrigg Common, and the stinting of the moor. A commissioner was appointed; notices of three attendances were pinned to the church door; the moorland boundaries were ridden, and the ground was surveyed by Thomas Bradley of Richmond. The Enclosure Award was made in 1817 and carried out from 1819 to 1820.

Then, as before and as now, land in Askrigg was owned by many people. There were twenty-four proprietors allotted ground in Askrigg Cow Close, fifteen in Newbiggin Cow Close, and fifty-three in the common. Many having land in all three, the number of owners totalled sixty-one. Lord Grantham was apportioned the most, one hundred and forty-three acres, followed by George Terry and C. A. Alderson of Woodhall Park. Others such as the Woods, the family of parsons, the Metcalfes, the surgeons and parsons, Sarah Lindsey's heirs inheriting the Smith property, and John Thomas Wharton, a newcomer and absentee landlord, came next; and lastly several who could claim no more than a few roods or even a few perches. These little bits were not worth the cost of walling round and were sold. Though there was not the dispossession that was a feature of the enclosure of arable land in other districts, these twenty or thirty poor people lost their ancient rights. Many were the craftsmen, and a few were women.

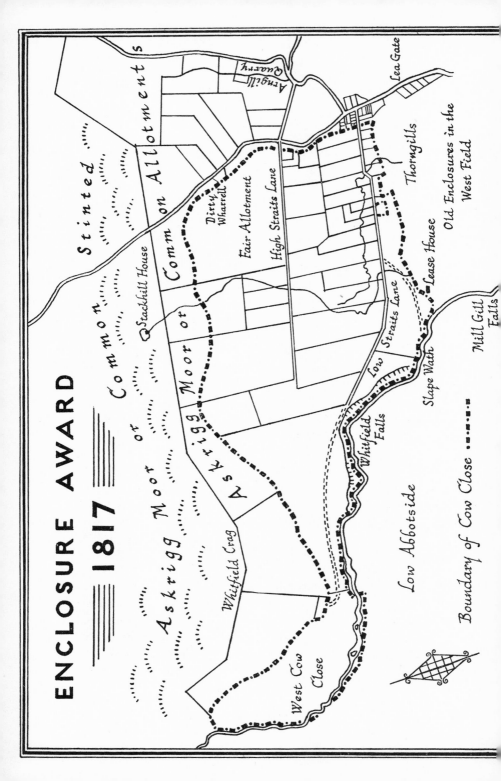

ENCLOSURE AWARD
═══ 1817 ═══

Common Moor or
Askrigg Moor or Common Stinted
Askrigg Moor or Common Allotments

Arngill Quarry

Lea Gate

⊙Stackhill House

Dirty Wharrell

Fair Allotment

High Straits Lane

Thorngills

Lease House

Old Enclosures in the
West Field

Low Straits Lane

Slape Wath

Mill Gill Falls

Whitfield Crag

Whitfield Falls

Low Abbotside

West Cow Close

Boundary of Cow Close ▪━▪━▪

The costs of the survey and the allotment of land were met by the sale of Bull Farmer and Bull Ing. Sold by auction, the first containing three acres realized £199 10s., and the second containing one acre and fourteen perches, £65 2s. Three quarries, Arngill, Dirty Quarry, and a third at Nappa were set apart for public use. (Dirty Quarry, usually called Dirty Wharrell, is now used as a council rubbish tip.) Fences were built by wallers, probably from the villages round Hawes, at prices such as 2s. 6d. per rood that only provided a bare living; yet the expense was heavy for small proprietors.

It was a time of severe agricultural depression, but the enclosures, and other trends, eventually led to better farming. Owners and tenants were encouraged to improve their land by draining and liming. One of the clauses in the Enclosure Act allowed for lime kilns to be built near outcrops of limestone. The ruins of these still remain, some in the pastures and others on the moor. Over the years the remaining small cowhouses were pulled down and two-storeyed barns built; stacks are now seldom seen. Man-made as it is the face of the land took on its present aspect.

An Act passed in 1830 to prevent inferior rams from being turned on to the commons allowed the improvement of breeds of sheep. In the eighteenth century, of the two breeds kept the moor sheep were described as horned and grey-faced with coarse open wool, and the enclosure sheep as horned and white-faced with 'dry, harsh, and thick-set wool.' The Askrigg farmers in 1816 had 414 of the former whose fleeces were valued at 2s. 3d. each, and 207 of the latter, the fleeces worth 4s. each. These breeds in course of time have been supplanted by Swaledale and Wensleydale sheep. A characteristic of the Swaledales is that they know their own 'heugh' and keep to their own ground on the moor.

In 1843 when the Wensleydale Agricultural Society held its first meeting for the exhibition of stock at Hawes there were classes for tups, ewes, shearlings, and lambs of Hard and Half-bred sheep, and for tups of Long-wooled sheep. In these years local fairs—Askrigg Hill Fair, where Scots black-faced sheep were bought, the October Beast Fair, Hawes Fair, and Brough Hill in Westmorland—provided marts for stock; but Hawes Auction Mart, ill-supported when first established in the 1880's, eventually replaced them.

The spread of a cattle plague (rinderpest) was feared in 1865. At a vestry meeting Guy Tiplady, the cow doctor, and John Chapman of Woodhall were appointed inspectors of cattle; and in February of the following year steps to adopt to keep 'this scourge as far as practicable from our borders' were discussed. The cattle murrain that raged for six years had caused alarm in the previous century. In 1750 inspectors who were empowered to search for hides sold without certificate visited the markets of the North Riding, including Askrigg; and the movement of cattle was regulated by licence.

In past times superstitious remedies were resorted to as cures for diseases. Sometimes a billy-goat was buried at the entrance to a cow-shed as a preventative of abortion, or a picked calf (a prematurely born calf) was left in a field corner; and witch-stones were hung in barns or tied to a cow's dewlap to ward off evil. But healthy stock is a feature of the dales farms.

In the early years of this century a further radical change took place. The sale of liquid milk sent to towns by train began, and cheeses gradually ceased to be made in the farm-houses. There were many farmers' wives and daughters who in spite of the work involved regretted the passing of a craft in which they took pride. Up to the first years of the last war Wensleydale cheese was made at outlying farms; in 1952 only two registered makers remained and those not in the dale itself.

The farms were run so that the cows calved in the spring, and from May to October whilst they were grazing in the fields cheese was made. There were two kinds, grass cheese eaten fresh, and Blue Wensleydale that had matured for several months, both made from the same recipe. In the 1840's three cheese fairs, at which prizes were offered, were held at Leyburn in August, October, and February, and within recollection cheeses were sold in bulk to dealers in the autumn or in small quantities to private customers. Those made at Colby Hall were carried by cart over the Stake Pass to Cray, near Buckden, where a Skipton shopkeeper with a load of groceries brought for exchange met the farmer.

Picture the kitchen at Nappa Mill Farm in the early morning fifty years ago—the hams and sides of bacon hanging from the beams, the oatcakes stored on a shelf suspended from the ceiling, the grandfather's clock ticking, the calceolarias and geraniums in the windows, the well-scrubbed stone floor, and the wide black gleaming kitchen range. A copper cheese-kettle, a pan measuring 2 feet in diameter by 18 inches in height, was hung on a crane over the fire. A man came in from milking, and lifting the kettle off, divided the milk into it and two more kettles. He poured in the morning's milk, making in all some seventy gallons. Then the farmer's daughter took charge. By late afternoon she had completed all the processes,[1] and had placed forty 1-lb. cheeses and perhaps seven others, ranging from eight to fourteen or even eighteen pounds, in the four presses; besides having turned those previously made, pickling in brine in lead vats or drying on the traves, the shelves in the upstairs cheese room.

This scene, varying with the numbers of cows kept, was repeated daily throughout the summer months at most of the farms. Cheese, like knitting, was a part of people's lives, and it inspired local sayings. An evasive reply to the inquisitive took the form 'There's a cheese on the cross'; or 'Not for a cheese' expressed reluctance to undertake an unwelcome task; or 'There's a cheese for the last' was said to the unpunctual.

The sale of liquid milk passed through a period of chaos. Farmers put their kits of milk on the 7.4 a.m. train (until about 1922) for the Wensleydale Pure Milk Society at Northallerton, or on later morning and evening trains for Durham towns, Leeds, Manchester, and Liverpool. But dealers frequently broke their contracts. Not until the Milk Marketing Board was

[1] See *The Story of Wensleydale Cheese*, by T. C. Calvert.

set up in 1933 was the disposal of milk placed on a sound footing. In September 1932 milk was last sent from Askrigg station, most of the 15,227 gallons dispatched that month having gone to the Express Dairy Company in London. From that date motor lorries, collecting the kits at the farms, carried them to the Express Dairy at Appleby and after 1937 to their newly opened dairy at Leyburn. In 1953 150,000 gallons were sent there from Askrigg township.

Meanwhile a dairy for the making of cheese had been set up at Hawes in 1897, and in 1919 one was started by Richard Mason in Askrigg. At first these experienced difficulties, and during the last war their survival was threatened for a time by rationing schemes. In 1943 Askrigg dairy became a branch of that at Hawes, the Wensleydale Creameries, now a large concern. Five men and two women are employed at Askrigg, and each day, except when milk is diverted elsewhere, they make some 56 cwt. of cheese from 800 gallons of milk collected from farms in the district. In this way the manufacture of Wensleydale cheese continues.

These changes went hand in hand with the gradual reduction in the numbers of tradesmen-farmers. A letter written in 1850 says: 'John Horner milks four cows and still carries on the shop and chandler's business. William milks three cows . . . and badging (corn-dealing) is very little worth.' The ownership of scattered meadows was slowly rearranged so that farms became more compact. By 1872 the fifty-four people who had had sheep gates allotted them in the enclosure award were reduced to twenty-five, and in 1953 to eleven. Six farmers only (some of them renting gates besides their own) graze flocks on the moor. Similarly in 1675 some sixty people in the township paid tithes on hay and stock, whereas to-day there are thirty-four holdings in the same area.

Farming is our background. Lambing time in April, clipping in early July followed by hay-time, sheep-dipping in August and October, mucking in winter: these mark the round of the seasons. It is highly individual farming. The farmer

Sheep clipper

himself works his holding; only on a few large farms are hired men employed. Some with their herds of shorthorns are 'cow proud,' some specialize in Swaledale sheep, and others without moor rights favour a cross of Swaledale ewes and a Wensleydale tup.

As we have remarked elsewhere, most of the farms of the

s

township are situated in the hamlets. At Askrigg there are
Lowlands, Lease House, Horrabank, and Thwaiteholme that
lie on the outskirts of the ancient townfields on land once
assarted, that is cleared by grant from the lords of the manors.
Some barns adjoin these houses and their meadows and pastures
stretch around them, whereas the buildings and fields of the
farmers who live in the village are often scattered.

In 1952 the holdings in the township were classified in acreages
of meadow and pasture, excluding rough grazings, as follows:

Under 20 acres	. .	9
20–50 acres	. .	13
50–100 acres	. .	9
100–150 acres	. .	2
300–500 acres	. .	1

At the same date the 4,700 acres of Askrigg township were
divided into 21 acres of temporary grass, 690 of meadow, 959
of permanent grazing, 925 of enclosed grazing, and in addition the moor. These lands supported 666 cattle of which
19 were bulls and 3,930 sheep, including lambs; and, witness
to the mechanization that has developed rapidly since the
war, there were only 17 working horses and 1 young horse,
compared with 39 in 1943.

Light tractors pull the few machines that are needed on
grass farms, muck-spreaders and harrows for manuring, and
mowing-machines, swathe turners, sweeps and rakes for hay-
making—implements that are comparatively recent innova-
tions. Wooden sledges or small wooden sweeps pulled by
horses, to carry loads of hay up steep hillsides to the barns in
the meadows, were formerly the chief aids, and the strewing
and turning was done by hand rather than by forks or wooden
hay-rakes.

Some of the oldest farmers remember the mowing of grass
with scythes before the change-over to machines began about
seventy years ago. Starting at two or three in the morning
to mow whilst it was cool, the foremen led six or seven scythers
across a field, with two or three boys following to strew and

dash out the grass.   The swathes were 11 feet broad by 1 to
1½ feet batt.[1]   If it was raining they sometimes tied old gig
umbrellas on to themselves to protect their backs.   An acre
was a day's mowing, and the best sharpeners were the best
scythers.   It is remembered that for a wager a man mowed a
four-acre meadow at Nappa without leaving it.   He started
in the middle and worked round and round.   Another, taking
a month to finish, mowed by himself the forty acres of meadow
land on his farm at Stalling Busk.

Usually several men and lads were employed for hay-time
on a large farm.   Many from Westmorland and Cumberland
came for this seasonal work and, at first in small numbers,
Irishmen appear to have come into the dale for over a hundred
years.   In July 1847 it is recorded in the *Wensleydale Advertiser* that hay-makers' wages had advanced and that one man
had asked £7 for a month, a horse to ride, plenty of gin and
water, and a lad to fetch it.   Gin was then the hay-time drink.
Before the last war Irishmen, hired at Hawes market in the
first week in July, were paid £10 for a month's work, a sum
that has risen until in 1953 up to £60 was asked.

'Finished hay-time after one day and one month's close
attendance,' wrote Alexander Fothergill on 13th August 1774.
'Hay is the grand object of the farmer,' said his son William
twenty years later.   Good seasons and bad seasons were and
are continually discussed.   On the quantity and quality of the
hay the foddering of cattle and sheep depends in the winter.
An old saying runs:

> On 14th February a good goose should lay
> And a fat hogg [2] should go without hay
> One third of your peats and half of your hay
> Will last till May Day.

Long and severe winters are fortunately rare.   The lessee
of the tithes in 1802 commented on the fluctuations of his

---

[1] The length and width of the stroke of the large scythes then used.   The batt
is the name of the wooden handle.   Here it means the depth of the swathe.
[2] A last year's lamb.

receipts caused by the loss of sheep and lambs due to storms. The year 1801 was 'uncommonly productive,' but in 1791 one-half of the moor sheep and two-thirds of the lambs were lost. At the present day the local hay crop is supplemented by that grown on farms in the Plain and brought into the dale by lorry. In the prolonged storms of the winter of 1947 hay was used up, and blocked roads prevented the transport of fresh supplies. Inevitably the farms at the head of the dale and in the side valleys suffered the most. A comparison of figures of the sheep population reveals the extent of the losses in that year.

	1946	*1947*	*1948*
Askrigg	3,547	3,408	3,751
Aysgarth	706	594	717
Bainbridge (including Raydale)	12,456	10,957	13,604
Hawes	18,662	14,442	16,160
High Abbotside	11,533	8,233	10,093
Low Abbotside	4,347	3,609	3,896

A farmer's wife has related to us her experiences in the winter of 1915. Aggravated by illness and war-time conditions, they are not typical, but they serve to show the hardihood and endurance sometimes needed. She and her husband had newly started farming at an isolated place near Camshouse. The husband fell ill with rheumatic fever; the farm man was called up, and for weeks she was milking fifteen or sixteen cows and feeding eleven or twelve small pigs. They had three hundred sheep overblown on Wether Fell, and when lambing-time came round forty died. 'We dug a platt—yer might have thowt we were planning a garden—and we buried 'em all in one grave.' In January they had bought fourteen calves. In time they changed from feeding them on milk and calf food to oil cake that, due to war-time troubles, contained a poison. 'In a week we'd killed 'em all off. We had a grave then to dig ah can tell yer.' For hay-time they required three horses, and to buy one at a reasonable price asked relatives to send a cab horse from Liverpool. Four days after its arrival the horse, that had cost over £30, was found dead, rigged, that is on its back, in a hollow in the pasture. Meanwhile the husband had had another bout of illness. 'Ah've heard 'em say they were brokken wi' ther losses'—but these two farmed for many years to come.

Farming as elsewhere has passed through good and bad times. Present prosperity contrasts strongly with the slump in the 1930's. Then milk was sold at 9d. a gallon and at a minimum of 4½d. in 1932, whereas in 1952 it was 3s. 2d.; wool that realized a minimum of 4½d. to 6d. a pound rose in the war to 6s. and is now 4s. to 4s. 7d.; a cow then sold for £20 and a Swaledale ewe for 30s. as against £60 and £4 at the present day. Wages and costs have risen by four and five times; but there are subsidies for cattle and sheep reared on hill grazings and for the improvement of land and buildings. After a long period of neglect pastures are being limed, and to fulfil modern requirements new cow-byres have been built. Placed near the farmhouses these tend to supplant the barns in the meadows, and they allow for the keeping of T.T. herds that will shortly be the only type of cattle kept in the township.

Young Farmers' Clubs started in the dale in 1937, and Farmers' Discussion Groups, a development of the war years, have diffused new ideas and provided contacts with varied aspects of agriculture. The Wensleydale Agricultural Show, restarted since the war, is held at Leyburn, and is supported by exhibitors from a wide area. It is worthy of record that R. M. Hodgson of Lowlands Farm was vice-chairman in 1950 and chairman in the two following years of the North Riding and South Durham County Branch of the National Farmers' Union, besides having undertaken the duties of secretary from 1933 to 1945.

In the 1952 returns of stock for Askrigg township 4,746 hens were kept. One specialist, Sam Outhwaite, runs a poultry farm of pedigree Exchequer Leghorns, and besides previous awards, in 1950 won the first prize in the North of England in the Accredited Farm and Stock Competition.

Stock has been sent to all parts of the world, including Australia and Canada.   First established at Carr End in 1915, the farm was transferred to Askrigg in 1946, and is equipped with the most modern appliances, such as the electric incubator that hatches some two thousand eggs each week during the winter and spring months.

From the time of the open fields to the present day new patterns have overlaid the old, yet much that is traditional remains.   Names derived from Norse words still distinguish parts of the byre—skell-boose (partition), boose (stall), groop (drainage channel), and barns are called laithes from the Norse hlaða.   Though 6th April, Lady Day, is the end of the term for the payment of rents, 'beck and boose,' that is water and stalls, may be claimed until May Day by a man who is giving up his tenancy.

The price of land is reckoned by twenty years' rent, a system of valuation used centuries ago.   Rented at £5 an acre, meadow land is worth £100 an acre, though in the war up to £200 was paid.   In 1950 the miller redeemed his fee farm rent on the mill and land.   It had been 53s. 4d., the same sum that Lucy Kettlewell paid in 1555.   One farm keeps up the mell, a celebration with sports, after the hay harvest. Cows still graze on the high pastures of the mountains when the grass is 'high and well waxen'; and flocks of ewes and lambs year by year patter up the moor road to the commons in spring.

Lady Hill

XI

WEATHER, FLOWERS, AND BIRDS

ON THE WEDNESDAY before June Fair Day 1908 the morning was stifling. The sun's heat beat down on the fronts of the houses and poured in at open doors. Most of the men had gone to the river to a meet of the otter-hounds, and the women were baking in readiness for the relatives and friends who would flock to the village next day.

About two o'clock a mason working on the south side of the valley noticed that a storm was gathering and, as he looked, a huge cloud hanging over Fair Hill above Askrigg seemed to divide and fall. Meanwhile in the village 'a blackness and dark fiery aspect brooded over all.' In a house above Moor Road Chapel the family suddenly heard a roar, and rushing to the window saw a torrent of brown water pouring down the road, carrying with it great boulders. After a few minutes the body of a cow was swept by. In a house at the top of Elm Hill a young girl who had been baking, alarmed by the darkness and noise, rushed to her elderly father asleep in another room.

Together they dashed to the door. To their horror they saw waves surging down the moor road and a swirling mass of water half-way up Elm Hill, whilst from a top storey window of one of the partly submerged houses a woman's figure gesticulated wildly. The nightmare was all the worse for those who witnessed the scene from the knowledge that the majority of the young men were far away.

It rained for three hours. Water lashed through the houses at Town Head. Articles of furniture, loaves of newly baked bread, and personal belongings floated away along The Gate, only to be found days later strewn across the fields. A neighbour carried Faith and Jane Cloughton out of their house, where the gable-end of a building had fallen and through whose lower storey flowed a muddy stream. At Grenada Hall a woman who was pregnant was found by her husband clinging to a bacon hook in the ceiling. In many houses the only means of entrance was by bedroom windows. Ten yards of metal were washed from the railway line by the flooded Paddock Beck, and the four o'clock train rocked as it was signalled to slow down by a chance passer-by.

Quickly as it had risen the water fell, leaving chaos behind it. Up the moor road a steam-roller was embedded in stones, the road itself was rent with a channel two yards deep filled with sand and rocks weighing several tons; the High Bridge was swept away, the Worton lane resembled a river-bed, and debris was piled up outside the houses. No lives were lost, but damage to council and personal property amounted to about £3,000, and, as after similar disasters elsewhere due to freak storms, some far worse than the Askrigg flood, a relief fund was opened. In time the buildings at the foot of the road were built up into the houses that we see there to-day.

The cloud-bursts that occur in the dales are fortunately rare phenomena; the most recent wrought considerable damage in Coverdale and Waldendale in 1949. On 12th August 1946 a minor storm caused Mill Gill Falls to swell into a savage muddy torrent from which spray was flung a hundred or more

Clearing up the debris left after the Askrigg flood on the 3rd June, 1908.

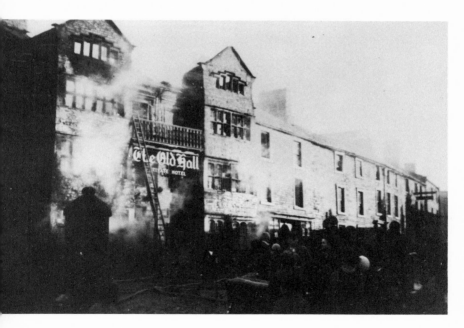

The scene on the 10th October, 1935, when Askrigg Old Hall burnt down.
Two fire brigades, one from Hawes and one from Catterick, fought the blaze,
but the fire spread so quickly that only the facade remained. Built in 1678 by
William Thornton, it was of great architectural interest, and was the focal
point in Askrigg market-place. At the time of the fire it was in use as an hotel.

yards. Below it boulders clashed together in the beck. Perhaps once a year heavy floods fill the valley bottom. On 15th February 1950 the river was lost in a rushing mass of water half a mile wide.

Conditioned to life on our 'cold and barren' ground we find the vagaries of the weather ever a fit subject for conversation. 'A nice day' is the greeting when it is still and warm, even if it is 'damping.' Or 'We're in for a hap-up' is the ominous remark when skies darken before snow. 'T' winds in Raydale 'oile—it'll rain,' we are told. And rain it does.

By the weather we mean conditions at a specific time. Climate on the other hand is adjudged chiefly by rainfall and temperature prevailing over long periods. Noting the average rainfall at the four stations where records are kept in Wensleydale, at Spennithorne in the lower dale, Bolton Hall, Askrigg, and lastly Mossdale Moor, we find a rise as altitude increases and as we move west. The average yearly rainfall at Askrigg taken at Yorebridge Grammar School, 670 feet above sea level, is 40·7 inches, a fairly heavy fall compared with the average at Spennithorne, 31·5 inches, or at York, for example, where it is 24·3; but less than that at Sedbergh, west of the Pennine watershed. A table, including mileages from Askrigg as the crow flies, will best show the divergences.

Place	Feet above sea level	Average rainfall
YORK 48 miles east	57	24·3 in.
SPENNITHORNE 12 miles east	358	31·5 in.
BOLTON HALL 8 miles east	420	32·6 in.
ASKRIGG	670	40·7 in.
MOSSDALE MOOR 9 miles west	1,125	75·0 in.
SEDBERGH 18 miles west	305	53·0 in.

T

It is calculated that temperature falls 1° for every three hundred feet of ascent, so that because of its high altitude the mean temperature at Askrigg, 45·4°, is low. A graph illustrates the coldness of our climate compared with that of York, and it shows that the growing period of vegetation (when the temperature is above 42°) is from the last quarter of March to the middle of October. It is a short growing season for the grass in the meadows and pastures and for the flowers and vegetables in the gardens.

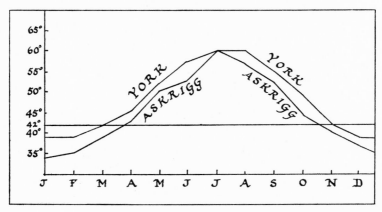

Comparison of mean average temperatures at York and Askrigg

Readings taken at Askrigg since 1932 record that the lowest temperature was −8° Fahrenheit in the last week in December 1939 or the first week in January 1940. At that time plumbing, especially the heating systems of public buildings, was severely damaged by frost. In contrast temperatures of 91° were twice reached in July 1934.

According to statistics from readings taken by F. E. Chevins at Yorebridge Grammar School from 1932 to 1950 we find that January is the stormiest month, November is the wettest, March is comparatively dry, that April heralds a cold wet time, and that May followed by June are the driest months. Contradicting these generalities the figures reveal that October

1938 with a rainfall of 10·49 inches was the wettest month of any in the above years. November 1945 was excessively dry, and as we know February and March of 1947 were remarkable for heavy snowfalls. Radiation taking place rapidly, nights are cold even in August. Early in this month we sense the first breath of autumn. In 1899 two farmers gave it as their sworn opinion that the average winter in these parts 'will be fifteen weeks.'

Statistics for the frequencies of snowfalls are not available. It is often assumed that if snow is reported anywhere in England, it will have fallen in the Yorkshire dales. This is not always the case. But a winter generally regarded as severe means a bad winter here. The passes fill with snow to a depth far greater than that in the valley or out on the Plain, and the attenuated lines of communication in these lands of sparse habitation are kept open with difficulty.

Our prevailing wind blows from the west, but often in spring, as throughout May 1935 and in March to mid April 1936, east winds bring fine cold days. Retarding growth, they are not welcomed. When wind from the south-west (from Raydale) wafts the chimes of the church clock clearly to Town Head, we expect rain. Breezes in summer, squalls in autumn, blasts in winter—we rarely enjoy long periods of still weather. On stormy nights the distant roar of a gale sweeping along the valley bottom accompanies a tumult of sound as gust after gust beats at the houses.

But the persistent smoke fogs of London or of industrial areas are unknown here, so that winters frequently compare favourably with those experienced in towns. Occasionally on autumn or winter mornings the land is shrouded in a white fog caused by radiation of heat from the earth, so that air in contact with the ground becomes cooled and forms mist. Usually the warmth of the sun disperses this during the morning. All day on 24th January 1951 a vast white fog blanketed the dale up to about 850 feet; above it the hillsides were bathed in sunshine. Low cloud lying on the hills and

ragged clouds blowing and breaking and forming again restrict
our vision, but seldom stretch lower than the high pastures.
We say:

> Mist on the hills
> Water for the mills.
> Mist in the hollows.
> Fine weather follows.

The weather brings skies that match the drama of the hill
country. There are slanting rays of the sun glancing from the
backs of clouds to creep round distant summits or to light up
bolsters of mist laid across the sides of the fells; January skies
green at the horizon rising to a blue vault that snow reflects
in long shadows; winter sunsets crowning Wether Fell with a
sea of flame; and in early spring galleons of cloud seeming to
carry off burdens of ice.

References to the weather experienced at Askrigg in past
centuries are few. There were the Michaelmas rains that
destroyed the crops of the monks at Fors in 1154. A witness
in a lawsuit in 1609 spoke of 'the contynuall coldnes lyinge in
these mountennes.' In 1740, a year in which the Thames was
ice-bound, Mill Gill waterfall froze to form a huge icicle behind
which twelve men took their luncheon. In February 1757
and in the winter of 1771–2 Alexander Fothergill was paying
wages to labourers to keep the turnpike open 'in the Great
Snows,' and two years later in February returning from York
he 'came to Rippon and found the waters [of the Ure] much
too high to ride.'

On 14th August 1844 the driver of the mail coach gathered
a basket of hailstones nearly as big as marbles. The storm
that on 27th February 1903 blew down a fine old sycamore
on Bainbridge Green was compared with the fearful gale on
Windy Monday, 7th January 1839. In 1895 poor people
suffered owing to all out-door work being suspended by the
frost. On a February evening of the same year a tournament
with the track lit by candles and lanterns was held on the ice-
bound river. Up the moor road, at that date used continually

by traffic from Swaledale to Askrigg station, Askrigg men on this side and Swaledale men on the other cut double tracks for cart-wheels through drifts fifteen to twenty feet high, and had at one point to desist as the overblow filled the channels as fast as the men opened them out. June of 1844 resembled a winter month, but the summer of 1896 was noted as the best hay-time within living memory.

Of all the seasons spring is here the loveliest. It reaches us suddenly. One week the fields are drab and desolate. The next they are dotted with ewes and lambs. Curlews call on the moor and the white wings of gulls flash against dark hills. There is the scent of growing grass, shoots point through frost-pocked soil, primroses are up Whitfield, bluebells in Grange Gill. The pattern of our lives shaped by winter changes.

Dorothy Wordsworth, writing in 1803, compared Wensley-dale favourably with Scotland. She said: 'At Wensley there is a unity, a softness, a melting together which in the large vales of Scotland I never perceived.' On warm June evenings when a faint pink sky meets creamy-blue hills and shadows softly define church tower and house and garden walls; when the greens shade from pale to dark, when cows graze high on Addlebrough, when the scent of lilac hangs in the air and flowers and fresh foliage are warmed by the glow of the sky; then this melting together is indeed perceptible.

A friend remembering an old saying bids us take farewell of summer, 'Ah think thou can put thi parasol away now.' Sometimes a warm spell 'puts the winter on.' But often in October we see Wether Fell blue-black under lowering skies, far away the glistening roofs of villages and the curve of a white wet road topping a knoll. We hear the rushing of becks whose peat-stained water leaves blobs of foam like the rolled-up fleeces of sheep. Uneasy sunshine flashes from ragged cloud. 'Ah reckon nowt to these bits o' gladdenings,' says our neigh-bour, 'they only strengthen t' storm.'

The winter of 1947 is nowadays our standard of comparison. From the first week of February to the third week in March

snow and frost gripped the land. Road traffic was at times
halted; buses did not run for seven weeks, and the railway,
save for a few stoppages, remained the life-line of the upper
dale.   Men battled helplessly, cutting roads open ten or eleven
times.   Hay and fuel supplies ran short.   Thousands of gallons
of milk that could not be collected were wasted, a few cattle
died, and sheep, overblown and starved, died in hundreds.
The snow stowering, that is driven by strong wind, blinded the
eyes and bewildered the mind.   Occasionally there were days
when the fields, polished like glass, mirrored the sun, when
rushes with crystal fringes bordered frozen becks, and evenings
when the scars of Ellerkin, reflecting the sunset, shone lemon,
apple-green, pink, and mauve.   The last heavy storm on
13th March was followed three days later by the beginning
of the thaw.   Roofs dripped, water-butts overflowed, and the
becks plunged down to the river.   The winter of 1947 had
ended.

Climate, soil, and a varied geological structure determine the
flora to be found in the township.   Carboniferous limestones,
shales, and sandstones, rich land in the Holmes, boulder clay,
the acid ill-drained soils of the high pastures, and peat on the
moor in a territory rising from 600 to 1,800 feet make for
distinction and variety of species.

With here and there solitary ashes and sycamores Askrigg
and its near surroundings are sparsely wooded.   The ash, a
native and the characteristic tree, is rivalled in numbers by the
sycamore, an introduction of the late Middle Ages.   More
trees are to be found at Woodhall, Nappa, and Mill Gill
(where many beeches were felled in the autumn of 1952); and
Hawbank adjoining the eastern boundary of the township is
clothed with the bushes of aboriginal woodland such as bird
cherry, hazel, wych-elm, and mountain ash.   Similar ancient
scrub, growing on the slopes below Whitfield Crag at 1,300 to
1,500 feet, forms one of the highest natural woods in Yorkshire.   Gooseberry and red and black currant are found near
the river and the lower reaches of the becks, and the former

The ash is the native and characteristic tree

lingering on by the overgrown ruins of houses is as sure a sign
of the habitations of men as the nettle.   Juniper, once native
to the district, was seen here by the botanist F. A. Lees, and
within recollection the shrub grew on Abbey Heads near the
river.

The moor, crossed by the two passes into Swaledale, is a

place of peat hags oozing sluggish streams of black-brown
water, sweet riggs of close-bitten grass on limestone outcrops, green-rimmed pools, bronze beads of ling flowers on
cropped tussocks, yellow patches of sphagnum moss, and bilberry plants below the Greets. Old peat pots, the ruins of
lead mines and limekilns, the green track that leads to the
disused coal pits on Blackstone Edge, hives of bees in a limestone quarry in August, shooting butts, and sheep rakes proclaim
the past and present occupations of men.

In winter the moor is visited by flocks of snow-buntings, a
lesser black-backed gull or ravens, and a rare fox or badger;
its denizens are mainly sheep and grouse. In February the
golden plovers return, in March the curlews cry of their alarm
or content, and black-headed gulls gather to nest at Summer
Lodge Tarn. Moths flutter amongst the hags; and the heath
rush, crowberry, ling, bell, and cross-leaved heather flower in
the short summer.

Crown property, the manorial rights leased for two and a
half centuries by the owners of Nappa Hall, this high land is a
valuable grouse moor, and was for fifty-three years, up to 1952,
in the charge of the keeper, Harry Storey. The record bag
for one day's shoot is 565 brace in 1902. In 1925 a fire burned
for three weeks, and laid waste fifty to sixty acres near the east
moor road. In a small paddock behind the shooting hut,
Stackhill House, rises a spring that provided a source of water
for driving the corn mill, and here a wind-swept copse of
ashes, sycamores, and mountain ash, planted in the last century, makes a landmark for many miles.

Similarly at the eastern corner of the township a copse of
pines on a bracken-covered knoll, called Lady Hill, is a landmark in Wensleydale. It is situated in what was a warren for
silver grey rabbits bred for their pelts. In 1757 Alexander
Fothergill, as agent for the Nappa Hall estate to which the
warren belonged, directed the rebuilding of a house for the
warrener. In the last century skins were sold to the tsar of
Russia and were dispatched to China. Now no longer closely

preserved, the rabbits are sold for food. The warren originally consisted of a hundred acres that since the coming of the
railway has been reduced to seventy-five. It is part of the
ancient Woodhall Park, and a length of the massive deer park
wall can still be seen alongside the river.

The flora of our territory may be classed roughly as flowers
of the moorlands, fields, streams, and verges of the lanes.
These categories tend to overlap; a few plants of the fields
invade the moor and some grow on the roadsides and the
edges of the woods. In this grassy land the weeds of cultivation form a class apart. Springing up in gardens and the few
waste places where soil is exposed, nettles, docks, petty spurge,
shepherd's purse, white and red deadnettle, and others may
seem abundant to the gardener, but compared with the rest
they are not numerous. Mill Gill and its continuation Whitfield Gill, and the course of Ellerbeck—a stream alien to this
country, for it meanders along a limestone terrace instead of
rushing down a slope—are the habitats of rare ferns and
flowers.

Below the moor, mat-grass, sheep's fescue, bent-grass, rushes,
some bracken, but few flowers cover the belt between 1,500
and 1,250 feet. Depending on drainage and deficiency of
lime in the soil due to leaching, one or the other predominates
—patches of mat-grass on the summit of Ellerkin, fescue
grass, common rush, and mat-grass on the upper slopes of
the Fair Hill Allotment; where on its lower border a long
terrace of dry short turf over limestone once made a suitable
terrain for the Hill Fair. Here and there are musk and
marsh thistle and tormentil, and near Woodhall mountain
pansies, and above Nappa Scar bracken.

But a distinctive flora blossoming in ancient pastures and
undisturbed meadow land between rough grazings and river
yields the most varieties; the one with plants such as milk-
wort, thyme, lousewort, tormentil, cinquefoil, and sheep's fescue
is close-matted; the other with pignut, yellow rattle, butter-
cups, goat's-beard, and wood geranium, to mention a few of

those mingled among the meadow grasses, might well be termed a flowery mead. Sometimes it is a buttercup year, often pignut predominates, or the red leaves of sorrel are conspicuous, or wood geranium diffusing a pink hue attracts the eye.

Herbs, once used for various purposes, are a feature of the district. Sweet Cicely borders the roadside at Town Head and a lane at Newbiggin, and is almost the commonest member of its family in Wensleydale; snakeweed flowers in damp places, and Good King Henry and comfrey grow near the houses and on the verges. In June the channel of Ellerbeck is lined with sea thrift that is said to be more profuse here than at any other inland station in England. Short lists of flowers with the most common omitted will be found in an appendix (page 308).

Like the flowers, and for similar reasons, the birds are remarkable for diversity of kind. They fall into six broad categories: birds of the moor and uplands, meadows and pastures, plantations and woods, tarn and river, open woods and copses, and habitations and gardens. These residents, and seasonal and rare visitors, noted over a period of years, add up to some ninety-five species. In the list in the appendix (page 311) it will be seen that some birds, such as the greenfinch, that would normally be resident in lowland country, leave here in the winter.

Of the moor birds the black-headed gulls far outnumber the rest. Comparative newcomers, they first appeared in the 1880's and now, arriving in hundreds in early March, they nest in the rushes on the west shore of Summer Lodge Tarn. Amongst the other spring visitors the curlews, so closely associated with wild country, often seek nesting grounds in the meadows. Of birds of prey, the peregrine, an occasional harrier, and the buzzard are rare vagrants, whilst kestrels and sparrow-hawks may often be met. We have seen an eagle owl on the moor, but this has not been verified by experienced ornithologists. Carrion crows, pipits, and wheatears are regularly seen.

In this village of sparse trees there are in consequence few birds. We think of swifts screaming over roof-tops on summer evenings, of swallows and martins packed on electricity wires ready for departure in late August, and of starlings imitating the curlew's calls as they perch in the churchyard trees in winter. Elsewhere, due to the lack of hedges and suitable bushes, many birds nest in crevices of the walls. Pied and yellow wagtails in the meadows; redstarts, tits, and finches at Woodhall, Nappa Scar, and Hawbank are typical, whilst tree-creepers and different species of owl are less often seen. By the river are sedge-warblers, sometimes corncrakes, and in recent years a few pairs of oystercatchers, and pitting the banks with their holes, sand-martins nest. The brilliant flash of colour of a kingfisher's back, a dipper skimming the water, the peewit of a green plover are familiar sights and sounds to the angler.

'Retired from the world, a man might here enjoy fly-fishing and grouse-shooting in the highest perfection,' wrote Lord Torrington in his diary in 1792. Both trout and grayling abound in the river, and fish weigh up to 2 lb. or more. The largest trout that has been taken, now stuffed and in a case at the Rose and Crown at Bainbridge, was caught by J. R. Hopper on 6th June 1931 and weighed 3 lb. 10 oz. The Wensleydale Angling Association, re-formed in 1920 from older clubs, restocks the river each season with one to two thousand yearling trout, and it has the fishing rights over five miles of the Ure, two miles east of Worton Bridge and three miles west, and part of Semerwater. In the river may be found cray-fish, as Camden recorded 'ever since Sir Christopher Medcalfe in our remembrance brought that kind of fish hither out of the south part of England.' Trout used to come down Askrigg Beck, that is now too shallow for them, so that people leaning over the parapet of the High Bridge could watch the fish in the shadow of the arch.

Speak to one of the older men of fishing, and he invariably looks back to boyhood, perhaps to a spring morning when playing truant from school he spent all day by a favourite beck or stretch of the river.   Watching the birds, fishing with a home-made rod—memory has given these simple delights a touch of magic.   Later in life on winter nights he ties his flies, Greenwell's Glory, Water Hen, Dark Snipe, or Early Brown, and the first spell of warm weather in spring draws him down to the river.

XII

THE VILLAGE AT NIGHTFALL

REMEMBERING the late autumn afternoon when the vision of the town in its heyday so easily grew in the mind, we return to our vantage point across the valley. The sun that set an hour ago behind the hills leaves its reflection in a clear sky, against which the slopes and terraces of land rising to Ellerkin appear as a grey-blue expanse. Askrigg itself is veiled in the smoke of fires being stoked ready for the night. Distant lights come on, in the grammar school to the left of the village, in a cow-byre near by. Three bright street lights, spaced apart, dim lights, and oblongs of light from house and Temperance Hall windows show plainly as darkness falls. The lit-up carriages of a train coming up the dale dart forward across the middle-distance of our view, and a little later a bus shines its headlights on the road at the far side of the valley.

It is the modern village that we visualize now. The bus that at six o'clock leaves the main street marks the time. Roadmen, quarrymen, joiners, electricians, clerks, dairymen, and lorry drivers return home to their firesides; the shop-keepers lock their doors; the garage closes down. The farmers are still milking in the barns, and from the post office sounds the thud-thud of letters being franked. The street empties; and for most people a few hours of leisure and amusement lie ahead.

Before returning to the village, we may review briefly the last thirty years. In 1923 the road through Askrigg was surfaced with tar, and the work of the stone-breakers who sat hammering stones all day at the top of Howgate and the moor

273

road gradually fell away. New methods of repair went hand in hand with the increasing use of motor transport.

Apart from small vehicles, privately owned, in the lower dale, Wensleydale had no buses until 1926. That year, like the railway companies before it, the Northallerton Omnibus Company Ltd extended its services to Leyburn, then to Hawes via Aysgarth. The following year the first bus taking a route on the north side of the valley to Hawes ran through Askrigg. These were linked shortly with others travelling out of the dale to Richmond, Darlington, and Ripon. In 1930 the company's buses in Wensleydale were taken over by United Automobile Services Ltd and now carry us to work, to neighbouring villages, to market, to school, and to distant towns.

Since 1924 the morning mail has been brought by road, first by a private contractor, and from 1933 by a post office van. The three postmen of Askrigg each walk or cycle daily one of the rounds of twenty-one, nineteen, and sixteen miles, the first covering the Bainbridge district, the second Askrigg and Abbotside to Litherskew, and the third Raydale to Marsett beyond Semerwater. Most isolated houses have to be visited regularly, for the farmers living off the road order newspapers by post. One retired postman covered the Marsett round daily for twenty-six years, and recollects many exhausting struggles through deep snow. Another, partly as a result of experiences that caused ill health in the winter of 1947, had to resign his job. Since September of that year the rounds have been undertaken in weekly rotation.

In 1919, on the retirement of William Balderston from the headmastership, the North Riding County Council took over the grammar school; girls were admitted, and, final break with the past, the Black Swan in York was sold, Anthony Besson's endowment passing eventually into the general funds of the education committee. The master appointed, R. C. Shorter, in 1931 saw the completion of a new building, not on the site at 'Yore's Bridge End' but set behind its playing-field a little west of Askrigg. The school now has a staff of four masters, two mistresses, and two part-time teachers, and can accommodate about a hundred scholars who, coming from all parts of the dale, travel to and fro by bus and train or board during the week in homes round about.

Besides this development strong cultural movements flourished throughout the 1920's. In 1911 T. W. Grubb, appointed by the Rowntree Trust for the furtherance of education, came to live at Bainbridge, and he began to conduct classes in English literature and French. As an outcome *Twelfth Night*, the first of what became known as the Easter plays, was given at Askrigg in 1913. *The Rivals*, *As You Like It*, and *The School for Scandal* were followed by many of Shaw's plays, and others by Pinero, Knoblock, Yeats, Dunsany, and Barrie. *Pygmalion*, produced in 1937, was the last of a remarkable series that ended from lack of leadership.

At a similar date the Askrigg Literary and Debating Society, an offshoot from the classes, met fortnightly, and the natural interest in music was stimulated by John Henry Lomax, a conductor of choirs, who had come to live in the village. Though these activities have ceased, their influence remains. Askrigg men and women have a more than average appreciation of books, plays, and choral performances; some possess real talent for acting, and one, Azariah Chapman, has a fine tenor voice.

The night of 10th October 1935, when the Old Hall was gutted by fire, is not to be forgotten. Moves to preserve the façade that was left standing proved impracticable. In time a new house was built on the site, and during that becalmed period of the inter-war years only one other house was built in the village. There have been a barn and two house fires in recent years. One home was saved, but the other, once Mary Middlemas's lodging house, was destroyed.

In 1930 the County Council took complete charge of the highways, and a central committee for poor relief replaced the Board of Guardians. From the inception of modern local government in 1894 the offices of the Rural District Council had remained at Askrigg, but in 1940 they were moved to new premises in Hawes. From 1939 to 1946 the Food Office for the area occupied a room in a house in the village until it too was transferred to Hawes.

We have reached the Second World War. Its impact on Askrigg was little different from that on other remote country places—the requisitioning of the Temperance Hall and of houses that chanced to be empty by the military; the billeting of evacuees who most of them eventually returned to their own homes; the sharing of grammar and elementary school premises with schools from Gateshead; and the accommodation of visitors who, unable to go to seaside resorts, flocked here for holidays. Hospitality was willingly given by those who appreciated that they were spared the full horrors of combat. Only one stick of bombs and a few incendiaries fell in the township. Forty-three men and six women either joined the forces or were engaged in war work, and seven men lost their lives.

The Askrigg and District Produce Association, started in 1942 to encourage home food production, ran a show each year (as it still does), and by sales of exhibits raised funds for the Red Cross. Our full energies were thrown into the efforts such as War Weapons Week; on 30th May 1944 for Salute the Soldier Week a pageant of local history was performed in the afternoon in Askrigg market-place and in the evening on Bainbridge Green. Written by R. C. Shorter and R. M. Chapman, the pageant was an event in the annals of Askrigg.

The troublous years ended. Once more, as in past centuries, celebrations and a service of thanksgiving for victory were held. Again those who had seen far-distant places came home; several of the girls married soldiers they had met and settled elsewhere.

During the last thirty years, and especially since the war, new developments and inventions have altered the equipment of homes. The first piped water supply brought from Worton Scar in 1877 proved inadequate, and in 1935 it was replaced

Celebrations of the Jubilee of George V. A procession led by the **Hawes Band** passes through the market place.

An ambitious pageant of local history was presented in 1944 at Askrigg as part of 'Salute the Soldier' week. The singers are from left to right: G Johnson, W Chapman, J H Lomax, C Simpson, J Gill, R Bushby, N Hutchinson (hidden) and A Chapman.

by a scheme that tapped a spring in Lanty Bog near the Fair Hill for collection in a small reservoir at Town Head—a reservoir built on the site of the pinfold. About 1880 the first water-closet had been put in a house. Then bath-rooms, without hot water, made their appearance, and within recent years bath-rooms with a hot-water system have been fitted in about half the houses. Small cottages usually have a water-closet in an outbuilding, and no more than half a dozen are without this amenity at the present day.

Gradually in the same period the stone floors have been replaced by wooden ones; the kitchen ranges (with vast surfaces to blacklead) have gone, and tiled fireplaces or, in some cases, closed-in cookers and water-heaters combined have taken their place. Since the national grid system reached Askrigg in 1948 electric cookers, heaters, and other appliances have been installed.

In the houses little is left of the oak and mahogany furniture of the seventeenth and eighteenth centuries. It was a heritage that mostly vanished with decline. Sixty years ago the Skidmores as antique dealers had two or three cottages filled with pieces needing repair; other dealers followed them. Auction sales, taking place either outside a house or in the Temperance Hall, are events; at them the best of the furniture that is left is sold and taken out of the dale.

In the shops the shelves are lined with tinned goods, with cakes, and with loaves of bread, some ready sliced. At most, six housewives bake their own bread, and no one regularly makes oatcake. The laundry van comes each week from Ingleton, an ironmongery shop on wheels tours the village, the fish-and-chip van arrives on Mondays. The full-time occupation of dressmaker has gone, and motor-vans from Darlington and Richmond stores, and the draper from Hawes in his car, stop at many houses on their rounds. In old days the women rose at four o'clock to finish the washing or the blackleading before breakfast; if 'it was all work i' them days,' it is no longer so to-day.

U

Girls leaving the grammar school take up a variety of occupations. To select a few examples from recent lists, there are a therapeutic dietician at Guy's Hospital, a children's welfare officer in Kent, a company manager of a mobile theatre, a prison wardress; and one flew to Canada and found work for herself. Another old scholar living in Askrigg is the district nurse, who thus continues the long line of those who have tended the sick. In 1684 Eden Geldart, and in 1749 Margaret Caygill, were licensed to practise as midwives. Barbara Ann Gill, who died aged ninety-three in 1949, after being left a widow trained in London as a midwife in the 1880's. Noted for her skill, she employed her gifts generously, and was for long the only nurse in the neighbourhood.

Outstanding amongst modern developments, Women's Institutes have widened horizons in rural places. That at Askrigg was formed on 20th October 1920, and now numbers a little over a hundred members. The institute has revealed women's capacity for leadership and organization, and, backed by a nation-wide federation, it is probably true to say that it is the most progressive and active body in the village.

A list of classes, lectures, and demonstrations held over the years makes formidable reading; and a striking feature is the number of charities regularly supported. The Second World War brought the movement into prominence. During this time Askrigg Women's Institute was instrumental in raising large sums of money for one cause or another. In War Weapons Week, Ladies' Day, held in the village, raised £240, and in the first ten years after its inception the Savings Group had passed through it £9,928.

Members gain awards at county exhibitions at York and successfully enter drama competitions. In 1948 one of them designed the Yorkshire page in the Federation of Women's Institute's Book presented to the queen, then Princess Elizabeth, on the occasion of her marriage. Another, a member of Bainbridge and Askrigg Institutes, whose work attains professional standards, besides other appointments is on the judge's panel for fruit preservation and horticulture, is group produce organizer for upper Wensleydale, and on the panel of demonstrators is called on to arrange exhibits at events such as the Great Yorkshire Show. One, a voluntary county organizer from 1944 to 1952, and several others holding offices for long periods, give their services freely.

In 1945, representing Askrigg and Carperby Institutes, a member of the latter was co-opted on to the Housing Committee of the Rural District Council; the following year two of our members were elected to the Parish Council.

Since the war the prosperity of farming, the building of two pairs of council houses and two bungalows, the effects of the 1944 Education Act and the National Health and Assistance Acts of 1948 have also brought change to village life. Canteens, started during the war, provide dinners at the schools, and harmonious colour schemes brighten the walls of classrooms. At the elementary school the children, now numbering about forty instead of the hundred of fifty years ago, leave at the age of eleven to continue their training at Hawes School.

Change has overtaken the workhouse since we viewed it. In March 1939 it was declared redundant and closed, but was reopened at the outbreak of war. Since 1948 the sick have been sent to hospital, casuals are no longer admitted, and the number of beds has been reduced from forty-four to twenty for men and sixteen for women. It is no longer called the workhouse, or the institute, or the vagrant's term for it 'The Spike,' but High Hall County Home for the Aged; and the master is the superintendent and the mistress the matron. In 1952 the interior underwent complete overhaul; the equipment was modernized, and the rooms were decorated with flowery wall-papers. Fires are lit in the bedrooms, all the food is cooked on the premises, radios may be switched on, and the pervading atmosphere is of warmth, comfort, and kindliness. On arrival the old people, if necessary, receive a complete outfit of clothes. They go out when and where they please, if they wish to work they are paid, and they all enjoy an annual holiday for which, if they cannot pay, about £5 a head is raised by whist drives and other efforts. The only sad note is that husbands and wives are still segregated.

Recreations, largely due to increased use of motor transport, have changed in character. Football as we have seen was played centuries ago, and local sports were an integral part of village life. Organized football was established by the formation of the Wensleydale League in 1920, and Askrigg United was started in 1936 as a continuation of a Bainbridge club. On Saturdays when there is a home match buses and cars throng the market-place and the roadside near the ground by the grammar school. Bainbridge Sports, that has developed into an important event since the war, draws a crowd of four to five thousand people, and the horse-trotting and motor-cycle races are entered by competitors from all parts of Yorkshire and even from Lancashire and Scotland. At the present time sports at Askrigg have lapsed.

In the summer months buses take us on annual outings organized by many bodies from the British Legion to the Angling Association. People journey to Grinton Sports, to the Wensleydale Agricultural Show held at Leyburn, and to other shows in Swaledale and farther afield.

Mention must be made of those people who have become known beyond the small village world. In 1918 George Metcalfe left Askrigg Elementary School to work first as a farm man, then as a railway porter, and in time as a signalman. Moved to York, he went to night school and in 1927 joined the police force. He was consistently promoted, and in 1951 at the age of forty-five was appointed Chief Detective Superintendent and head of the West Riding C.I.D. The following year, for the apprehension of an armed man who had shot a police inspector and a constable, he was awarded the M.B.E.

At Askrigg in 1942 Ella Pontefract completed *Yorkshire Cottage*, her last book written before her death in 1945, and in the years 1940 to 1946 whilst he lived in the village, Thomas Armstrong wrote *Dover Harbour* and *King Cotton*.

The church looms dark beyond leafless trees

In 1765 Ann Fothergill writing from London to her brother Alexander said '. . . doubtless you may also have ample imploy. But one wou'd rather hope in that quiet retreat remoat from the intrusions of hurry and noise, you might sometimes injoy an abstracted hour and both body and mind have some moments of quiet recess.' Ann's kindly thoughts were as wide of the mark as is the townsman's view of the countryman in the twentieth century.

Crossing over to the village, we find many people enjoying some moments of quiet recess in their homes, perhaps listening to the wireless or watching television. But seldom a night passes without event, especially in the winter months. There are the Toc H for the men, the Women's Institute for the women, lectures organized by the Workers' Educational Association, the Wesley Guild, and one night each week the pictures. The young men and girls journey to dances held in villages all over the dale. The men gather at the inns (only two now, the Kings Arms Hotel and the Crown Inn), or at the two clubs to play billiards and to read the papers.

The newspapers have changed since we last noted them. The *Northern Echo* is the most widely read paper in the neighbourhood, next come in a group the *Yorkshire Post*, the *Daily Mail*, and the *Daily Express*, followed by the *Daily Telegraph*. The *Darlington and Stockton Times* has for long been the weekly newspaper, the farmers' bible as it is often called, and in 1950 it was joined by the *Thirsk Bedale and Northallerton Times*.[1]

Focus for many of our activities is the Temperance Hall. Here may be heard the thud of the feet of the badminton players, the ring of a bell as the players move on at a whist drive, and the rollicking tunes to which the square dancing enthusiasts whirl and skip. There may be in progress a concert featuring local talent or the Swaledale singers or a choir from a distance, or a production of a three-act play by the Hawes or West Burton Players. Sometimes the room is thronged for the Women's Institutes' Group Drama Festival, that lasting from two o'clock to ten at night is a feat of endurance for adjudicators, performers, and audience.

Once a year we hear a speech from the Member for the Parliamentary Division at the Conservative Reunion that, as in the days of the Conservative Ball, includes a supper and a

---

[1] The *Darlington and Stockton Times*, established in 1847, was amalgamated with what had been originally the *Ripon and Richmond Chronicle* in 1894, since when it has circulated in Wensleydale. The *Thirsk Bedale and Northallerton Times*, established in 1856, was issued in the dale until its amalgamation with the *Ripon Gazette and Observer* in 1914. It was republished under its old title in 1950.

dance attended by people from all over the dale. Now it is sometimes a three-day event with a whist drive and supper and a tea for the children. Men and women flock to the institute's new year's party, that is followed by one for the children—one of the many arranged for them by the schools and Sunday schools at this time of the year.

At all these events we shall have heard Yorkshire voices, but little of the pure ancient speech of the North Riding. Everyone is bilingual, and dialect is put aside for life on the farms. But to illustrate the shrewd philosophy of our neighbours, the following remarks made to us within the last year or two are worth recording :

> Pride's painful.
> Your life looks short when you look back.
> Short reckonings make long friends.
> Folk are queer, especially t'wick 'uns.
> You can put up wi' owt except being hung.
> The worst of work is, it waits.
> She talks as she warms (said of a gossip).
> She never looked side I was on (said after being ignored).
> You want more on than your shoe-laces (said of a bleak place).
> You've had the truth, and truth goes farthest.

Before the evening ends and the lights go out let us join in at one or two events.

On November the Fifth in the dark of a moonless night chimneys and roofs are silhouetted against an orange glow. A shaft of light falls across the market-place as a door opens; a sneck clicks, and a man disappears up Pudding Lane. Other people follow him, in ones and twos, in family parties, the children clutching boxes of fireworks. Behind the blacksmith's shop at the end of the lane a field slopes down to the bonfire, a blazing tower of branches, cartons, rubbish, and old tyres, capped by smoke that balloons upwards in ever-changing patterns. The glow reveals people standing in groups and children eagerly lighting squibs and sparklers. Loud reports punctuate the burble of talk and excited shouts. Faces turn upwards as a rocket pours its handful of colour into the night sky.

Thirty or forty years ago it was customary for the men to carry a blazing tar-barrel, poised shoulder high on poles, up and down the main street. Gates and water-butts tended to disappear overnight. Even recently there has been a change; for since a new signpost was erected in the middle of the market-place, the traditional setting for the celebration, the bonfire has been lit in the field behind the smithy, a field at the side of which lies the funeral pyre of the Old Hall, a long heap of burnt stones dumped here out of the way.

Warmth bathes our shins and faces; the night air blows chill on our backs, and a drizzle of rain seems to evaporate in the heat as it falls. Like us, in every village in the dale people watch the flames of a communal fire. Perhaps we commemorate the ritual lighting of the midsummer fires of the Norsemen rather than a plot hatched out in a distant place. 'Penny for the guy,' cries the Cockney child, but here the children ask 'Have you anything for the bonfire?'

Or approach the village on a bright frosty evening after a day of snow showers on the second Monday in March. People now turn up the West End on their way to the annual meeting of the Parish Council held at the elementary school. The first-comers sit on forms in the classroom with their backs to walls adorned with friezes of cut-out farm animals. Ten minutes or more pass before the late-comers arrive and the meeting starts. Unless there is a reason, such as the time in 1946 when the women came in force to press for representation, only the five councillors, a handful of men, and two or three women are assembled.

The clerk reads the minutes of the previous annual meeting, and the chairman explains the current distribution of the charities, Wetherill's and Alderson's Dole. Methods of raising money for the upkeep of the church clock are discussed, and, as in 1749 when a new clock was needed, voluntary subscriptions are agreed on. The vicar states the cost of the winding. Two collectors offer their services, the one to cover the east side of the street, the other the west, not forgetting the ginnels, some with old names, Wapping, and Seen Wynd.

At the time of this meeting the original electric wiring of the village still serves, but the new scheme of the North Eastern Electricity Board is planned. We talk of wayleaves and posts, and urge that the latter be fixed at the backs of the houses. The number of street lights, increased since the first lamps were bought with the last of the proceeds of the market tolls, receives notice.

By now, in the room clouded with tobacco smoke and well warmed by the big grey enamelled stove, the meeting has become a family conclave. When complaints are raised as to the condition of the pavement in front of a house, we listen sympathetically to the householder who pleads the difficulty of obtaining kerbstones. He makes no demur that a stretch of public pavement is his responsibility, for the arrangement goes back to 1758 when the street was paved. The clerk announces that the footpaths have to be marked on the maps now in his charge, those age-old tracks trodden hard by the footsteps of men. So year by year parish business, apparently modern, still has its roots in the past. On one occasion we deplored the loss of the town seal, and on another expressed dissatisfaction with our postal address, that since 1933 has been 'Askrigg, Leyburn, Yorkshire.' 'Why Leyburn?' we asked in turn, well aware of our ancient status as a market town. 'Yorkshire is enough.'

Lastly, see the village as daylight fades on Christmas Day. The church, where that morning communicants have gathered, looms dark beyond leafless trees, and the cross stands deserted. The market-place is still, as it was when we saw it at dawn. In the main street a single figure steps out of one doorway to enter another near by. Sprays of holly lie along the ledges of the sash windows of the houses, whose upper storeys merge into the darkening sky. Below, curtains are drawn in many lighted rooms, living-rooms and little-used parlours, gay with

Christmas-trees, paper streamers, children's toys, and blazing fires. Everyone, as on the festivals in the calendar of the medieval village, entertains the others 'with arguments of love, freedom, and hospitality.'

The New Year with its climax of parties follows. We search for the arc of the January moon in the night sky over the hills. 'I allus feel sad at the end of the old year,' says our neighbour. 'You know what's passed, but you don't know what's to come.' The lives of individuals, village life and national life, inextricably linked, move on into the future.

M. H.

J. I.

Askrigg, 1950–1953.

ACKNOWLEDGMENTS AND SOURCES

INTEREST in local history is not new to this village. In 1890 Canon Whaley wrote his *History of Askrigg*, a good book if restricted and modest in scope. J. J. G. Lodge devoted himself to church matters and transcribed the parish registers, Mr R. M. Chapman accumulated a fund of knowledge, and Ella Pontefract, collecting material for her book *Wensleydale*, spurred on interest. In spite of this background, from which we have benefited, the piecing together of the story of the village was barely started; no single large mass of documents lay to hand, and facts had to be searched for in a multitude of places.

We thank Mr R. M. Chapman for his generous co-operation throughout the writing of this book, for reading the manuscript, for particulars on which the map of prehistoric times is based, for the loan of papers, and for reminiscences of childhood days. We are grateful to Mr C. K. Croft Andrew at the County Record Office, Northallerton, for the infinite trouble he has taken in making documents available and in answering queries. Similarly we have been fortunate at the York Diocesan Registry in the help of the Rev. Dr J. S. Purvis, who brought much to light for us and also read the chapter 'St Oswald's Church.' Mr W. V. Wade, lecturer in Romano-British archaeology at Leeds University, has kindly written the note on and supplied the plan of the Roman fort at Bainbridge (page 294) where he is conducting excavations.

Our thanks are due to the Senior Bursar of Trinity College Cambridge, Mr H. Thornley at County Hall, Northallerton, and Colonel Innes N. Ware at the York Diocesan Registry for courteously allowing us to see the documents in their charge, and to Mr O. Errington Wilson at the Ripon Diocesan Registry for the considerable trouble he took in giving us similar facilities. Miss C. Rob clarified and enlarged our knowledge of the flora and reorganized our list of flowers, and

Mr J. Kirby added to it. Mr J. P. Utley checked the list of birds and amended our classification. Mr J. H. B. Taylor, head postmaster at Northallerton, gave us postal information. Dr A. Raistrick loaned photographs on which two drawings of details of the Old Hall are based, and the Rev. W. Oliver assisted with the list of vicars. We thank many librarians for their unstinted help. We also thank the following for information: the Public Relations and Publicity Officer of the North Eastern Region of British Railways, the secretary of the North Riding Agricultural Executive Committee, the secretary of United Automobile Services Ltd, and the managers of Barclays Bank, Hawes, and the Express Dairy Company, Leyburn, and solicitors in the dale.

We would not have cared to undertake this book without the co-operation of our neighbours, to whom we offer thanks. Mr R. W. L. Bankes loaned us a large and valuable bundle of deeds; and Mr F. E. Chevins allowed us to use his meteorological statistics. The following gave us access to documents: the Rev. J. T. R. Steele, Mr E. W. Webb and the governors of Yorebridge Grammar School, Mr J. J. Willan at the offices of Aysgarth Rural District Council, Hawes, Mr S. A. Dickinson at High Hall, Bainbridge, and the secretaries of local societies. We particularly thank those who have loaned their deeds and ledgers. We have constantly relied on Mr T. Weatherald's excellent memory, and have been told many details of the old days by Mrs Balmer. The following similarly have answered queries: the Rev. J. H. Benson, vicar of Aysgarth, Mr T. T. Calvert, clerk to the Parish Council, Mr R. M. Hodgson, Mr H. and Mr J. Storey, Mr W. H. Burton, Mr E. Dinsdale, Police Constable C. Jackson, Miss C. Bell, Mrs F. Kettlewell, Mr and Mrs A. Robson, Mr R. Hugill, Mrs W. Sharples, Miss J. Little, Miss K. Cloughton, Mr D. Daykin, and many others too numerous to mention by name.

We wish to thank Mr E. F. Bozman of Messrs J. M. Dent for the interest that he has shown and the encouragement he has given us during the writing of this book.

MANUSCRIPT SOURCES

THE PUBLIC RECORD OFFICE

Records of the Chancery

Chantry of St Anne, Askrigg Church (1467). Askrigg Corn Mill (1555). Grant of Market at Askrigg (1587). Tithe dispute between Trinity College Cambridge and Sir T. Metcalfe (1618). Manor of Bainbridge sold by Charles I to citizens of London (1628). Dispute about the township bulls (1682). Inheritance of Colby estate (1689). Grant of market at Hawes (1700).

Records of the Exchequer

Book of horses and mares taken off the field of Branxton (Flodden Field, 1513). Dispute between the Crown and the Countess of Lennox *re* the title to the Manor of Wensleydale (1573). Askrigg Mill (1579–80–1607). Dispute between the Duke of Lennox and his tenants *re* the title to the Manor of Wensleydale (1607). Hay tithe suit brought against Sir T. Metcalfe by the tenants in the forest (1609). Hay tithe suit between Sir T. Metcalfe and tenants in the forest (1611). Colbys and the Manor of Wensleydale (1616). Felony of Peter Thornton (1620–1–2). Bernard Smith's hay tithe suits (1661–2). Askrigg market toll dispute (1733).

Records of the Court of the King's Bench

Felony and homicide of Peter Thornton (1609).

Records of the Court of Common Pleas

Agreement between James Lightfoot and Robert and Sarah Killinghall *re* estate of Grace Thornton (1748).

Records of the State Paper Office

Report on knitting trade in Richmond (1595). The Yorkshire Plot (1663–4); Petition by T. Metcalfe for lease of manorial rights in order to mine for lead (1664). Petition of inhabitants of Hawes for a market and fairs (September 1699).

BRITISH MUSEUM

Material about the Forest of Wensleydale. A pamphlet published 1647 *re* a fight between forces under Sir T. Fairfax and the Clubmen of the dales in Richmondshire.

TRINITY COLLEGE CAMBRIDGE

Rectory of Aysgarth tithe books, assessments, moduses, customs, and depositions in the tithe suits. Particulars of leases, decrees, petitions, terriers, correspondence.

BORTHWICK INSTITUTE, YORK

Archbishops' Visitation and Court Books (including Yorebridge Grammar School case, 1626).

YORK MINSTER LIBRARY

Copies of Askrigg Court Rolls.

LEEDS ARCHIVES DEPARTMENT

Wills and Inventories of the Archdeaconry of Richmond.

OFFICES OF BRITISH RAILWAYS, YORK

Minute books and time-tables.

YORKSHIRE ARCHAEOLOGICAL SOCIETY LIBRARY, LEEDS

Box of deeds relating to Askrigg (including the cotton mill). Photostat of Easby Abbey Chartulary.

BROTHERTON LIBRARY, LEEDS

Metcalfe deeds.

RIPON DIOCESAN REGISTRY, LEEDS
(also material from Chester)

Bishops' Visitation Books, Act Books, Register Books, terriers. Tithe Award and map; Archdeaconry of Richmond Consistory Court records (now at Leeds Public Library).

COUNTY HALL, NORTHALLERTON

Original records of the N.R.Q.S. (selected material). General pardon granted to Anthony Besson (1603). Maior Norton's appointment to Forestership of Wensleydale. Justices order *re* bastardy case at Thornton Rust. Turnpike Road Acts. Alexander Fothergill's diary (1751, June 19–July 29; 1754, May 4–1757, Feb. 24; 1773, Dec. 28–1775, Jan. 11) and turnpike papers. Seventeenth- and eighteenth-century deeds relating to Askrigg. Copy of complaint *re* eighteenth-century postal services in Wensleydale. Police in the North Riding (N.R.Q.S. Records). Copy of the Highway Act to divide North Riding into districts. Reports of commissioners concerning charities in England and Wales (1819–37).

HAWES COUNCIL OFFICES

Enclosure Award and map. Rate Book, 1839–40. Valuation, 1847. Broderick Valuation, 1872.

YOREBRIDGE GRAMMAR SCHOOL

Papers relating to school history, lawsuits, etc. Township books deposited at the school—The Book of the Four Men. Poor Rate Book. Churchwardens' Book. Minute books of Select Vestry and Parish Council.

HIGH HALL, BAINBRIDGE

Ledgers and minute books.

PARISH CHEST, ASKRIGG CHURCH

Documents, registers, terrier, etc.

ASKRIGG

Minute books of local societies.

PAPERS IN PRIVATE HANDS

Mr Robert W. L. Bankes—Documents relating to various families: the Thorntons, Lightfoots, Lindseys, Pratts, Smiths of Camshouse, and Christopher Alderson. Other papers relating to property at Camshouse, and in Askrigg, in particular the Old Hall. Woodhall mines dispute. Dr J. Lightfoot's prayer. *Mr J. Scarr*—Documents relating to Terrys, Pratts, Colbys, and prices of land, cattlegates, etc. *Mr R. M. Chapman*—Transcripts made by R. A. Scott Macfie of Lunds at Chester Diocesan Registry. Record of pre-railway era written by Major J. Skidmore. *Miss M. E. Metcalfe*—deeds of Woodhall. *Mr T. Weatherald, Mr W. Chapman, Mr A. Chapman, the Misses Williams, Mr J. Tennant,* of Camshouse, *Mrs J. Scarr, senior,* and *Mr J. Dinsdale*—deeds of property. *Mr T. C. Calvert* of Hawes —files of the *Wensleydale Advertiser* and books. *Mrs S.* and *Mrs F. Outhwaite*—post office and Fothergill papers. *Miss W. Percival*— Nappa Mill ledger. *Mrs A. N. Pym* and *Miss E. Leyland*—Bainbridge constable's account-book and staff. *Mr William Calvert* of Gunner-side and *Mr Calvert Chapman*—blacksmiths' ledgers. *Miss M. A. Calvert* and *Miss P. Banks*—cutting books. *Mr J. H. Lomax*—Lodge account-book. *In the authors' possession*—Bainbridge Mill and shoe-maker's ledgers.

PRINTED SOURCES

Calendar of Charter Rolls.
      ,,   *Inquisitions.*
      ,,   *Patent Rolls.*
      ,,   *Close Rolls.*
      ,,   *State Papers Domestic.*
Domesday Book for Yorkshire, translated by Robert H. Skaife.
Kirkby's Inquest, 1286–7 and *Nomina Villarum for Yorkshire, 1316* (Surtees Society, vol. lxix).
Early Yorkshire Charters, vols. iv and v, edited by Charles Travis Clay.
Feet of Fines, 1218–31 (Y.A.S. Record Series, vol. lxii).
Yorkshire Inquisitions (Henry III and Edward I) (Y.A.S. Record Series, vol. xii).
'Yorkshire Deeds,' *Y.A.S.J.*, vol. xii.
'Bishops' Visitations, Archdeaconry of Richmond,' *Y.A.S.J.*, vol. xiv.
'New Taxation, 1318,' *Y.A.S.J.*, vol. xxv.
Manwood: *Lawes of the Forest.*
J. Charles Cox: *The Royal Forests of England.*
Ripon Chapter Acts (Surtees Society, vol. lxiv).
John Leland: *Itinerary.*
Camden: *Britannia.*
J. S. Purvis: *Tudor Parish Documents in the Diocese of York.*
Quarter Sessions Records, edited by the Rev. J. C. Atkinson (North Riding Record Society).
Seventeenth-century Yorkshire Surveys, edited by T. S. Willan and E. W. Crossley (Y.A.S. Record Series, vol. civ).
The Journal of George Fox.
Rev. Henry Gee: 'The Derwentdale Plot, 1663,' *R.H.S. Third Series*, vol. xi.
Owen's Book of Fairs.
Sir John Fortescue: 'A Quaker Critic of an Engagement in the "Forty-Five,"' *The Army Quarterly*, vol. xl.
John Dupont: *The Loyal Miscellany* (sermons and tracts).
John Wesley: *Journal.*
The Hon. John Byng (later Fifth Viscount Torrington): *The Torrington Diaries* ('A Tour of the North,' 1792).
E. R. Brinkworth: 'The Study and Use of Archdeacons' Court Records,' *R.H.S. Fourth Series*, vol. xxv.
T. S. Whitaker: *History of Richmondshire.*
C. Clarkson: *History of Richmond.*
Walter C. Metcalfe and Gilbert Metcalfe: *The Records of the Family of Metcalfe.*
John Orton: *Annals of the Turf.*
Deed of Settlement of the Swaledale and Wensleydale Banking Company.
Directories (1823, 1840, 1848, 1867, 1890).
Captain F. Chapman: *The Wensleydale Hounds.*

Christopher Whaley: *History of Askrigg*.

Ella Pontefract and Marie Hartley: *Wensleydale*.

William Weaver Thompson: *The North Eastern Railway, its Rise and Development*.

M. W. Beresford: 'The Lost Villages of Yorkshire,' *Y.A.S.J.*, vol. xxxviii.

Eilert Ekwall: *The Concise Oxford Dictionary of English Place-Names*.

P. W. Matthews and Anthony W. Tuke: *History of Barclays Bank Ltd.*

Several books have been generally useful: *The Victoria County History of Yorkshire, North Riding*, vol. i; *The Parish Chest*, by W. E. Tate (reprint 1951); *The Justice of the Peace and Parish Officer*, by Richard Burn; *English Local Government* (various volumes), by Sidney and Beatrice Webb; and *Handbook of British Chronology*, by F. M. Powicke.

We have adhered to the New Style for dating.

APPENDIX A

THE ROMAN FORT AT BAINBRIDGE

THE Roman occupation of this island began in A.D. 43 and Britain remained a province of the Roman Empire for nearly four centuries.

The control of the highly Romanized areas of the lowland south and east of the province, where settled agriculture was generally practised, could safely be left to the local tribal authorities; and the surviving relics of the Roman occupation in those parts are almost entirely civilian in character.

But the highlands of the north and west were an entirely different problem. The inhabitants were much less highly organized and led a semi-nomadic pastoral life or, at best, practised a very poor kind of agriculture. Such people were always prone to brigandage and insurrection; and beyond the Solway–Tyne frontier and the Irish Sea were hostile tribes, ever ready to take any opportunity of raiding the province. In such circumstances direct military control was essential and these highland zones were covered with a network of forts and roads which divided them into areas of convenient size for supervision and administration.

The garrisons of the forts consisted of regiments, 500 or 1,000 strong, of auxiliary infantry or cavalry drawn from many parts of the Roman Empire. Behind these frontier networks lay the great fortresses of the three legions of Britain— at York, Chester, and Caerleon-on-Usk.

The fort on 'The Brough' at Bainbridge is a typical example of an auxiliary infantry fort and formed a part of a system designed to keep in check the Brigantes, whose territory covered a large part of northern Britain, including the Pennines. It is rectangular with rounded corners and has a gate in each side, placed centrally on the east and west, but a little east of centre on the north and south sides. Outside the rampart is a V-shaped ditch, some 18 feet wide by 7 feet deep. The fort measures about 330 feet by 270 feet internally, i.e. about two acres, and is large enough to hold an auxiliary cohort of five hundred infantry. In fact, we know from an inscription seen there in the sixteenth century that the garrison of the fort in the early third century A.D. was the sixth cohort of the Nervii, which came originally from what is now Belgium.

Excavation at Bainbridge has revealed that the fort, first built probably in the seventies or eighties of the first century A.D., was originally defended by a rampart of earth, which would be surmounted by a wooden palisade. The gates and towers of the fort and its internal buildings would be of timber at this period. At a later date, not earlier than the middle of the second century A.D., the defences were strengthened by the addition of a stone wall to the front of the earth rampart and the heightening of the rampart behind the wall. The gates and internal buildings were rebuilt in stone. The evidence of coins, pottery, etc., shows that the fort was occupied until late in the fourth century A.D.

Inside the fort a road, called the Via Principalis, ran from the north to the south gate; fronting on to the west side of this road and equidistant between the north and south gates stood the Headquarters Building, facing east. From the Headquarters Building to the east gate ran a road known as the Via Praetoria. The east gate was excavated in 1926 and 1931 and its masonry is still exposed to view.

An entrance in the east side of the Headquarters Building led into a courtyard, probably surrounded by a colonnade. An opening in the west side of the courtyard led into the Cross-Hall, which ran the full width of the building from north to south. In the Cross-Hall the commandant of the fort would hold his courts-martial, and a raised dais was provided for him at one end of the hall. The foundations of this dais were uncovered in the north-west corner of the Cross-Hall at Bainbridge in 1951. West of the Cross-Hall the rear portion of the Headquarters Building was occupied by a range of five rooms, of which the central and largest was the Regimental Chapel, where were kept the standards and the statue of the emperor. Beneath the Regimental Chapel at Bainbridge, as at many other forts, was a cellar or strong-room for the safe

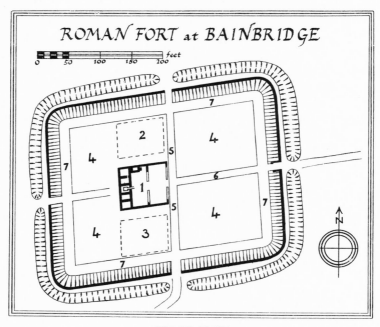

ROMAN FORT at BAINBRIDGE

KEY TO PLAN:

1. Headquarters Building   5. Via Principalis
2. Granaries   6. Via Praetoria
3. Commandant's House   7. Intervallum Road
4. Barracks, etc.

custody of the pay chest, soldiers' savings, burial fund, etc. This was excavated in 1926 and its site may still be seen, now filled in with stones for reasons of safety.

North of the Headquarters Building stood the granaries, long stone buildings with raised floors and buttressed walls, parts of which were uncovered in 1950 and 1951.

South of the Headquarters Building was the Commandant's

House, which has not yet been examined but will doubtless prove to be, as in other similar forts, a square building with ranges of rooms set around a central courtyard.

Most of the remainder of the fort will be occupied by the barracks of the soldiers, six long, narrow buildings, each divided into ten double rooms holding eight men apiece, with slightly wider centurion's quarters at one end.

The ramparts still stand up well on the hill-top and the remains of the Regimental Chapel with its cellar and those of the east gate may still be seen. The positions of the four gates are marked by dips in the ramparts and the courses of the Via Principalis and the Via Praetoria are clear on the ground. For the rest, we must wait until the spade has laid bare the remains of the other buildings and has enabled us to draw out in full the plan of the whole fort.

W. V. W.

APPENDIX B

LISTS OF INHABITANTS OF ASKRIGG

FROM YORKSHIRE LAY SUBSIDY, 1301 [1]

Askerigg

De Johanne Carpentario		vd
De Alano Carpentario		iiijd
De Johanne garcione Capellani	iiijs	
De Johanne filio Roberti	iijs	ijd
De Ada Bercar' (shepherd)	ijs	
De Johanne Fabro (smith)	vs	
De Elya Mouse	iijs	viijd
De Elya Fraunceys	vs	ijd
De Elya Haustewyk'		xiijd
De Radulpho Textore (weaver)	iijs	vjd
De Petro del Kragg	iijs	
De Thoma Wayte	iijs	iiijd
De Elya Preposito (reeve)	vjs	iiijd
De Willelmo de Askerigg'	iijs	
De Thoma filio Gamelli	ijs	iijd
De Grangia de Neubigging (Easby Abbey)	xs	
Summa tocius quindecime	lxs	ijd

[1] Ref. *Yorks. Arch. Soc. Record Series*, vol. xxi, 1896.

ASKRIGG MEN WHO ATTENDED MUSTERS TAKEN BY
CHRISTOPHER LORD CONYERS AND 'SIR JAMYS METKALF,'
KNIGHTS, ON MIDDLEHAM MOOR, 23RD JANUARY 1535 [1]

Archers

George Mason horse & harness
Richard Besson, Junr. horse
Gawdon Thirnbek horse
Richard Tutyng horse
Robert Tutyng horse
Oswald Metkalf horse
Ninian Metkalf horse & harness
Henry Bladde horse
Edmund Laffeld horse & harness
Jamys Pratt horse
Francis Braidrig horse & harness

Thomas Pekrang, Junr. horse
George Metkalf horse & harness
Symon Rawlinson horse
Geffrey Thwaitt horse & harness
Anton' Yngram horse
John Metkalf horse & harness
Olyn Fawcett horse & harness
Martyn Fawcett horse
Mawe Metkalf horse & harness
Alexandre Metkalf horse
Richard Duke horse & harness

Pikes

John Mason horse
George Wedderhelde horse & harness
Jamys Wedderhelde horse
Francis Clerkson horse

Richard Besson, Senr. horse & harness
Christ[opher] Mason horse & salett [2]
Edmund Gollan' horse

Bills

Peter Smyth horse
Walter Metkalf horse
Jamys Metkalf horse
Gwan Cowton horse
Bryan Rawlinson horse
Jamys Robinson horse & harness
Robert Crakell horse
Francis Metkalf horse
Rawffe Rawlinson horse & harness
Simon Alderson horse
Richard Tirrye horse
Thomas Mason horse
Jamys Thompson horse & steilcapp

Richard Wedderheld horse & steilcapp
Thomas Clerkson horse
George Cole horse & sallet
Stephen Thorneton horse & harness
Jamys Garathwait horse
Thomas Pekiring horse
Christopher Tuting horse
William Wright horse & sallet
Francis Rog' horse & sallet
Adam Metkalf horse & harness
Francis Metkalf horse & harness
Rawlin Gristhwait horse & harness
Thomas Battyson horse & harness

[1] Ref. P.R.O. E36/44 Musters.   [2] Salett = helmet.

LIST OF INHABITANTS WHO PAID OR WERE EXEMPT FROM HEARTH TAX ABOUT 1663 [1]

Askrigg

Thomas Metcalfe	1	John Outhwaite	1
Reynold Jefferson	3	James Metcalfe	1
George Atkinson	1	Edward Clarkson	1
John ffoster jun.	2	George Clarkson	1
Bezehan? Mason	1	Alex: Wetherill	1
William Metcalfe	1	James Beezon	1
Symond Metcalfe	1	Thomas Beezon	2
Thomas Lupton	1	Gyles Metcalfe	1
James Blythe sen.	1	Dorothy Waire	1
Robert Lambert gent.	4	Chr. Metcalfe	1
George Browne	2	Edward Bell	1
John ffoster senr.	3	James Pearse	1
Ann Mayson	1	Ewan Wetherill	1
Abraham Metcalfe	1	Tristram Janson	1
William Thornton	5	Joseph Mason	1
John Mayson	1	Stephen Wood	1
Abraham Metcalfe jun.	1	Richard Besson	3
William Lawkeland	2	Cuthbert Hird	1
William Tomlinson	1	William Atkinson	1
William Parkin	1	Chr. Warricke	1
Edmond Metcalfe	1	Feorge ffryer	2
Richard Metcalfe	1	John Hunter	1
Edm. Pratt	1	Vincent Bradricke	2
Thomas Pearson	1	John Atkinson	3
John Clarkson	1	Widdow Smith	3
James Wetherill	2	James Bradricke	2
Chr. Dawson	—	Thomas Burton	2
George Metcalfe	1	Chr. Alderson	2
Anthony Dinsdale	1		

Newbiggin

James Clerkson	1	George Bradrick	1
William Harker	1	John Kendall	1
ffrancis Rogers	1	Thomas Watson	1

Nappa

James Metcalfe Esq.	6	William Wharton	1
Thomas Metcalfe Esq.	5	William Barwicke	1
Addam Battyson	1		

[1] Ref. P.R.O. Lay Subsidy E 216/474.

Woodhall

William ffranckland gent.	2	ffrancis Dodsworth	3
Tristram Blaydes	2	John Story	1
George ffawcett	1	George Fawcett jun.	2

ASKRIGG NOT LYABLE AS AFORESAYDE

George Metcalfe	1	James Dinsdale	1
Chr. Clarkson	1	Peter Pratt	1
Richard ffisher	1	Thomas Blayds	1
James Hird	1	James Hawe	1
Richard Hutchinson	1	John Lupton	1
John Watson	1	Alex: Spence	1
Edward Guy	1	Chr. Spence	1
Jo: Warricke	1	Mathew Terry	1
Uxor Ingram	1	Abraham Metcalfe	1
Uxor Stanley	1	John Mayson	1
Thomas Backson	1	John Pearson	1
Richard Metcalfe gent.	1	Leonard Lupton	1
James Wetherill	1	Uxor Blagthorne	1
James Spence	1	William Spencly	1
Henry Alleiyne	1	Edm. Blaydes	1
James Weatherill	1	Richard Mayson	1
George Carr	—	George Hutchinson	1
John Nicholson	1	Widdow Blythe	1
Robert Hodgson	1	John Bland	1
Thomas Towson	1	Leonard Jaques	1
John ffoster	1	Edward Scaife	1
John Wetherill	1	Thomas Scaife	1
Robert Cloughton	1	Richard Webster	1
James Clarkson	1	ffrancis Walker	1
Thomas Clarkson	1	Thomas Nicolson	1
John Winn	1	Uxor Battyson	1
Jam. Tettersall	1	Uxor Carter	1
Tho. Thrailkelt	1	Rich. Broadley	1
William Robinson	1	Thomas Metcalfe	1
John Kendale	1	Thomas Watson	1
James Wadeson	1	Wm. Hutchinson	1
Richard Dowthwaite	1	John Dendale	1
John Crostes	1	Jo: Hutchinson	1
John Dawson	1	Jas. Bradricke	1
Robert Kendall	1		

NAMES OF THE FOUR MEN OF ASKRIGG (Incomplete)
(Appointed yearly in October)

1668	Thomas Pearson	James Beezon	Thomas Metcalfe	—
1673	Simon Metcalfe	John Beezon	—	—
1703	Christopher Walker	—	—	—
1724	John Alderson	William Terry	John Halliday	George Terry
1725	William Alderson	Leonard Terry	Richard Dixon	Thomas Cloughton
1726–32	William Alderson	Leonard Terry	Miles Dixon	John Cloughton
	George Robinson	Thomas Watson	John Halliday	Jeffrey Wood
	Richard Terry (continued to appoint one another)			
1733	John Alderson	Warwick Terry	Mr Rudstin	—
1741	Matthew Caygill	George Smith	John Garnett	Ambrose Garth
1742	Thomas Metcalfe	George Smith	John Tiplady	John Garnett
1743	Warwick Terry	Matthew Smith	James Little	John Wilson
1744	Miles Alderson	Thomas Wilson	William Terry	Robert Dixon
1745	John Adinson jnr.	Anthony Fearon	John Sagar	Anthony Metcalfe
1756	Alexander Metcalfe	Thomas Wood	Thomas Harker	John Hoggart
1757	John Robinson	Jeffry Wood	Matthew Blyth	Anthony Fearon
1758	John Pratt Esq.	John Robinson	James Calvert	Anthony Fearon
1759	John Pratt	J. Calvert	A. Metcalfe	J. Wood
1821–9	Miles Robinson Parke	John Lodge	John Thompson	William Terry
1830–1	James Lightfoot	John Lodge	John Thompson	William Terry
1832–6	James Lightfoot	John Thompson	William Terry	—
1837–8	James Burton Wood	James Lightfoot	John Thompson	William Terry
1839	James Lindsey Brougham	Wood Metcalfe	George Winn	Samuel Sykes
1840–1	James Burton Wood	Wood Metcalfe	George Winn	Samuel Sykes
1842	Wood Metcalfe	George Winn	George Terry	Samuel Sykes
1843–4	Wood Metcalfe	George Winn	George Terry	Samuel Burton
1845	Wood Metcalfe	George Winn	John Ryder Wood	George Terry
1846	Wood Metcalfe	George Winn	George Terry	Thomas Moore Parke
1847–50	Wood Metcalfe	George Winn	Jonathan Robinson	George Terry
1851	James Lightfoot	George Winn	George Terry	Guy Tiplady
1852	James Lightfoot	George Winn	George Terry	Guy Tiplady
1853–6	Simpson Little	John Graham	George Terry	Guy Tiplady
1857–65	Azariah Chapman	Simpson Little	John Graham	Guy Tiplady
1866–70	Simpson Little	Richard Tiplady	John Graham	Guy Tiplady
1871–75	Simpson Little	Richard Tiplady	Metcalfe Graham	Guy Tiplady
1876–80	Simpson Little	Stockdale Thompson	William Winn	Guy Tiplady
1881	Simpson Little	William Winn	Richard Mason	Guy Tiplady
1882–88	Simpson Little	William Winn	Richard Mason	Robert Mason
1889–93	Metcalfe Graham	William Winn	Richard Mason	Robert Mason
1894	Metcalfe Graham	James Trotter	Richard Mason	Robert Mason

FIRST MEMBERS OF ASKRIGG PARISH COUNCIL

Thomas Lodge   Rev. Christopher Whaley   Timothy Spensley
Thomas Metcalfe   James Yelland

VICARS OF ASKRIGG

1175	Uctred the Priest.
1301	Robert the Chaplain.
1523–5	Roland Sagarwhayte.
1548	Percival Atkinson.
15??–1601	Tristram Janson, probably a son of the vicar of Aysgarth (1573–1617).
1633	Henry Hodges.
1665	William Colden (or Calton), deacon and priest at Durham 1630.
1674–9	Cuthbert Allen, deacon and priest at Richmond, Sept. 1673.
1684–5	Peter Alcock, deacon at Ely 1681, priest at Peterborough 1684.
1691	William Thompson, licensed schoolmaster at Yorebridge Grammar School 1688, deacon at Carlisle 1689, priest at Chester 1691.
1697	James Metcalfe, B.A., son of Augustine Metcalfe, gent., born at Sedbusk, school Yorebridge, admitted Sizar (age 17) at St John's College Cambridge 9th May 1692, matric. 1692, B.A. 1695–6, probably ordained deacon Chester 19th Sept. 1696.
1751	Thomas Metcalfe, M.A., son of John Metcalfe, born at Askrigg, school Richmond, matric. 1703, probably admitted Sizar (age 17) at Christ's College Cambridge 14th June 1703, Scholar 1704–5, B.A. 1706–7, M.A. 1710, Fellow 1707–16, Tuxor 1714, priest at Ely 25th Sept. 1709, Rector of Toft, Cambridge 1715, chaplain to Bishop of Ely, Rector of Childerley 1717–23, Rector of Hardwick 1723, J. P. for Cambridge, died 26th Jan.1777, aged ninety.
1754	Thomas Morland, came from Darlington, ordained priest 15th Oct. 1752.
1761	James Lamb, M.A., came from Westmorland, master of Winton School, stipendiary curate of Lunds 1745, curate of Lunds 1755.
1797	John Taylor.
1800	Robert Bowman, at first resident, but in 1811 lived at West Witton and was stipendiary curate there. He had a curate at Askrigg whom he paid £40 a year. Assistant curate at Hawes 11th Nov. 1797.
1821	William Plues, M.A.
1823	Richard Wood, M.A., Corpus Christi Cambridge, B.A. 1822, deacon 1822, priest 1823, M.A. 1825, vicar of Woollaston with Irchester, Northants. 1829, died 1868.

1868   Jacob Tomlin, B.A., author, St John's College Cambridge, B.A. 1818, deacon 1845, priest 1846, curate of St Augustine's, Liverpool 1845–6, Tunstall near Kirby Lonsdale 1847–8, Tankersley 1849–53, Great Coates 1854–6, Brodsworth 1860–1, Crossall 1865–6; vicar of Woollaston with Irchester 1868, Dacre 1868.

1869   Christopher Whaley, M.A., Hon. Canon of Ripon, Rural Dean of Catterick West, died 8th July 1905, aged sixty.

1906   Frederick Morris Symonds Squibb, B.A.

1924   John Henry Stewart Bayley, B.Sc.

1933   Arthur Thurston Pain.

1946   John Thomas Robson Steele, B.A.

1953   William H. Dale Chapman.

METCALFE CHANTRY PRIESTS

1468   Henry Herryson.
1523   John Dynley.
1535   John Bowmer.
1546–8   Roger Kendall.

ASSISTANT CHAPLAINS

1523–5   Thomas Metcalfe   Arthur Kettywell   Galfridus Stokdall
       Adam Mason   Thomas Mayson   Henry Mowne
       Thomas Swandell   Thomas Wyn

ASSISTANT CURATES AND CURATES IN CHARGE

1755–61 Daniel Addison
1785–7 James Sagar
1789–90 William Armstrong
1792–4 Anthony Wharton
1794–6 George Mounsey
1796–7 William Richardson
1798 Robert Lambert
1801 John Garnett (?)
1808–11 William Richardson
1811–17 Samuel Lindsey Brougham (and again in 1820–3)
1829–32 Warren Metcalfe
1834 William Nugent Bree
1857–68 Richard Wood, jun.
1868–9 Christopher Whaley

LAY READERS

Feb. 1930 A. G. Keswick
Dec. 1930 — Boulton
July 1931 S. C. Caygill
Nov. 1931 John H. Platt
Oct. 1934 John C. Bond
Feb. 1942–51 Wilfred M. Case, F.Ph.S. (Eng.)

MASTERS AT YOREBRIDGE GRAMMAR SCHOOL

1601–14	Richard Leake
16 —	— Dobson
16 —	— Taitham
16 —	Richard Smith
16 —	Thomas Swadling
1626–33	Adam Foster, senr.
16 —	— Foster, junr.
16 —	— Motley
1668	John Stephenson
1672	Michael Metcalfe
1688	John Horner
1688	Rev. William Thompson
1696	John Nelson, B.A.
1708	Rev. James Metcalfe, B.A.
1720	Rev. Anthony Clapham, B.A.
1752–8	Robert Thistlethwaite, B.A.
1758–9	Rev. Thomas Morland (duties carried out by John Thompson)
1759	James Ellwood
1794	Rev. Anthony Wharton
1843	Thomas Darnton Milner, LL.D.
1846	Rev. William Balderston, M.A.
1891	William Balderston, jun., M.A.
X 1919	Rennie Charles Shorter, M.A. X ← SISTER'S HEAD
1949	Ernest William Webb, M.A., M.Sc.
1953	Philip H. Edmonds, M.A.

MY SISTER WAS THE FIRST SCHOLAR TO GO TO CAMBRIDGE

WENT TO TEA @ YOREBRIDGE, MASTER'S HOUSE @ BAINBRIDGE.

ASKRIGG CLOCK-MAKERS [1]

c. 1681 JOHN OGDEN.
A Quaker, probably from Halifax. Later joined his son John in Darlington.

22nd April 1693–29th Jan. 1776 MARK METCALFE.
Apprenticed to John Ogden. 18th Feb. 1739 married Margaret Heslop of Richmond, who died 15th Nov. the same year. 8th Aug. 1750 married Dorothy Harland of Newbiggin.

c. 1769 JOHN ADDISON.
Apprenticed to Joseph Hindley of York, watch- and clock-maker.

Died 18th May 1781. JAMES WILSON.
Apprenticed to Mark Metcalfe.

4th March 1738?–5th Jan. 1803 CHRISTOPHER CAYGILL.
Apprenticed to Mark Metcalfe. 26th March 1769 married Alice Tomlin.

MATTHEW CAYGILL.
Voted at York 1807.

Born 2nd July 1748 WILLIAM SMITH.
Son of George Smith. 5th June 1774 married Elizabeth Pratt of this parish. Not known to have worked in Askrigg.

BENJAMIN LAWSON.
18th March 1786 married Isabel Slinger of this parish. Not known to have worked in Askrigg.

29th May 1746–1805 EDMUND SAGAR.
Son of John Sagar, parish clerk. 4th Dec. 1769 married Jane Horsefield of this parish. Moved to Skipton.

c. 1770 WILLIAM TERRY.
Came from Bedale. Apprenticed to James Wilson.

1783–7th April 1850 JOHN STANCLIFFE.
Apprenticed to Christopher Caygill and married his daughter Mary.

1757–18th Jan. 1850 JAMES PRATT.
Apprenticed to Christopher Caygill. 24th Nov. 1787 married Mary Hutton.

10th March 1784–1855 GEORGE LEE.
Son of George Lee, blacksmith. Went to Skipton to learn clock-making from Edmund Sagar whom he succeeded in business in 1805.

JAMES METCALFE OF HALIFAX.
7th April 1788 married Christiana Smith of Askrigg parish. Not known to have worked in Askrigg.

[1] Most of the dates are based on entries in the parish registers.

c. early nineteenth century WILLIAM THOMPSON.
Left the neighbourhood.

c. 1814 JOHN HARKER.

9th Dec. 1788–12th March 1857 WILLIAM PRATT.
Son of James Pratt. Trained in Liverpool. 12th Dec. 1835 married Elizabeth Skidmore of this parish. Worked in partnership first with his father, later with his brother John.

21st April 1799–25th Sept. 1861 JOHN PRATT.
Son of James Pratt.

1832–26th Feb. 1914 JOHN SKIDMORE.
20th April 1857 married Mary Hannah Preston of Bainbridge.

APPENDIX C

SOME FLOWERS IN THE TOWNSHIP OF ASKRIGG

Fields

Meadow Crowfoot	*Ranunculus acris* (L)
Bulbous Buttercup	*Ranunculus bulbosus* (L)
Ragged Robin	*Lychnis flos-cuculi* (L)
Meadow Cranesbill	*Geranium pratense* (L)
Wood Cranesbill	*Geranium sylvaticum* (L)
Red Clover	*Trifolium pratense* (L)
White Clover	*Trifolium repens* (L)
Tuberous Pea	*Lathyrus montanus* (L) Bernh.
Great Burnet	*Sanguisorba officinalis* (L)
Pignut	*Conopodium majus* (Covan) Lor. and Barr.
Knapweed (Hardheads)	*Centaurea nigra* (L)
Common Hawkbit	*Leontodon hispidus* (L)
Goat's Beard	*Tragopogon pratensis* (L)
Yellow Rattle	*Rhinanthus minor agg.* / *R. Crista-galli*
Ribwort Plantain (Ribgrass)	*Plantago lanceolata* (L)

Typical Meadow Flowers

Milkwort	*Polygala vulgaris* (L)
Pearlwort	*Sagina procumbens* (L)
Rest Harrow	*Ononis repens* (L) / *O. arvensis*
Barren Strawberry	*Potentilla sterilis* (L) Garcke.
Tormentil	*Potentilla erecta* (L) Rausch.
Lady's Bedstraw	*Galium verum* (L)
Mouse Ear Hawkweed	*Hieracium pilosella* (L)
Harebell	*Campanula rotundifolia* (L)
Eyebright	*Euphrasia officinalis agg.*
Lousewort	*Pedicularis sylvatica* (L)
Thyme	*Thymus serpyllum agg.*
Betony	*Stachys officinalis* (L) Trev.
Hoary Plantain	*Plantago media* (L)
Sheep's Sorrel	*Rumex acetosella agg.*
Creeping Buttercup	*Ranunculus repens* (L)
Goldilocks	*Ranunculus auricomus* (L)
Marsh Marigold (Kingcup)	*Caltha palustris* (L)
Spring Whitlow Grass	*Erophila verna* (L) Cheval. / *Draba verna*

Typical Short-turfed Pasture Flowers

Rockrose	*Helianthemum chamaecistus* Mill.
	H. vulgare
Bladder Campion	*Silene cucubalus* Wibel.
Purging Flax	*Linum catharticum* (L)
Kidney Vetch (Ladies' Fingers)	*Anthyllis vulneraris* (L)
Meadow Sweet	*Filipendula ulmaria* (L) Maxim.
	Spiraea ulmaria
Lady's Mantle	*Alchemilla vulgaris agg.*
Water Avens	*Geum rivale* (L)
Agrimony	*Agrimonia eupatoria* (L)
Grass of Parnassus	*Parnassia palustris* (L)
Heath Bedstraw	*Galium pumilum* Murr.
Common Valerian	*Valeriana officinalis* (L)
Devil's Bit Scabious	*Suaecisa pratensis* Moench.
	Scabiosa sueccisa
Carline Thistle	*Carlina vulgaris* (L)
Marsh Thistle	*Cirsium palustre* (L) Scop.
Creeping Thistle	*Cirsium arvense* (L) Scop.
Melancholy Thistle	*Cirsium heterophyllum* (L) Hill.
Toadflax	*Linaria vulgaris* (L)
Foxglove	*Digitalis purpurea* (L)
Snakeweed	*Polygonum bistorta* (L)
Early Purple Orchid	*Orchis mascula* (L)
Fragrant Orchid	*Gymnadenia conopsea* (L) R Br.
	Habenaria conopsea
Spring Woodrush	*Luzula campestris* (DC)

Rare

Herb Christopher	*Actaea spicata* (L)
Alpine Penny Cress	*Thlaspi alpestre* (L)
Rock Hutchinsia	*Hornungia petraea* (L) Rchb.
	Hutchinsia petraea
Treacle Mustard	*Erysimum cheiranthoides* (L) adventive
Wood Starwort	*Stellaria nemorum* (L)
Spring Sandwort	*Minuartia verna* (L) Hiern.
	Arenaria verna
Meadow Saxifrage	*Saxifraga granulata* (L)
Yellow Mountain Saxifrage	*Saxifraga aiziodes* (L)
Mealy Primrose (Bird's Eye)	*Primula farinosa* (L)
Butterwort	*Pinguicula vulgaris* (L)
Water Ragwort	*Senecio aquaticus* Hill.
Butterbur	*Petasites hybridus* (L) Gaertn. female plant
Hemp Agrimony	*Eupatorium cannabinum* (L)

Y

Marsh Hawk's Beard	*Crepis paludosa* (L) Moench.
Toothwort	*Lathraea sqaumaria* (L) parasitic on Hazel and Wych Elm
Spear Mint	*Mentha spicata* (L) emend Huds.
Long-leaved Dock	*Rumex longifolius* (DC)
Tea-leaved Willow	*Salix phylicifolia* (L)
Yellow Star-of-Bethlehem	*Gagea lutea* (L) Ker-Gawl
Herb Paris	*Paris quadrifolia* (L)

BIRDS IN THE TOWNSHIP OF ASKRIGG

R = Resident birds
S = Summer breeding visitors
W = Winter visitors

L = Local
V = Vagrant
* = Uncommon

Uplands and Moorland

Raven (V)
Snow Bunting (W)
Meadow Pipit (S)
Ring Ousel (L S)
Wheatear (S)
Short-eared Owl (L R)
Common Buzzard (V)
Peregrine (V)

Merlin (L R)
Curlew (S)
Golden Plover (S)
Black-headed Gull (S)
Red Grouse (R)
Black Grouse (L R *)
Green Plover (S)
Stock Dove (R)

Meadows and Pastures

Greenfinch (S)
Skylark (R)
Mistle-thrush (R)
Redwing (W)
Fieldfare (W)
Hedge-sparrow (R)
Partridge (R)
Carrion Crow (R)

Magpie (R)
Tree Pipit (S)
Long-tailed Tit (R)
Common Whitethroat (S)
Garden Warbler (S)
Cuckoo (S)
Corncrake (S *)
Brambling (W)

Plantations and Woods

Coal-tit (L R)
Marsh-tit (L R)
Tree-creeper (R)
Nuthatch (L R)
Goldcrest (V)
Green Woodpecker (L R)

Great-spotted Wood-
  pecker (L R)
Long-eared Owl (L R)
Tawny Owl (R)
Wood Pigeon (R)
Siskin (W)

Rivers and Tarns

Pied Wagtail (S)
Grey Wagtail (R)
Yellow Wagtail (S)
Sedge-warbler (S)
Reed-bunting (L R)
Dipper (R)
Sand-martin (S)
Kingfisher (R)

Common Snipe (R)
Jack Snipe (W)
Redshank (S)
Common Sandpiper (S)
Oystercatcher (L S)
Herring Gull (V)
Lesser Black-backed Gull
  (V)

Mallard (R)
Teal (R)
Common Heron (R)

Common Tern (V)
Moorhen (R)
Coot (L R)

Open Woods and Copses

Willow-warbler (S)
Redstart (S)
Pied Flycatcher (L S)
Tree-sparrow (L R)
Nightjar (L S *)
Little Owl (L R)
Sparrow-hawk (R)
Kestrel (R)

Woodcock (L R *)
Pheasant (R)
Goldfinch (L V)
Linnet (S)
Whinchat (S)
Lesser Redpoll (L R)
Blackcap (S)
Chiffchaff (S V)

Habitations and Gardens

Jackdaw (R)
Starling (R)
House-sparrow (R)
Chaffinch (R)
Great-tit (R)
Blue-tit (R)
Song-thrush (R)
Blackbird (R)

Robin (R)
Wren (R)
Spotted Flycatcher (S)
Swallow (S)
House-martin (S)
Swift (S)
Barn Owl (R)

INDEX

313

197, 205, 207, 227, 241, 242, 247, 268; Manor, 7; Scar, 6, 7, 45, 50, 61, 105, 130, 170, 194, 214, 238, 255, 266, 269, 271

Neville, 49, 56, 202

Newbiggin, 6, 7, 41, 54, 128, 130, 142, 156, 184, 203, 238, 270

Newspapers, 24, 30, 119, 124, 156, 166, 177, 181, 282

Norsemen, 12, 240

Northallerton, 24, 36, 121, 150, 180, 234, 251

Northern Lights, 117

Oatmeal, 104, 128, 233

Occupations, 28, 91, 94, 102, 121, 141, 183, 221, 226, 235, 236, 273

Ogden, John, 87, 229

Outhwaite, 178, 257

Pack-horse route, 157, 158

Paddock Beck, 71, 132, 260

Parish: clerk, 64, 177, 216, 220, 221; registers, 26, 60, 126, 199, 212–14, 218

Parke, 136, 142, 147, 159, 177

Paveior, 96

Pearson, 49, 61, 76, 242, 243

Penhill, 5, 8, 147, 149

Pennines, 3, 17, 131

Pilgrimage of Grace, 56

Plumbers, 96, 121

Poaching, 50, 73

Pococke, Dr, 14

Poets, 165, 166

Police, 161, 162, 165, 185

Poor: Act of Settlement, 128; Aysgarth Union, 155; gifts, 93; Gilbert's Act, 149, 153, 155; guardians, 149, 150, 154, 275; house, 128; Laws, 70, 140, 149; oatmeal funds, 128, 156; outdoor relief, 154–6; overseers, 29, 70, 72, 128, 131, 149, 150, 154, 194; people, 167, 187; rates, 70, 71, 72, 94, 102, 128–31, 150, 153; work-

house, 101, 153, 154, 155, 187, 228, 279

Population, 26, 86, 126, 140, 183

Post, 23, 24, 157, 177, 178, 182, 188, 189, 274, 285

Pratt, 15, 58, 61, 91, 94, 99, 114, 122–5, 126, 146, 148, 158, 159, 209, 210, 221, 223, 228, 230

Prices, 94, 96, 104, 114, 116, 117, 120, 153, 163, 164, 181, 184, 198, 233, 235, 257

Quakers (see SOCIETY OF FRIENDS)

Quarries, 86, 117, 225, 246, 249, 268

Quarter Sessions, North Riding, 29, 65, 67, 70–4, 80, 88, 89, 211, 219

Queen Anne's Bounty, 92, 199, 205, 212

Railway, 29, 140, 148, 157, 168, 169, 179, 181, 182, 260; station, 6, 179, 182, 165

Rainfall, 261

Raydale, 54, 55, 61, 67, 68, 127, 157, 201, 274; Riot, 65

Recusants, 82, 218

Redmire, 105, 109, 116, 122, 146, 162, 238, 240

Reeth, 36, 94, 195

Reform Bill, 139, 147

Richmond, 22, 37, 39, 40, 48, 57, 59, 67, 69, 70, 105, 107, 111, 115, 116, 122, 123, 127, 147, 157, 158, 162, 167, 213, 216, 232, 233, 234, 274, 277; Archdeaconry, 44, 199; Castle, 37, 40, 43, 162; Honour of, 37, 39

Richmondshire, 37, 43, 44

Ripon, 51, 264, 274; Diocese, 199, 200, 213

Rising of the North, 56

Roads: common way, 41, 68, 105; Highway Board, 149; highway rates, 94; occupation, 141; repair, 71, 273, 275; surveyors, 29, 70, 98, 105–14, 137, 150; turnpike, 29, 91, 105–14, 168; waywardens, 150

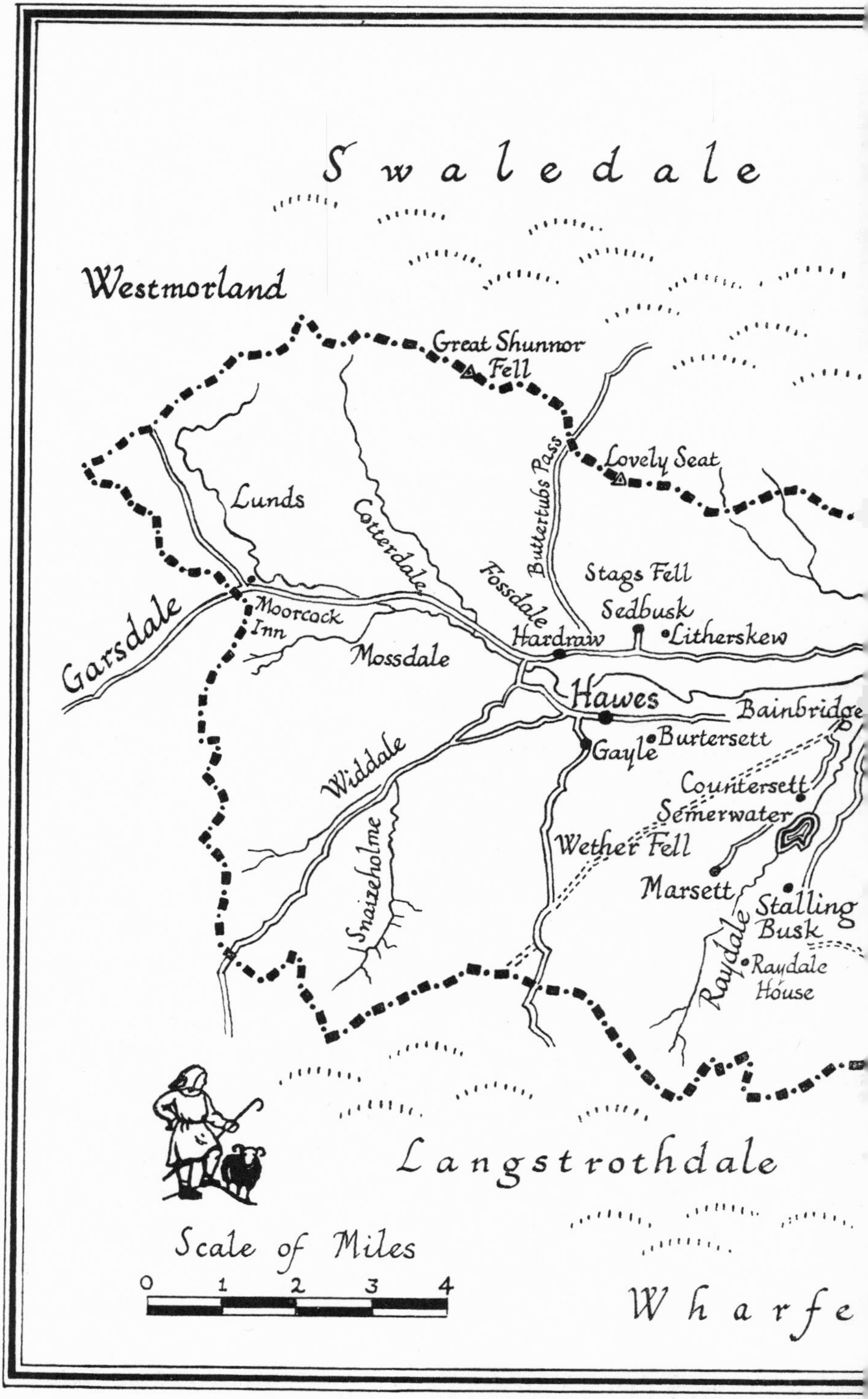

S w a l e d a l e

Westmorland

Great Shunnor
△ Fell

Lovely Seat
△

Lunds

Cotterdale

Butertubs Pass

Fossdale

Stags Fell
Sedbusk
• Litherskew
Hardraw

Garsdale

Moorcock
Inn

Mossdale

Hawes
Bainbridge
• Burtersett
Gayle

Countersett
Semerwater

Widdale

Wether Fell

Marsett

Snaizeholme

Raydale

Stalling
Busk
• Raydale
House

L a n g s t r o t h d a l e

Scale of Miles

0   1   2   3   4

W h a r f e